Oh My Goddess!

ああっ女神さまっ

39

STORY AND ART BY
Kosuke Fujishima

TRANSLATION BY
Dana Lewis and Christopher Lewis

LETTERING AND TOUCHUP BY
Susie Lee and Betty Dong
with Tom2K

DARK HORSE MANGA™

CHAPTER 243

Let Me Grant Your Wish

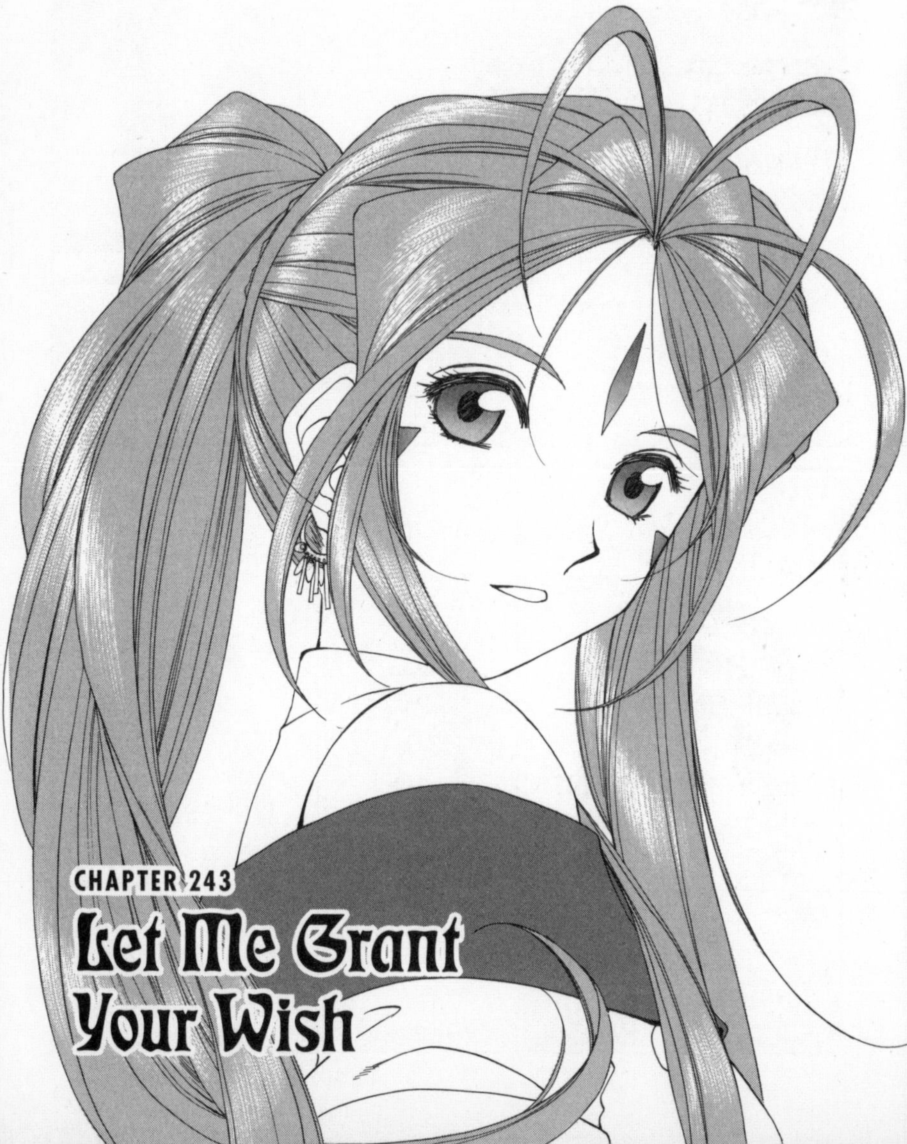

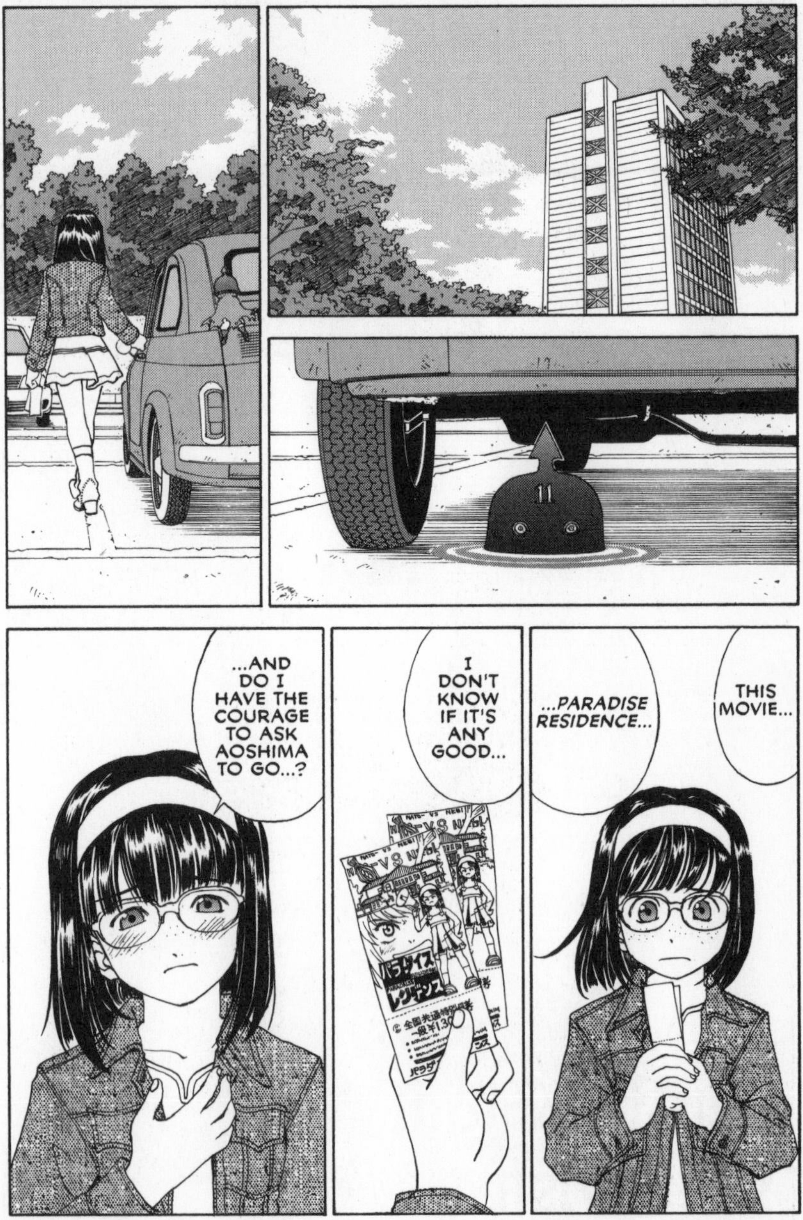
THIS MOVIE...
...PARADISE RESIDENCE...
I DON'T KNOW IF IT'S ANY GOOD...
...AND DO I HAVE THE COURAGE TO ASK AOSHIMA TO GO...?

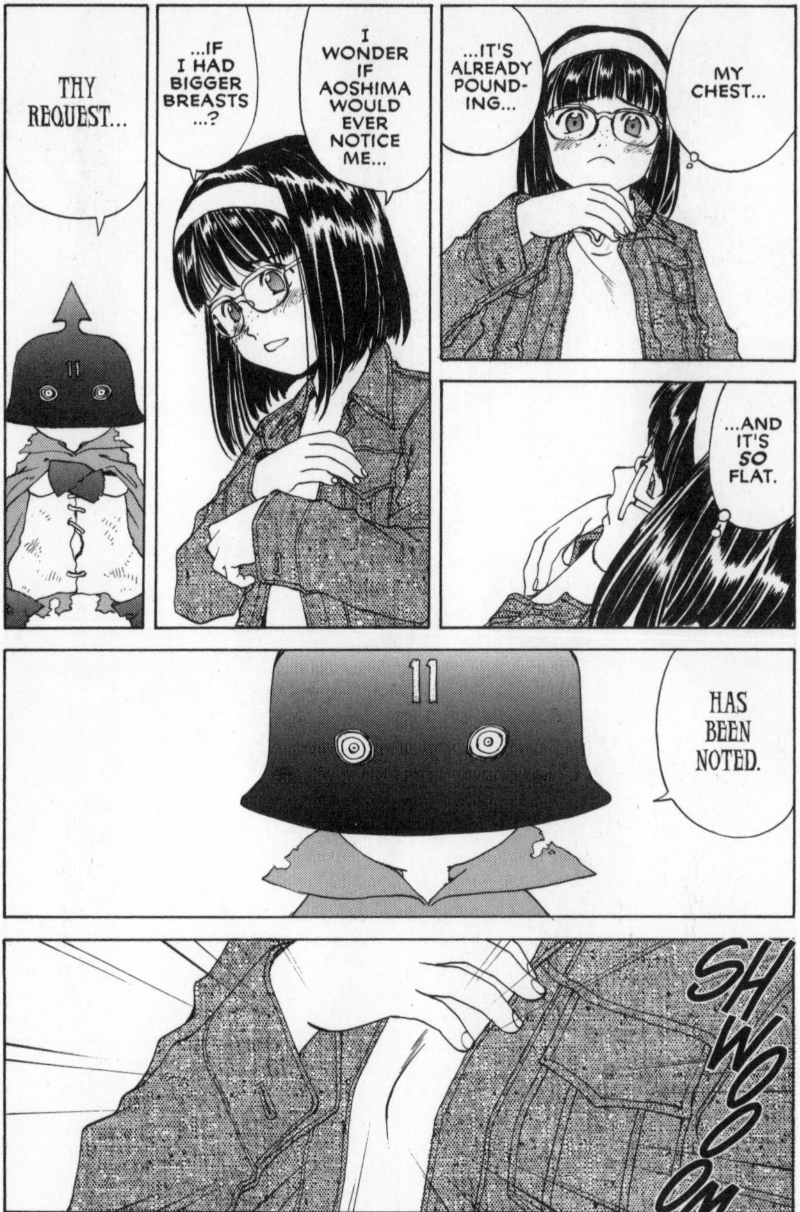
MY CHEST...
...IT'S ALREADY POUNDING...
...AND IT'S SO FLAT.
I WONDER IF AOSHIMA WOULD EVER NOTICE ME...
...IF I HAD BIGGER BREASTS ...?
THY REQUEST...
HAS BEEN NOTED.
SHWOOOOM

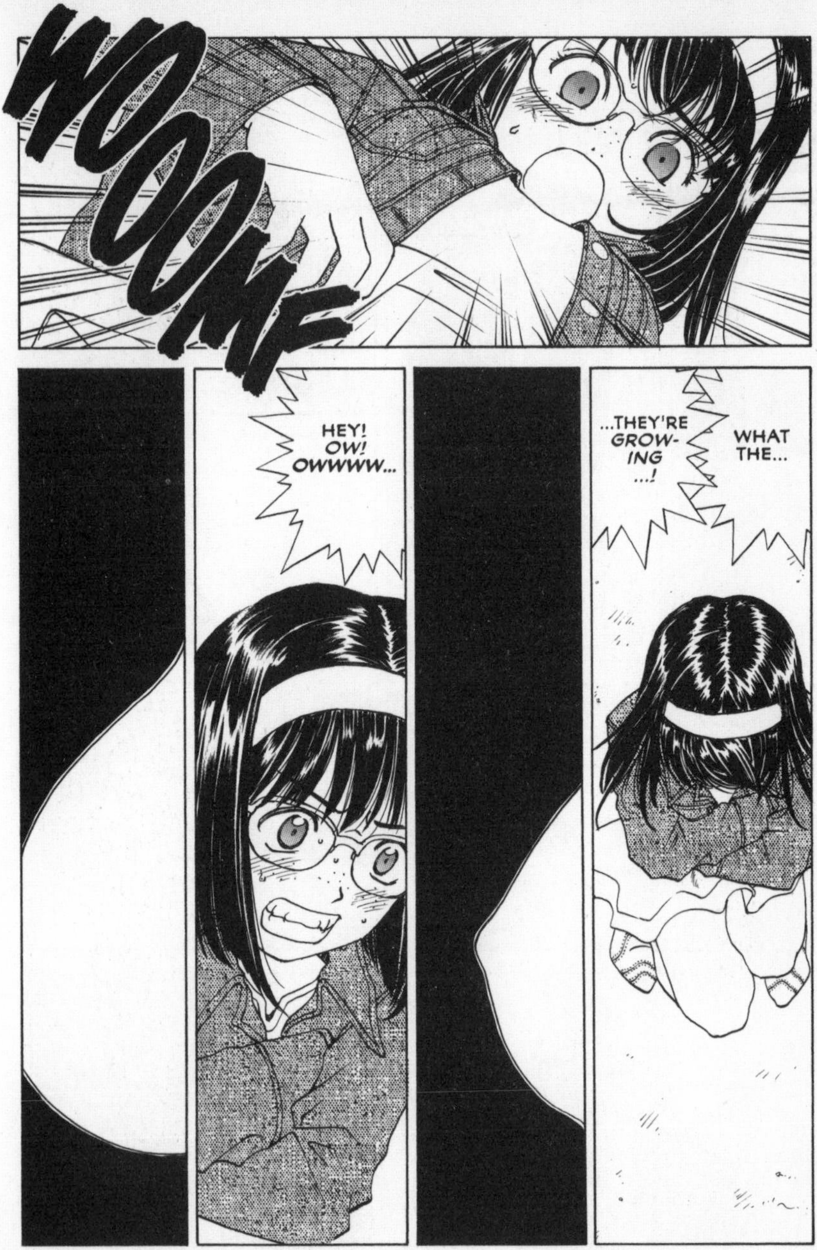
WOOMF
WHAT THE...
...THEY'RE GROW-ING ...!
HEY! OW! OWWWW...

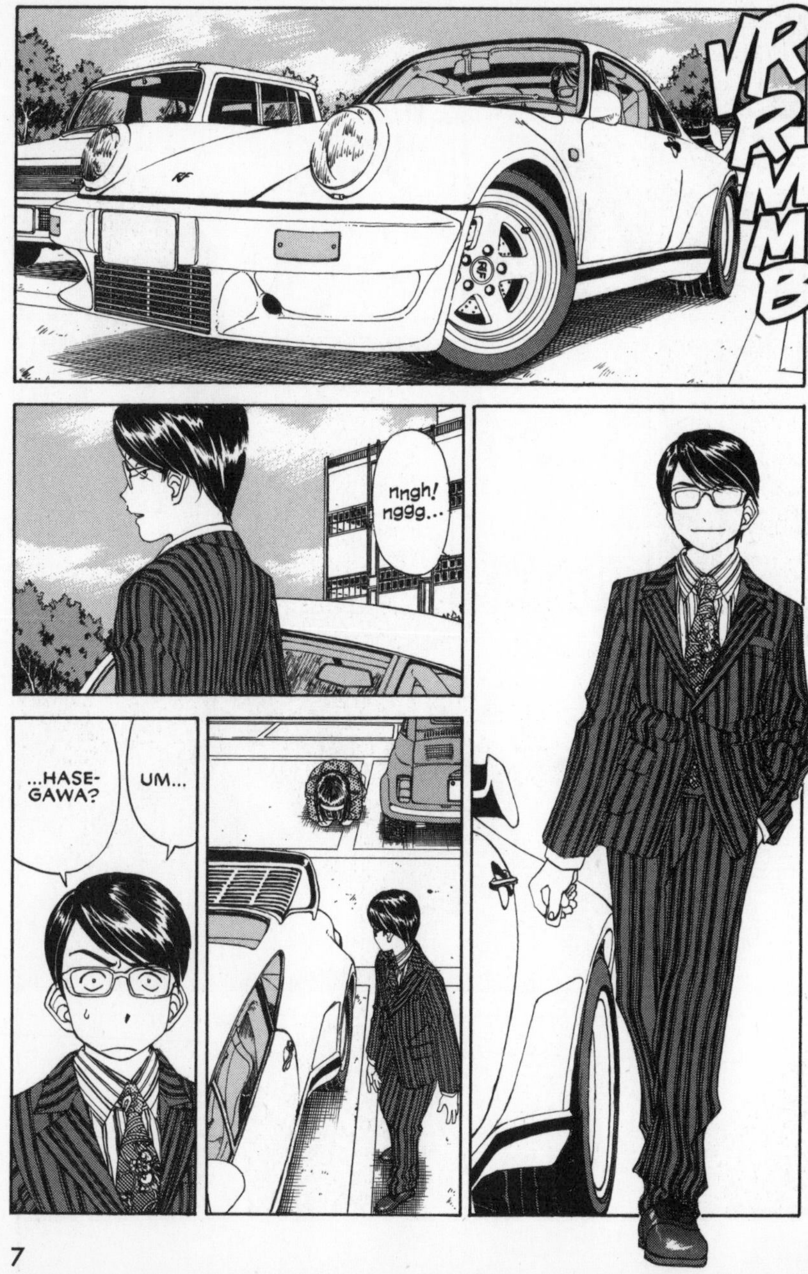
VRRMMB
nngh! nggg...
UM...
...HASE-GAWA?

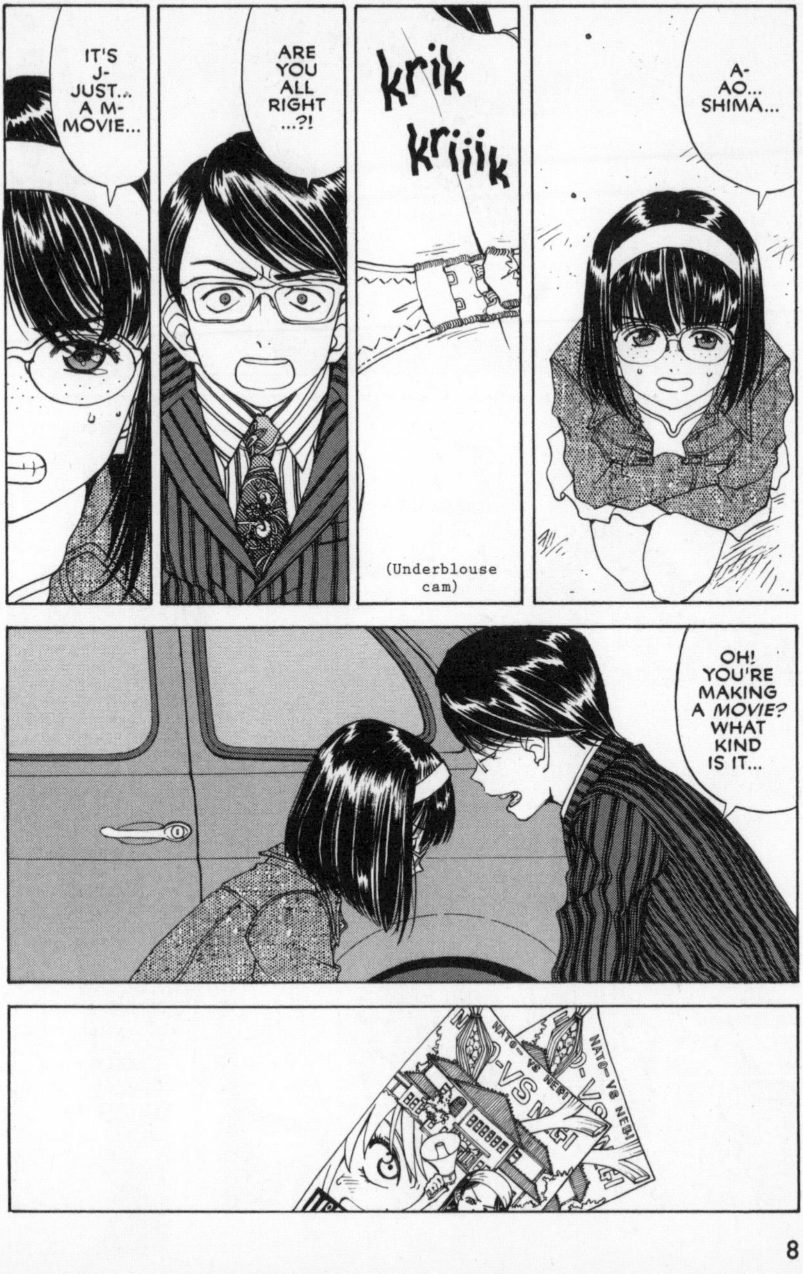
A- AO... SHIMA...
krik
kriiik
(Underblouse cam)
ARE YOU ALL RIGHT ...?!
IT'S J- JUST... A M- MOVIE...
OH! YOU'RE MAKING A *MOVIE?* WHAT KIND IS IT...

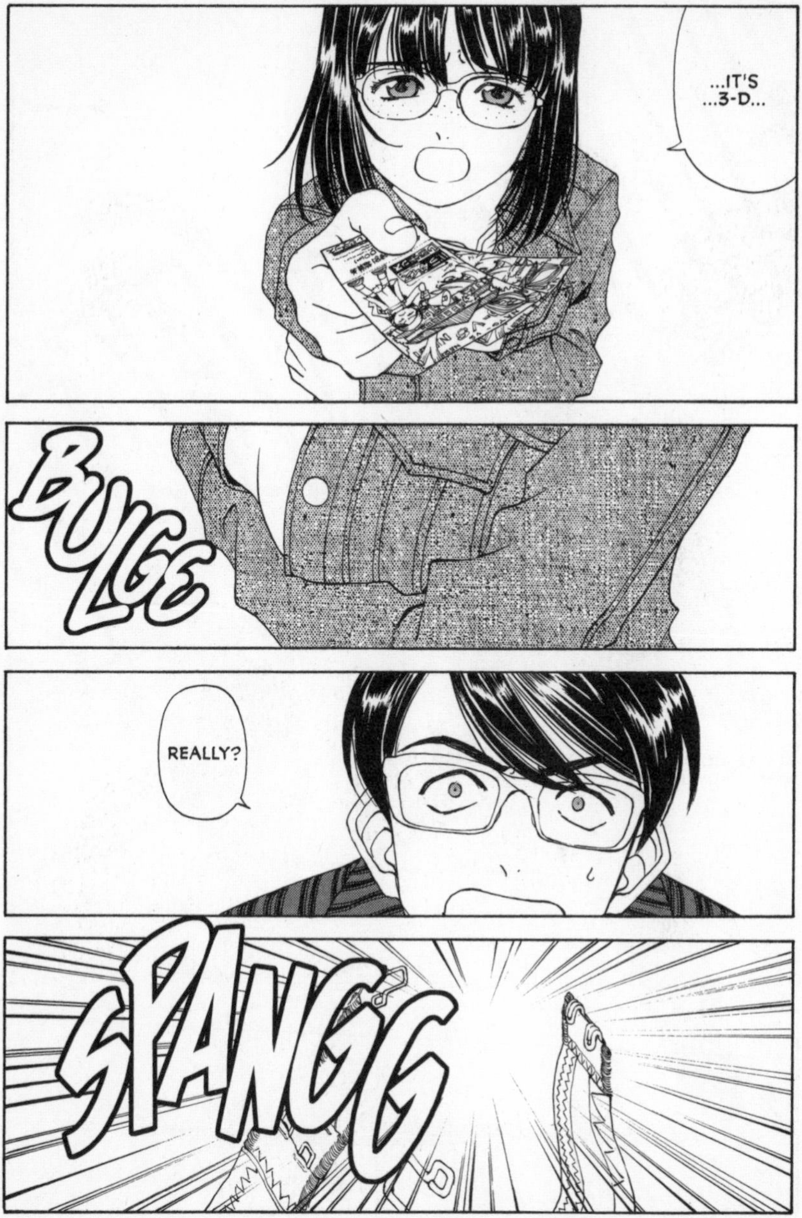
...IT'S ...3-D...
BULGE
REALLY?
SPANGG

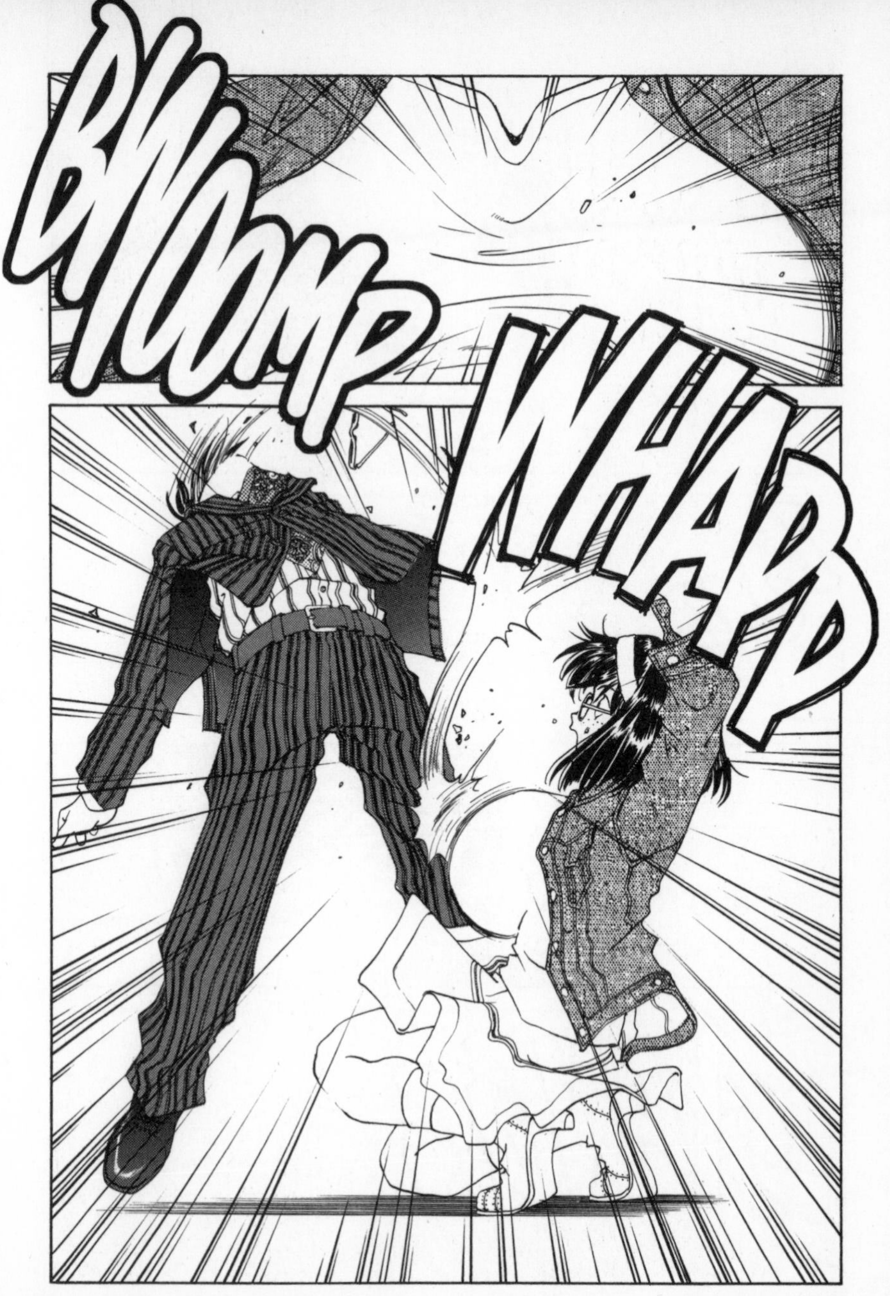
BWOMP
WHAP

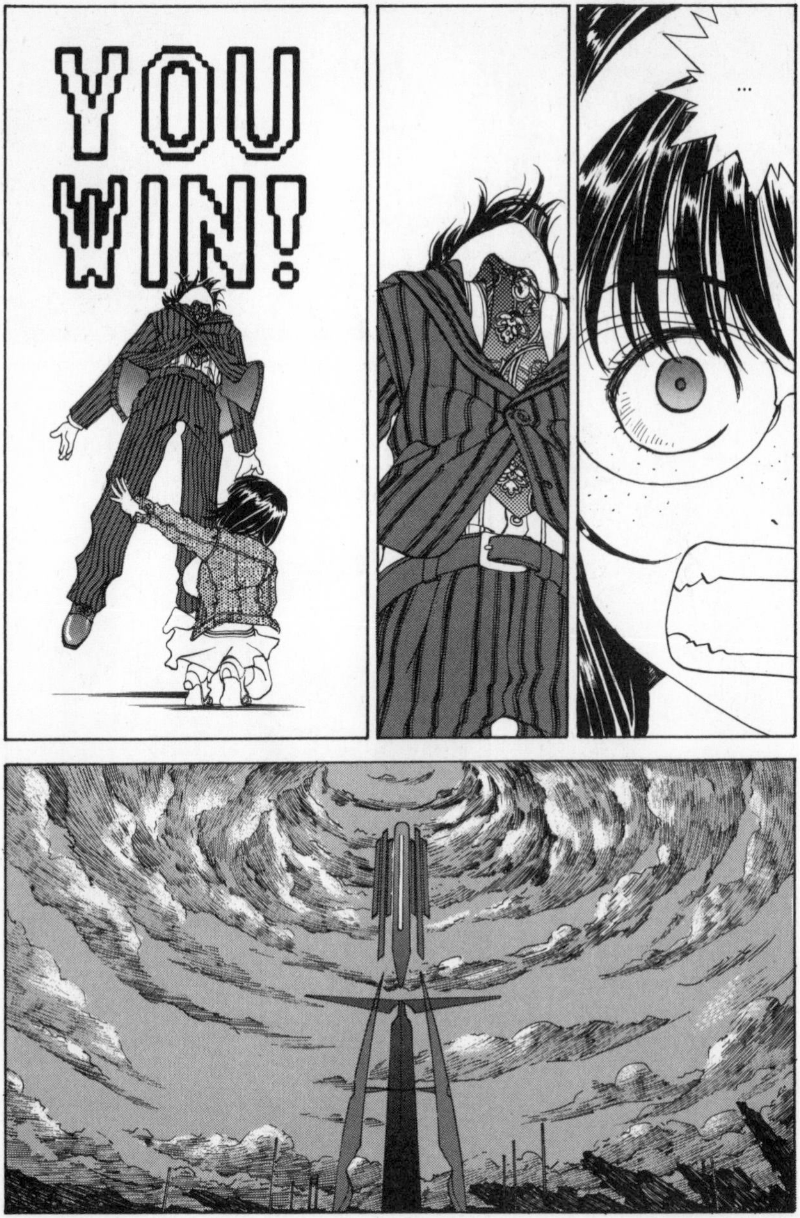
...
YOU WIN!

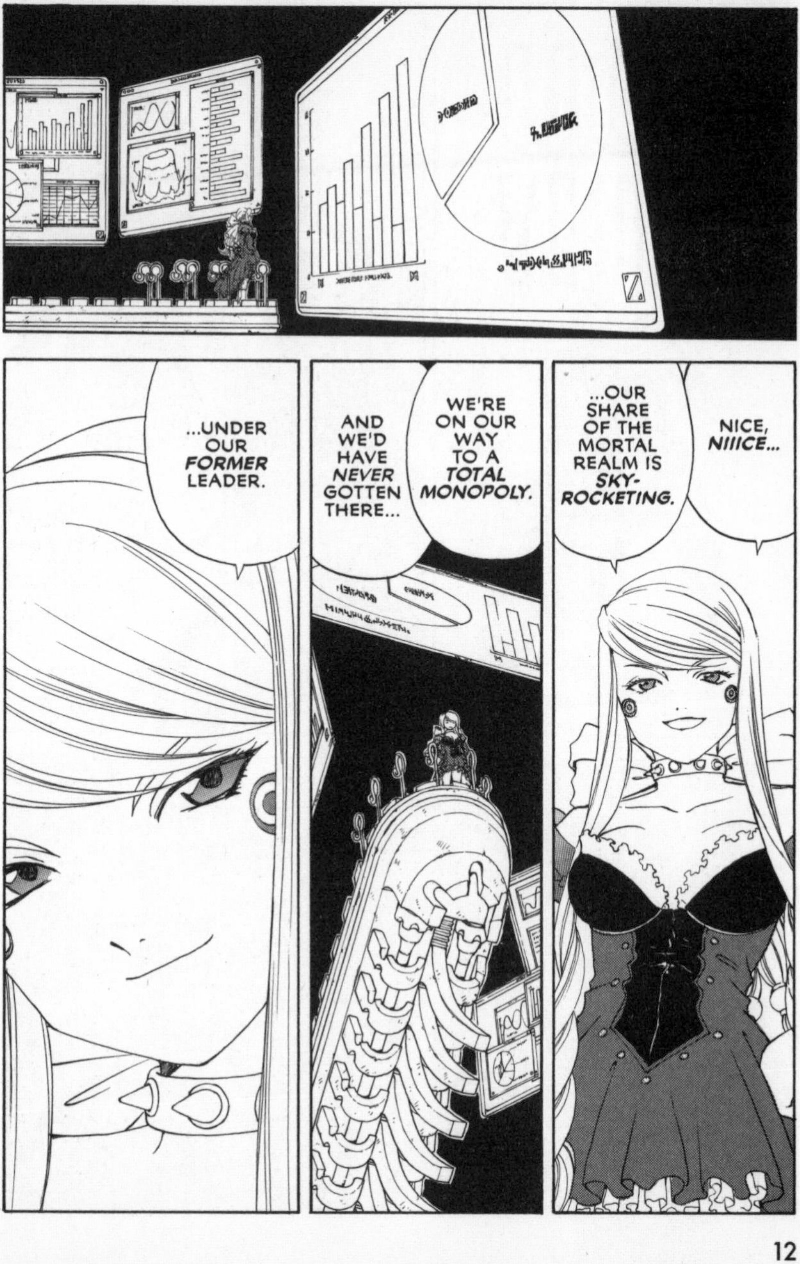
NICE, *NIIICE...*
...OUR SHARE OF THE MORTAL REALM IS *SKY-ROCKETING.*
WE'RE ON OUR WAY TO A *TOTAL MONOPOLY.*
AND WE'D HAVE *NEVER* GOTTEN THERE...
...UNDER OUR *FORMER* LEADER.

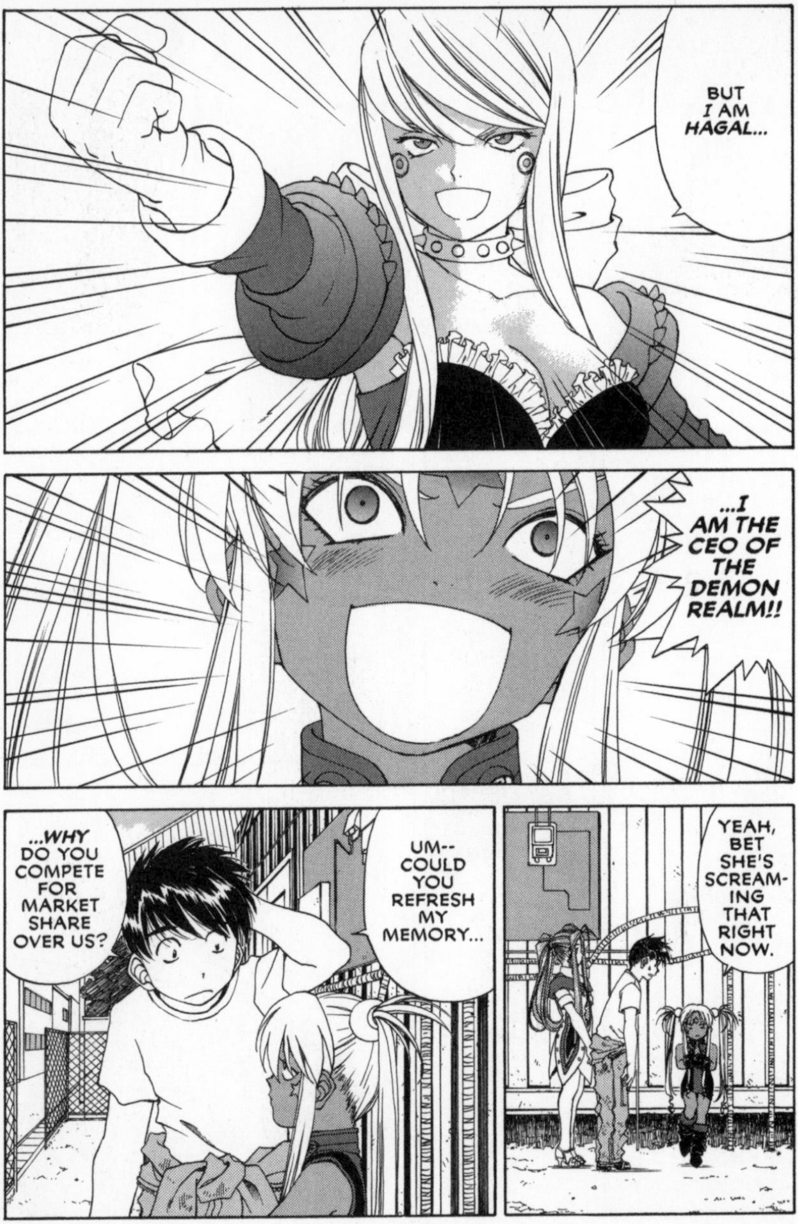
BUT I AM HAGAL...
...I AM THE CEO OF THE DEMON REALM!!
YEAH, BET SHE'S SCREAM-ING THAT RIGHT NOW.
UM-- COULD YOU REFRESH MY MEMORY...
...WHY DO YOU COMPETE FOR MARKET SHARE OVER US?

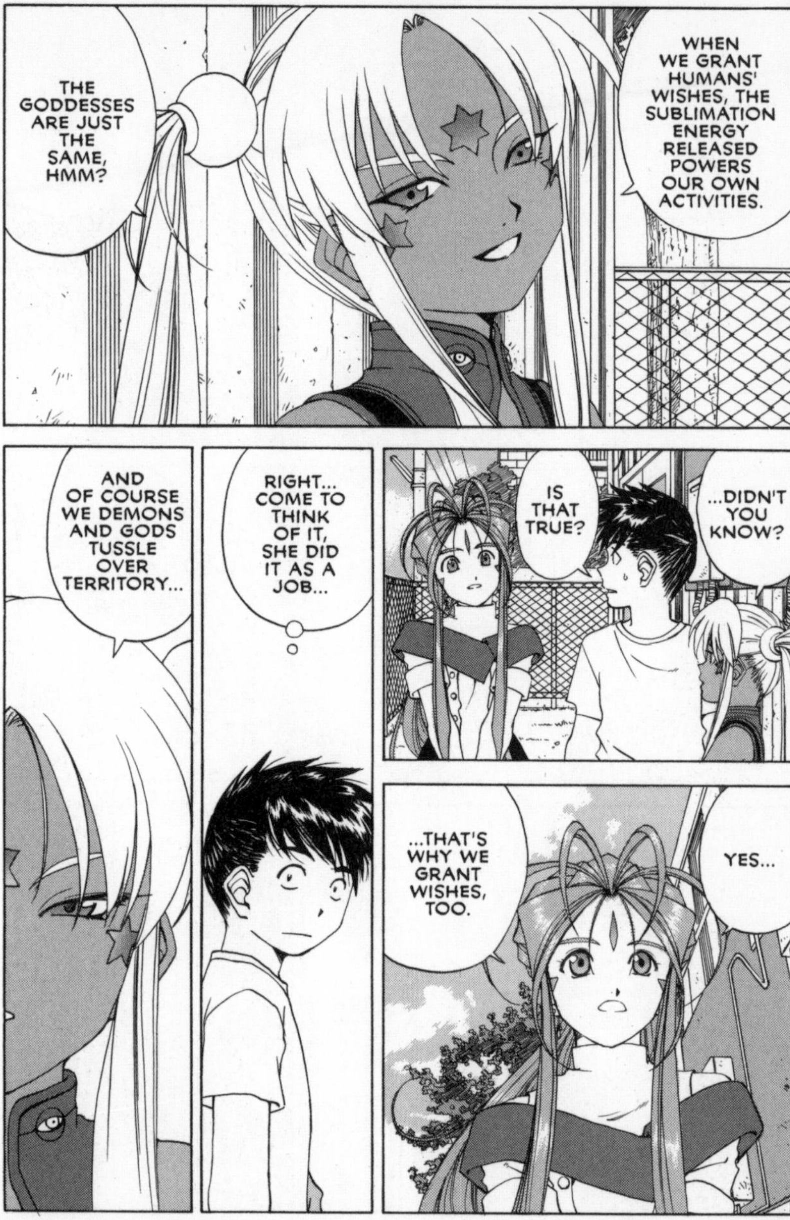
WHEN WE GRANT HUMANS' WISHES, THE SUBLIMATION ENERGY RELEASED POWERS OUR OWN ACTIVITIES.
THE GODDESSES ARE JUST THE SAME, HMM?
...DIDN'T YOU KNOW?
IS THAT TRUE?
YES...
...THAT'S WHY WE GRANT WISHES, TOO.
RIGHT... COME TO THINK OF IT, SHE DID IT AS A JOB...
AND OF COURSE WE DEMONS AND GODS TUSSLE OVER TERRITORY...

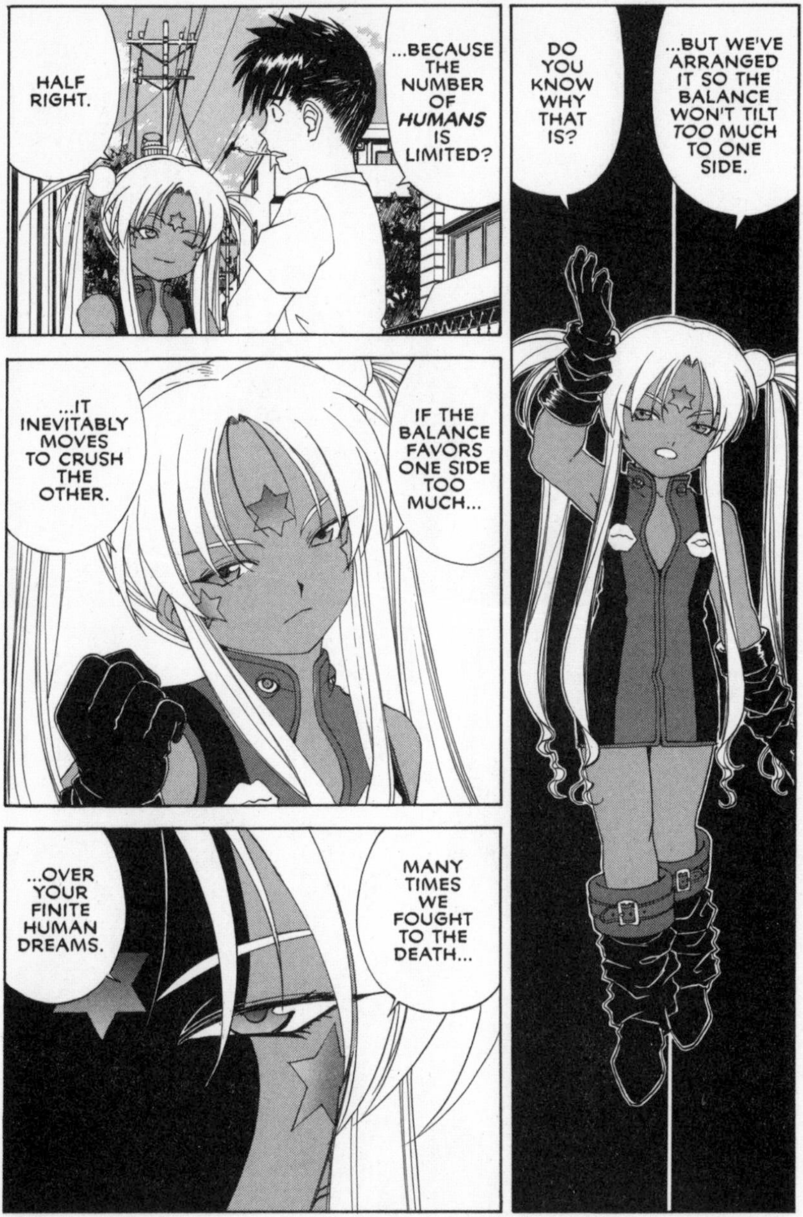
...BUT WE'VE ARRANGED IT SO THE BALANCE WON'T TILT *TOO* MUCH TO ONE SIDE.
DO YOU KNOW WHY THAT IS?
...BECAUSE THE NUMBER OF *HUMANS* IS LIMITED?
HALF RIGHT.
IF THE BALANCE FAVORS ONE SIDE TOO MUCH...
...IT INEVITABLY MOVES TO CRUSH THE OTHER.
MANY TIMES WE FOUGHT TO THE DEATH...
...OVER YOUR FINITE HUMAN DREAMS.

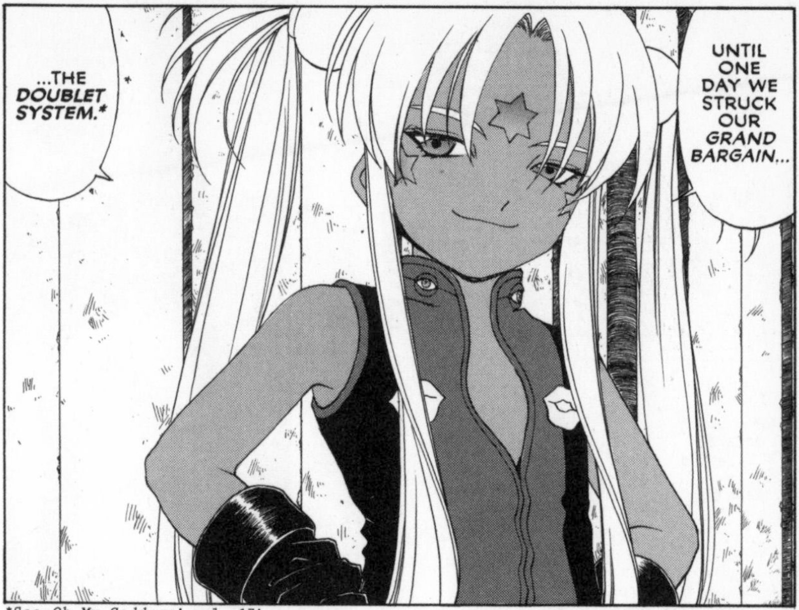
UNTIL ONE DAY WE STRUCK OUR *GRAND BARGAIN*...
...THE *DOUBLET SYSTEM.**

*See *Oh My Goddess!* vol. 17!

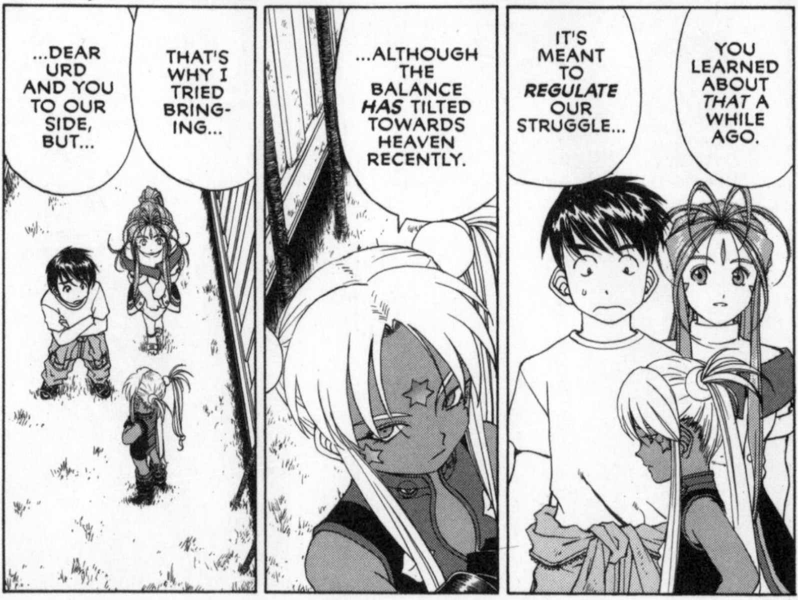
YOU LEARNED ABOUT *THAT* A WHILE AGO.
IT'S MEANT TO *REGULATE* OUR STRUGGLE...
...ALTHOUGH THE BALANCE *HAS* TILTED TOWARDS HEAVEN RECENTLY.
THAT'S WHY I TRIED BRING-ING...
...DEAR URD AND YOU TO OUR SIDE, BUT...

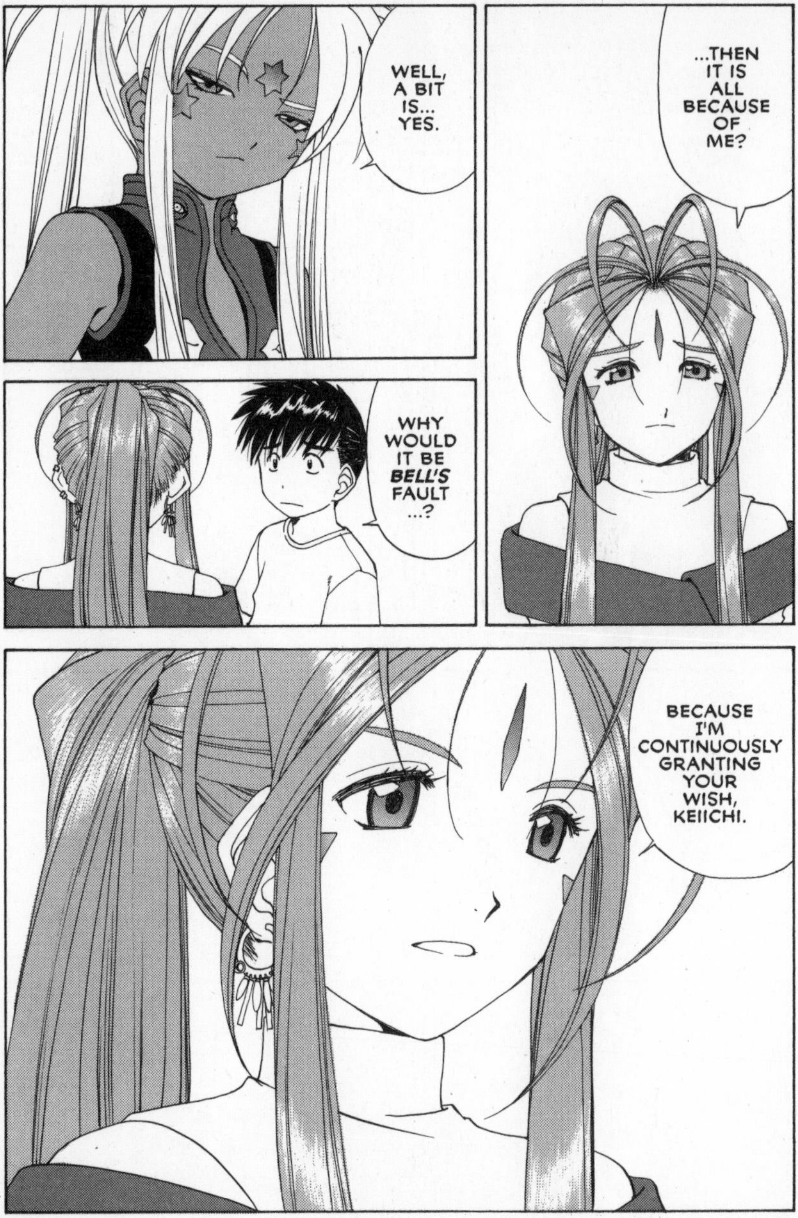
...THEN IT IS ALL BECAUSE OF ME?
WELL, A BIT IS... YES.
WHY WOULD IT BE *BELL'S* FAULT ...?
BECAUSE I'M CONTINUOUSLY GRANTING YOUR WISH, KEIICHI.

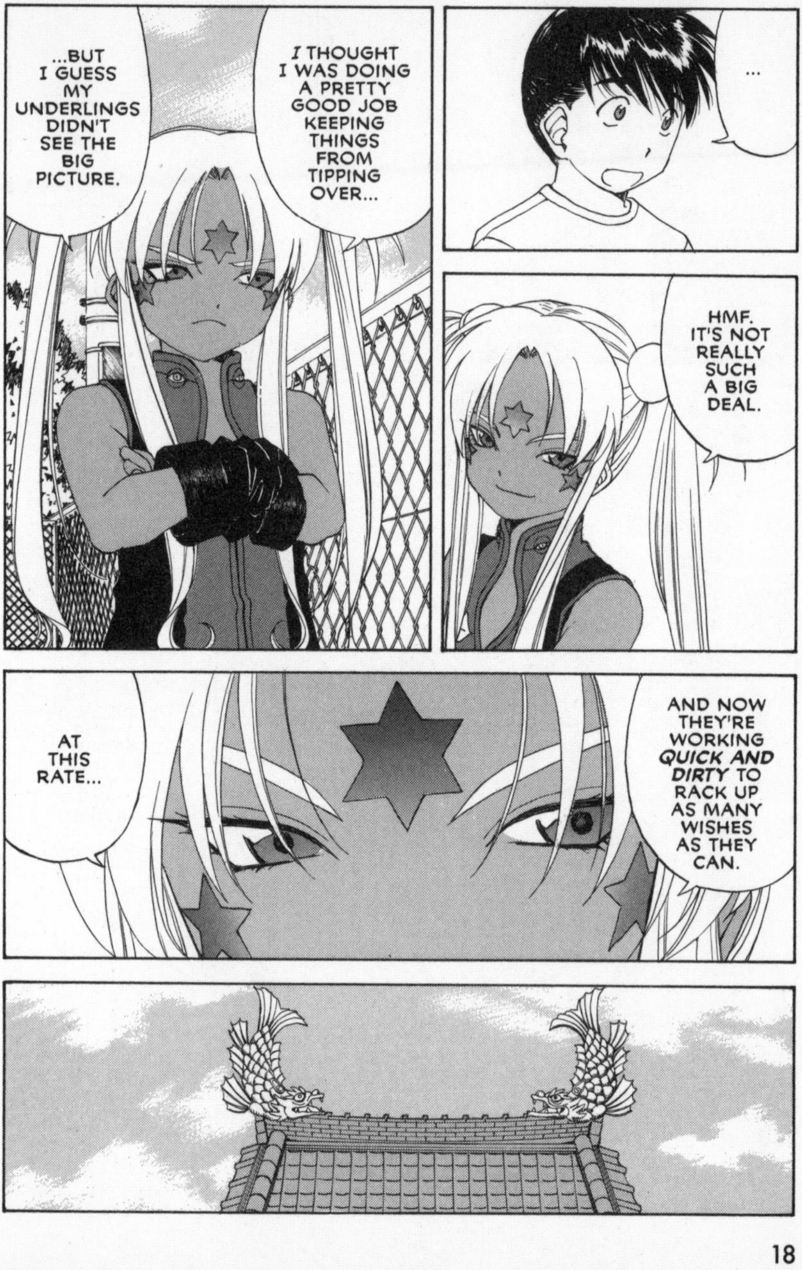
...
HMF. IT'S NOT REALLY SUCH A BIG DEAL.
I THOUGHT I WAS DOING A PRETTY GOOD JOB KEEPING THINGS FROM TIPPING OVER...
...BUT I GUESS MY UNDERLINGS DIDN'T SEE THE BIG PICTURE.
AND NOW THEY'RE WORKING ***QUICK AND DIRTY*** TO RACK UP AS MANY WISHES AS THEY CAN.
AT THIS RATE...

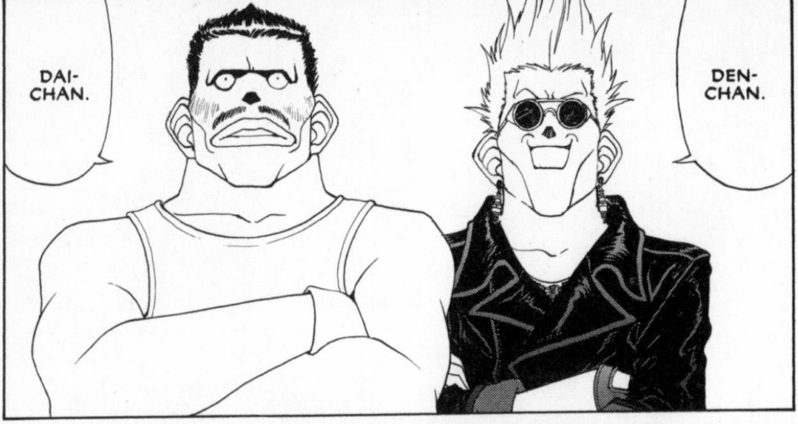
DEN-CHAN.
DAI-CHAN.

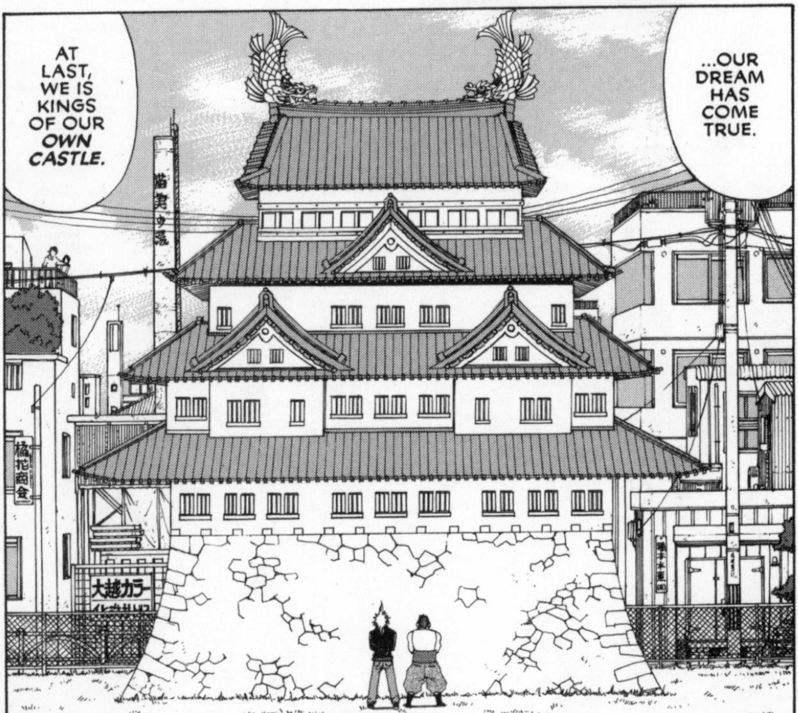
...OUR DREAM HAS COME TRUE.
AT LAST, WE IS KINGS OF OUR *OWN CASTLE.*
大越カラー

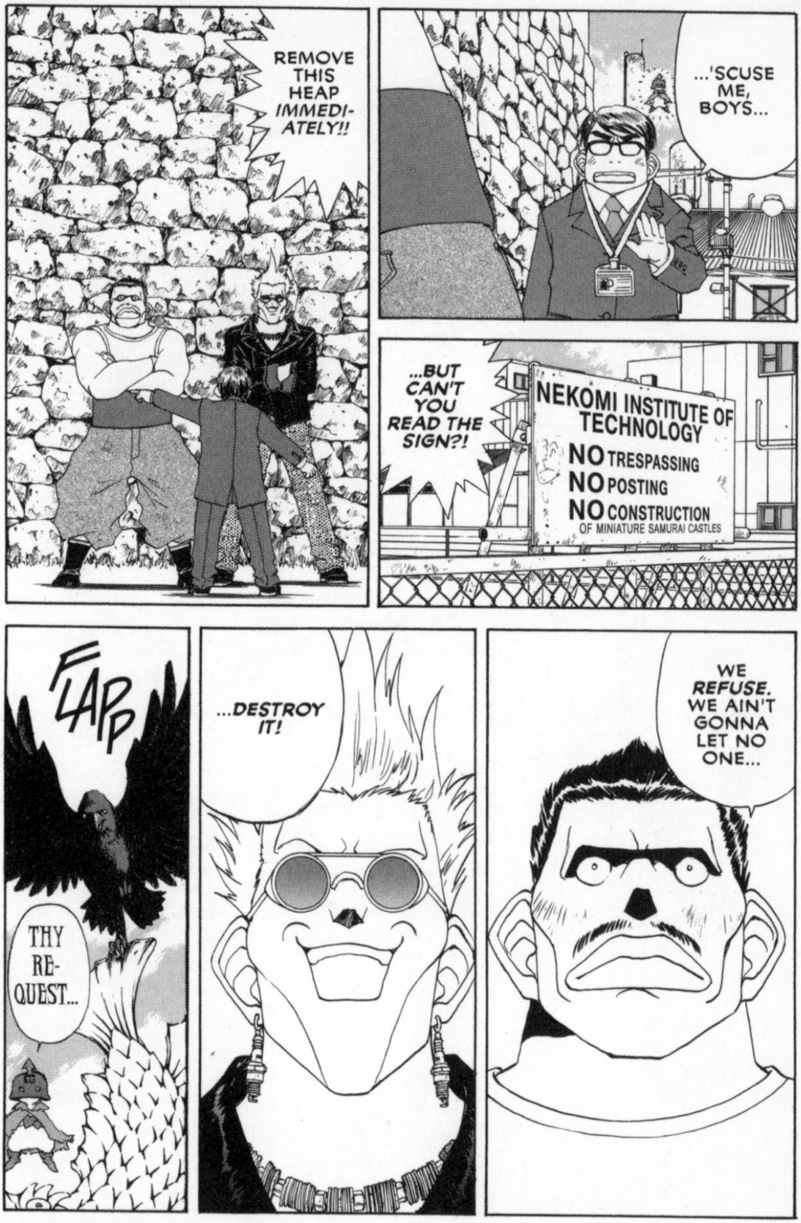
...'SCUSE ME, BOYS...
...BUT CAN'T YOU READ THE SIGN?!
NEKOMI INSTITUTE OF TECHNOLOGY
NO TRESPASSING
NO POSTING
NO CONSTRUCTION OF MINIATURE SAMURAI CASTLES
REMOVE THIS HEAP IMMEDIATELY!!
WE REFUSE. WE AIN'T GONNA LET NO ONE...
...DESTROY IT!
FLAPP
THY REQUEST...

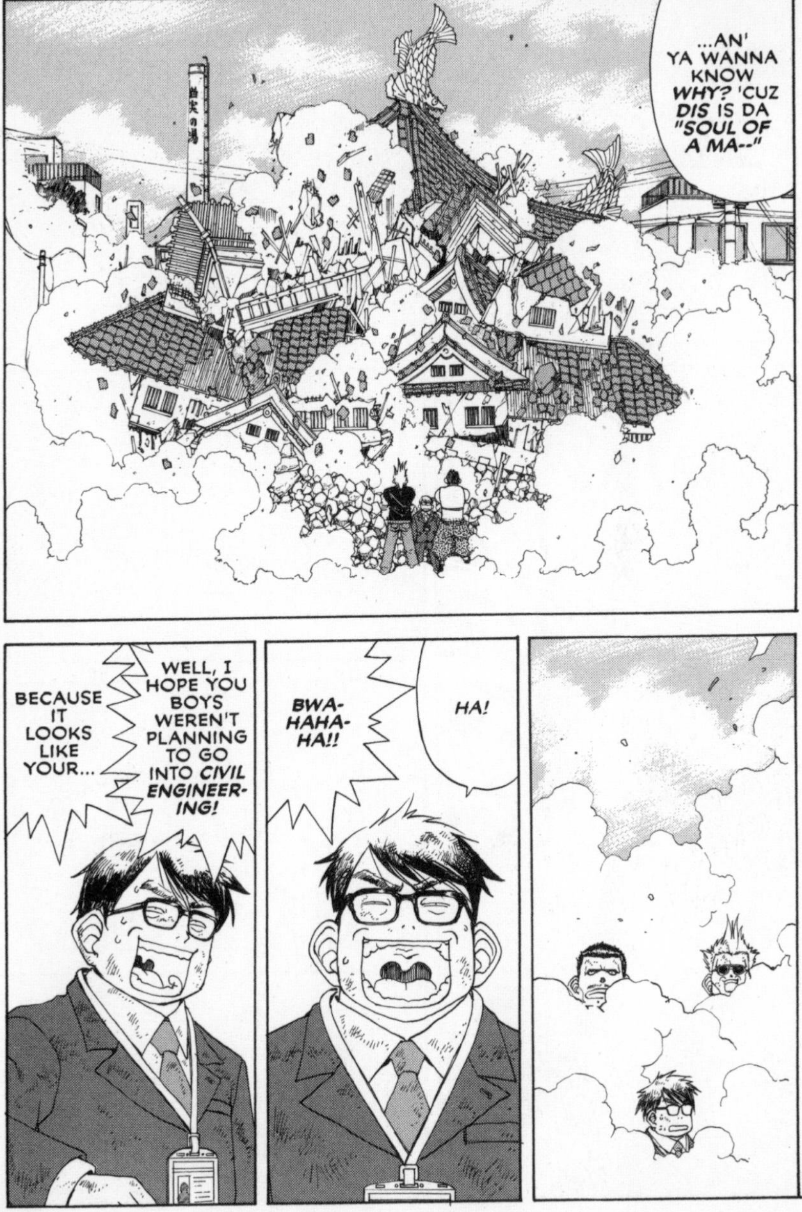
...AN' YA WANNA KNOW *WHY?* 'CUZ *DIS* IS DA *"SOUL OF A MA--"*
HA!
BWA-HAHAHA-HA!!
WELL, I HOPE YOU BOYS WEREN'T PLANNING TO GO INTO *CIVIL ENGINEERING!*
BECAUSE IT LOOKS LIKE YOUR...

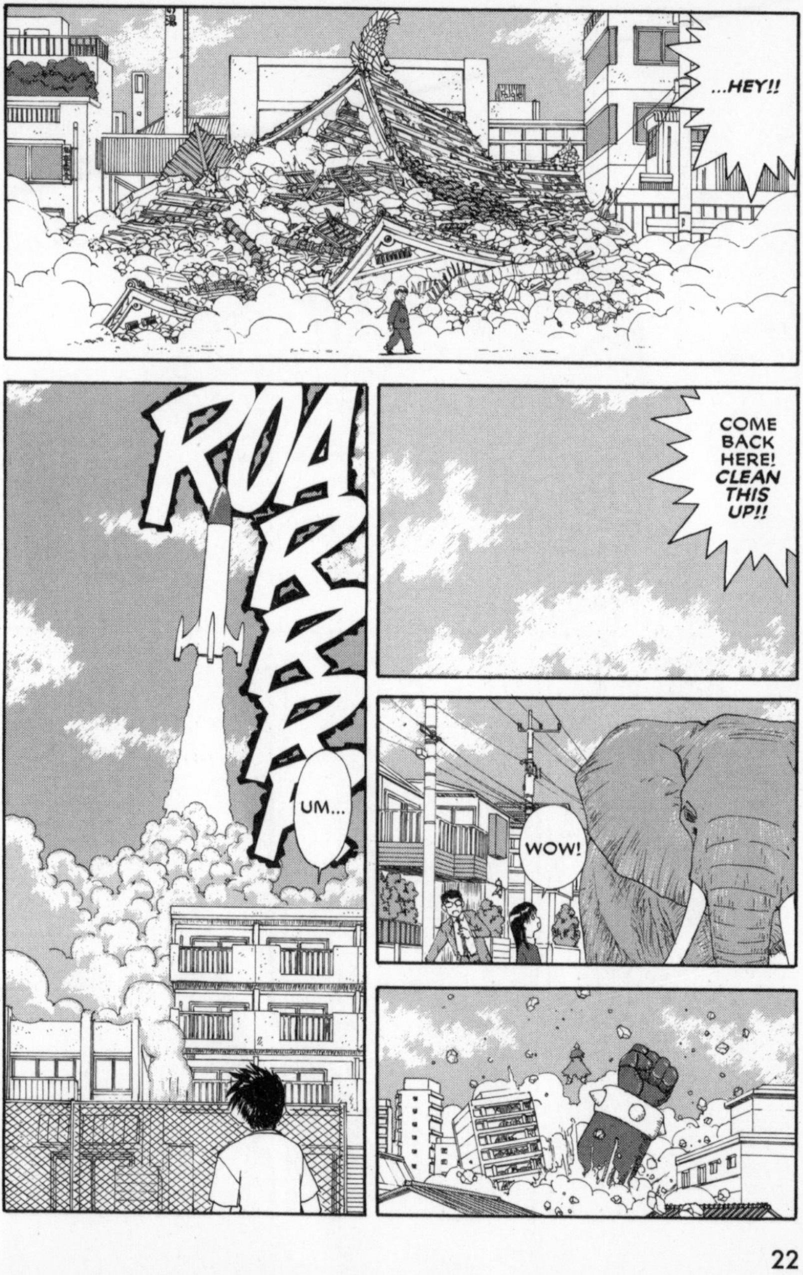
...HEY!!
COME BACK HERE! CLEAN THIS UP!!
WOW!
ROARRRR
UM...

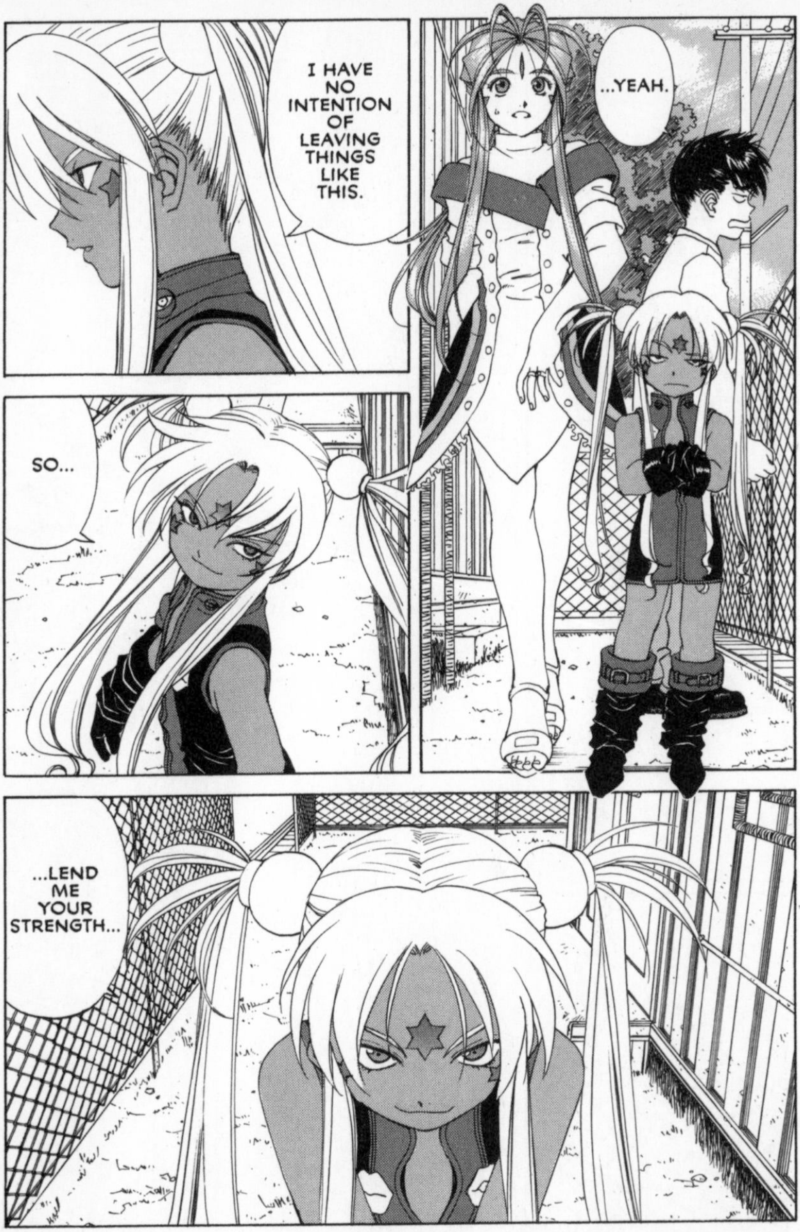
...YEAH.
I HAVE NO INTENTION OF LEAVING THINGS LIKE THIS.
SO...
...LEND ME YOUR STRENGTH...

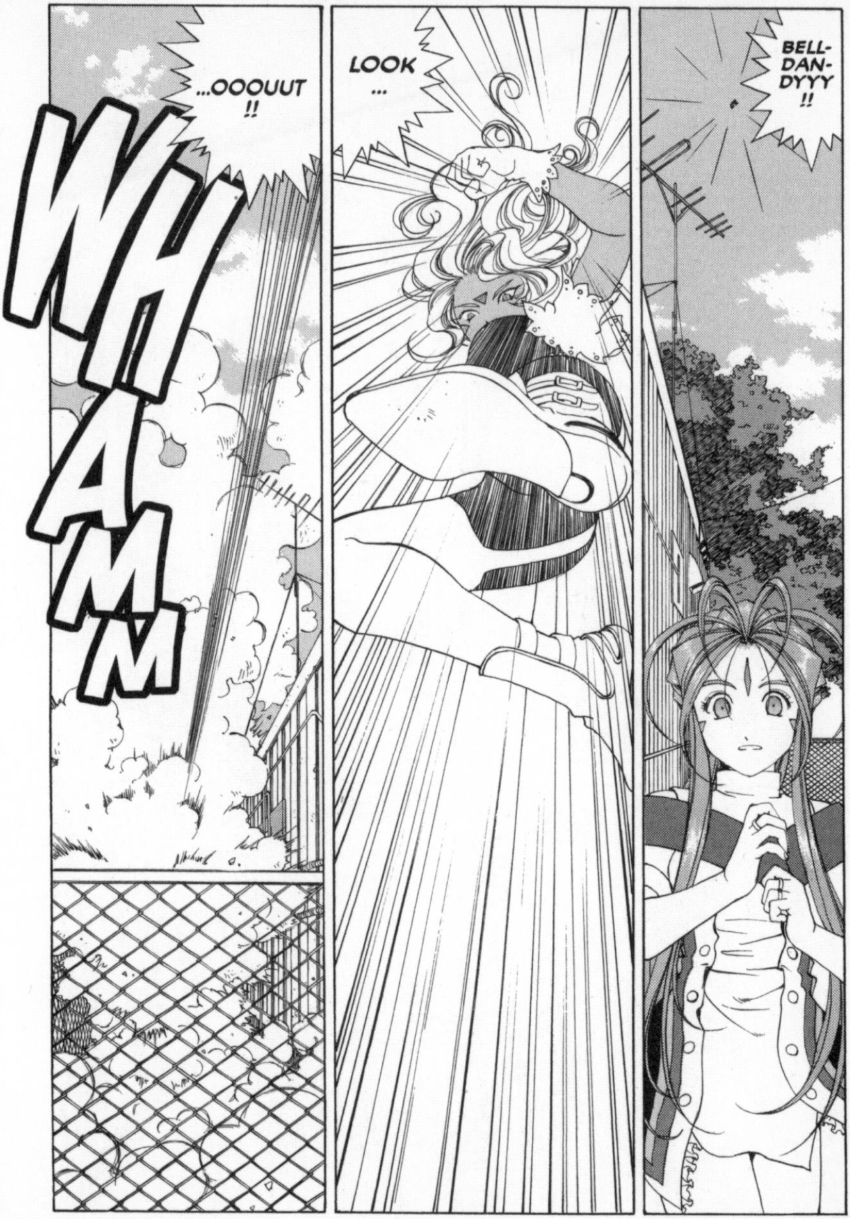
BELL-DANDYYY !!
LOOK ...
...OOOUUT !!
WHAMM

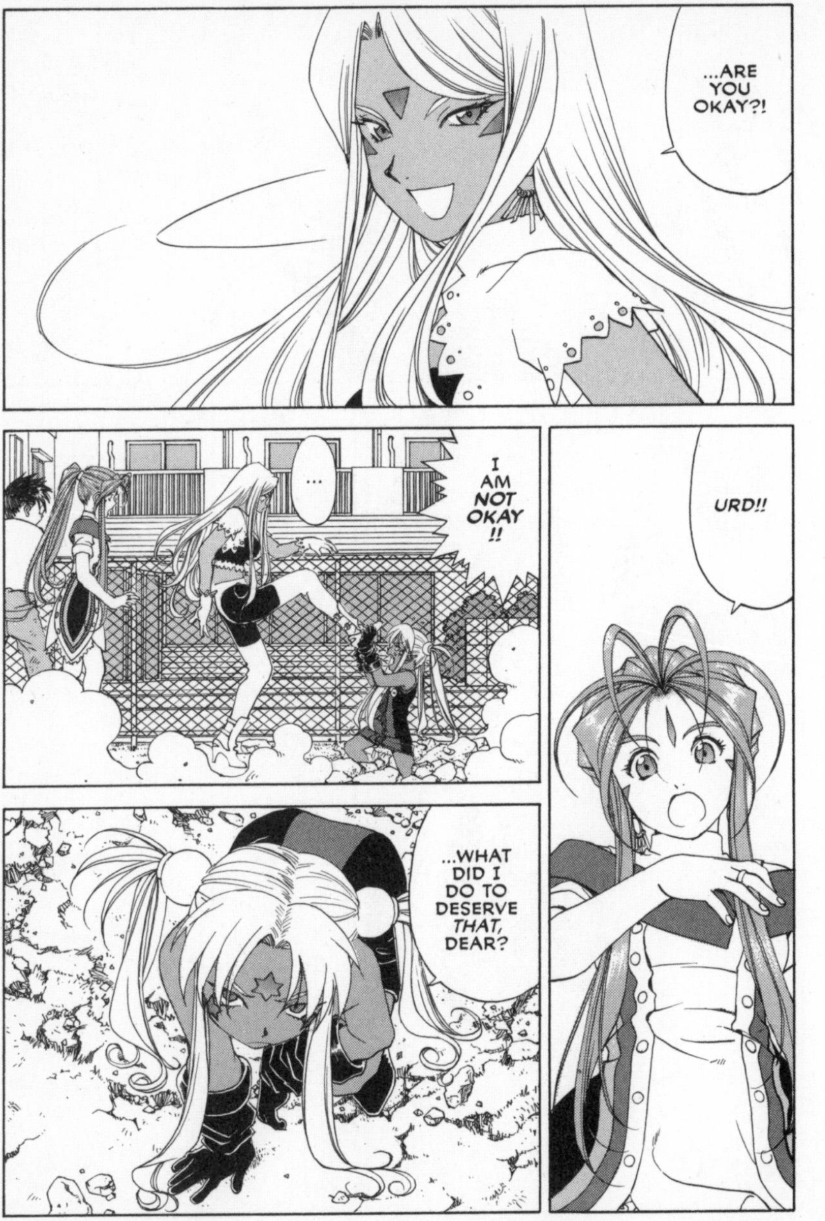
...ARE YOU OKAY?!
URD!!
I AM *NOT OKAY* !!
...
...WHAT DID I DO TO DESERVE *THAT*, DEAR?

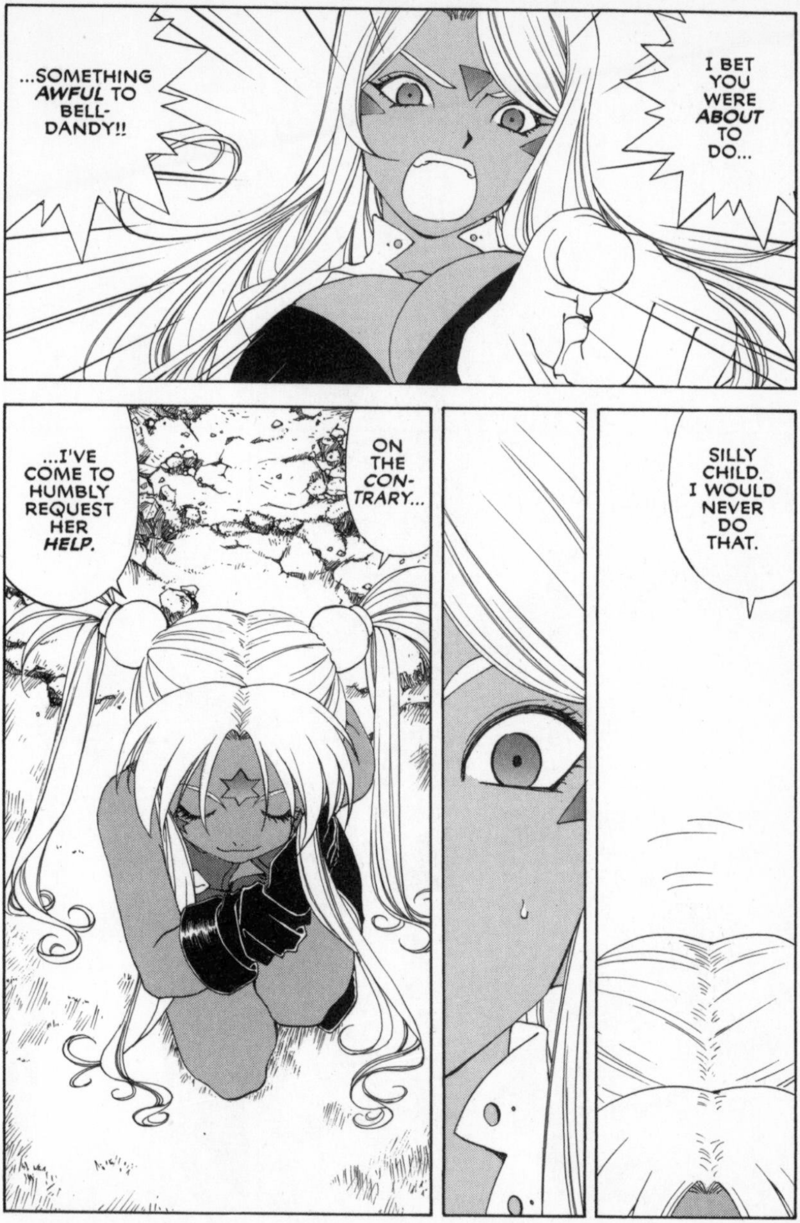
I BET YOU WERE ABOUT TO DO...
...SOMETHING AWFUL TO BELL-DANDY!!
SILLY CHILD. I WOULD NEVER DO THAT.
ON THE CON-TRARY...
...I'VE COME TO HUMBLY REQUEST HER HELP.

CHAPTER 244

The Closing World

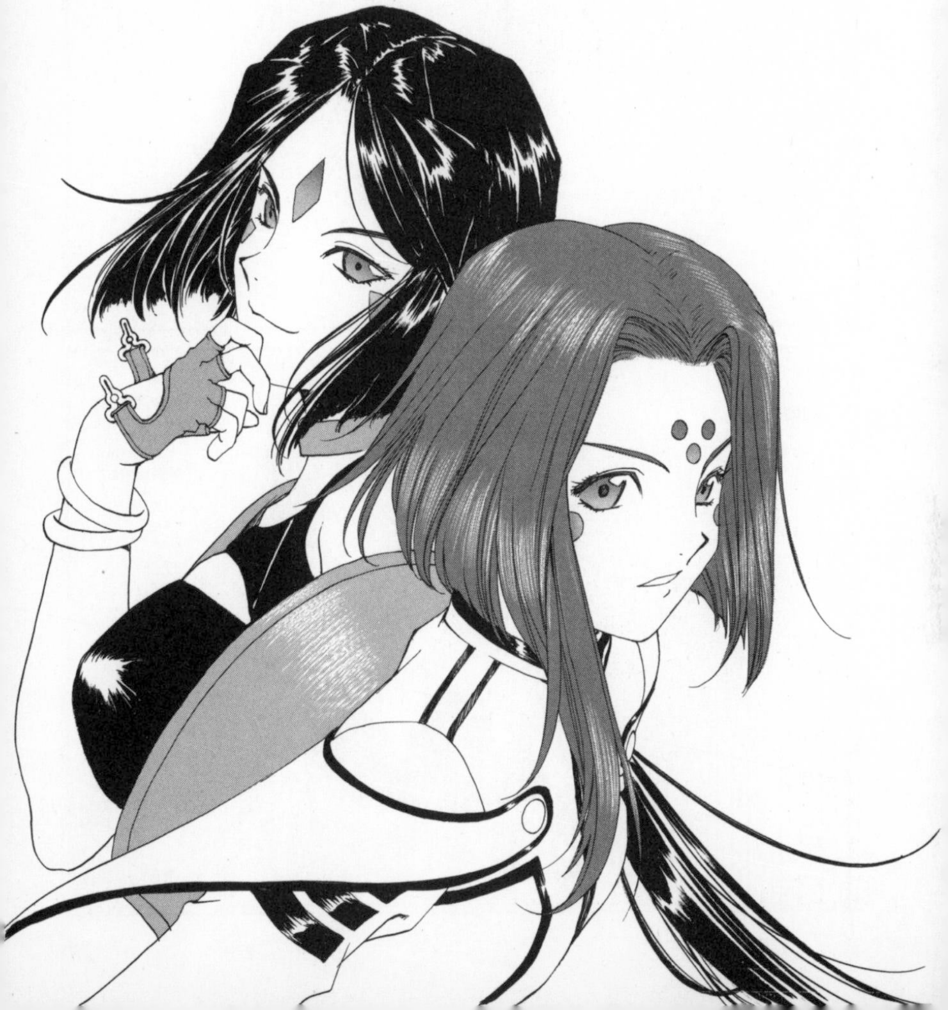

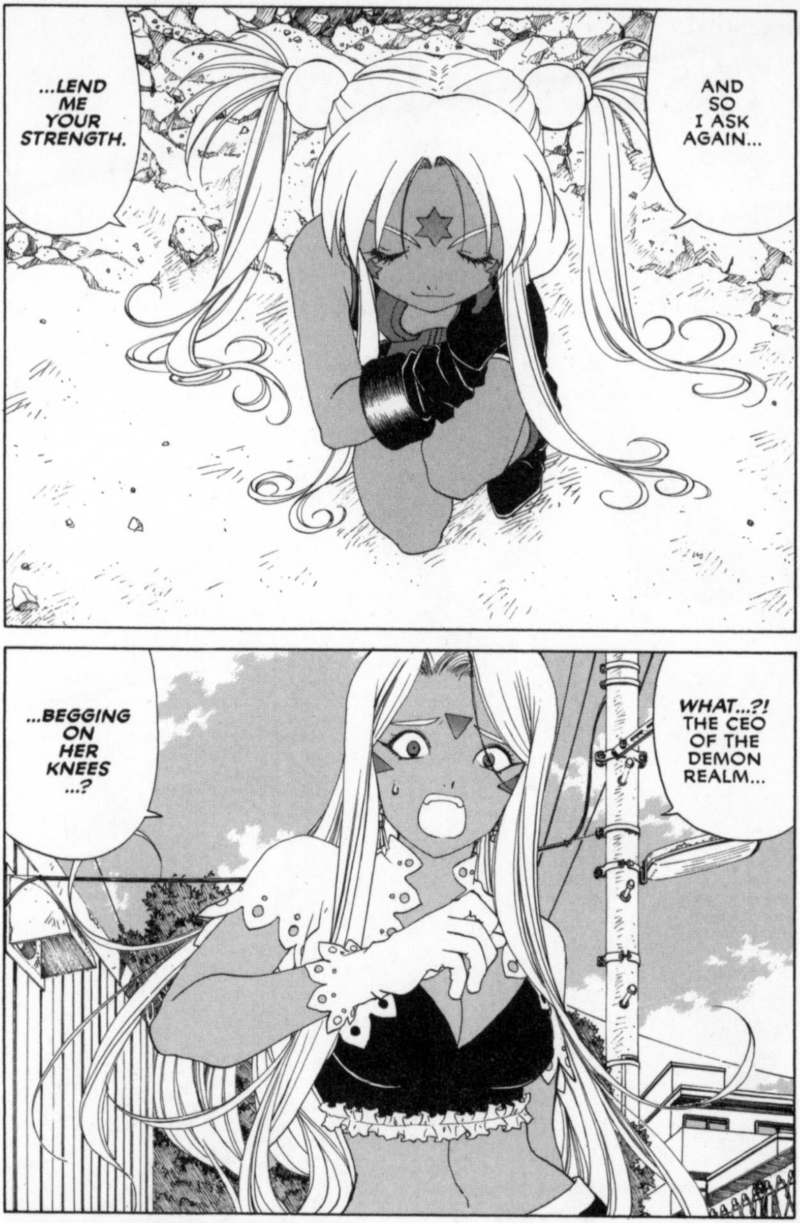
AND SO I ASK AGAIN...
...LEND ME YOUR STRENGTH.
WHAT...?! THE CEO OF THE DEMON REALM...
...BEGGING ON HER KNEES ...?

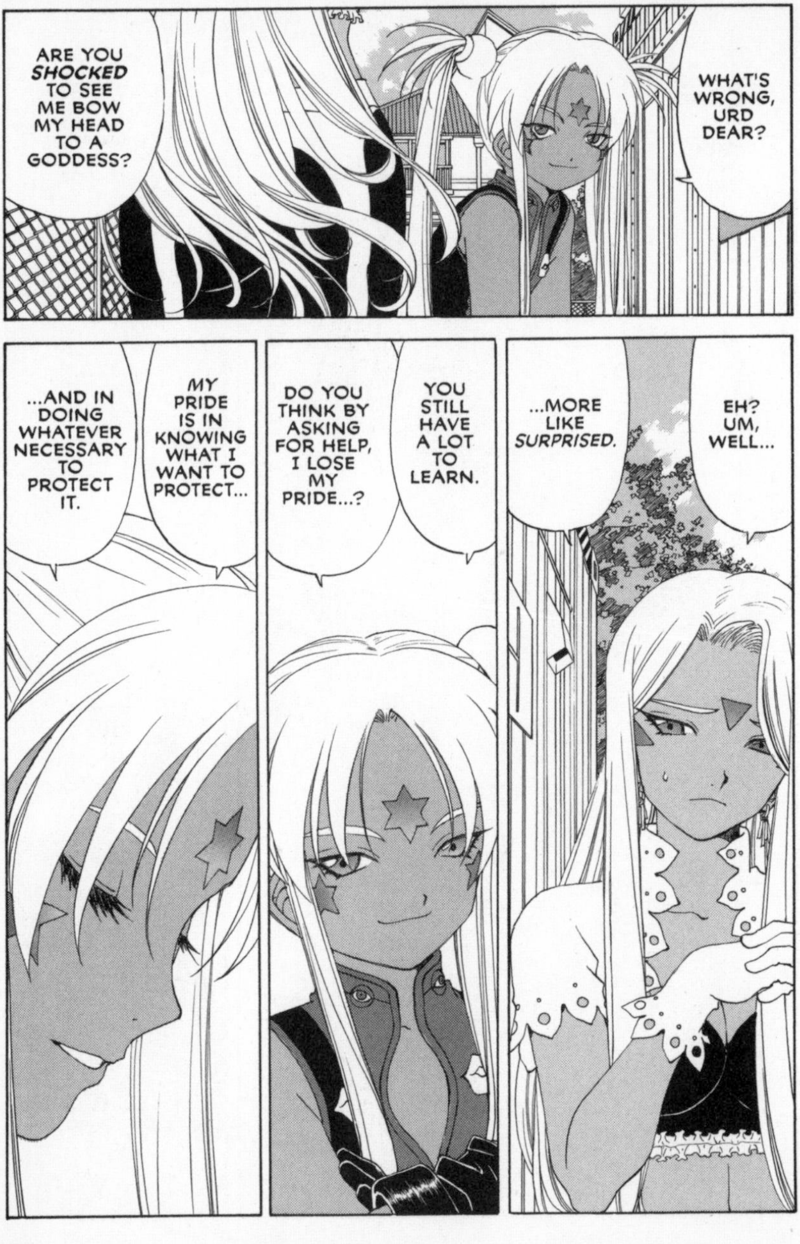
WHAT'S WRONG, URD DEAR?
ARE YOU *SHOCKED* TO SEE ME BOW MY HEAD TO A GODDESS?
EH? UM, WELL...
...MORE LIKE *SURPRISED.*
YOU STILL HAVE A LOT TO LEARN.
DO YOU THINK BY ASKING FOR HELP, I LOSE MY PRIDE...?
MY PRIDE IS IN KNOWING WHAT I WANT TO PROTECT...
...AND IN DOING WHATEVER NECESSARY TO PROTECT IT.

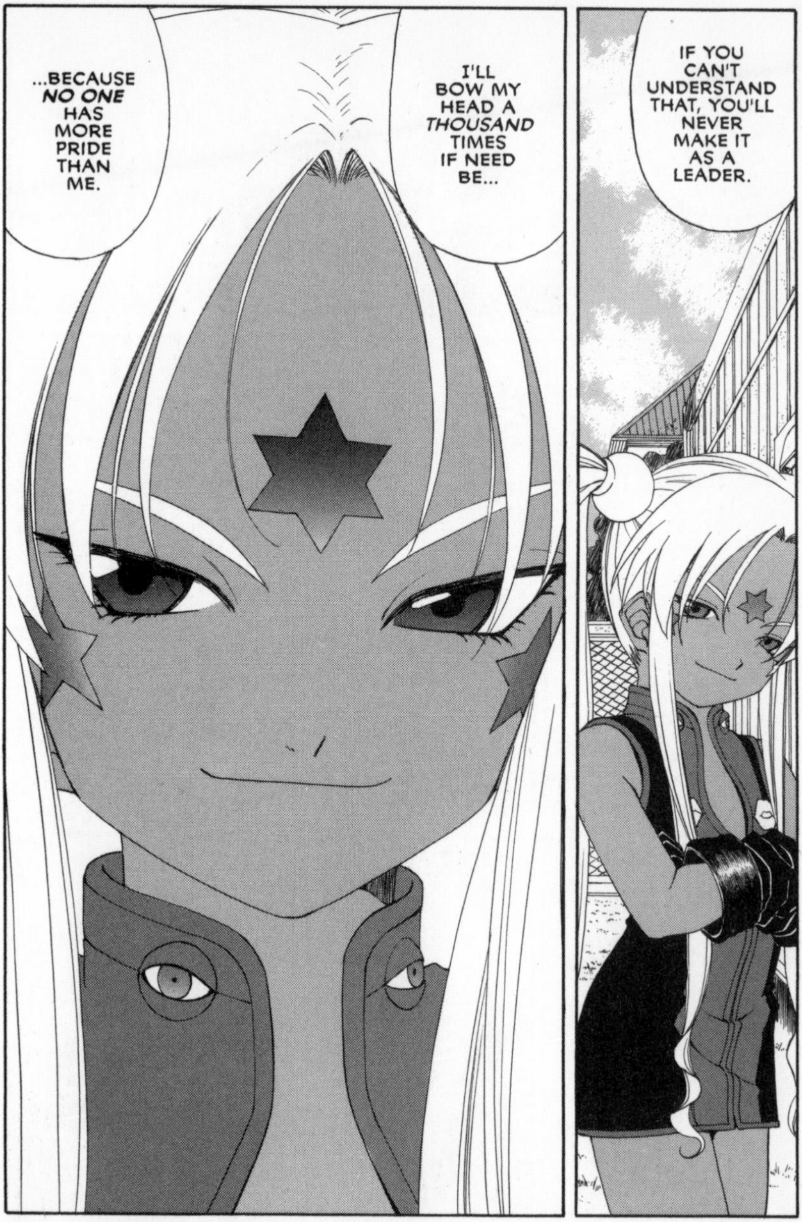
IF YOU CAN'T UNDERSTAND THAT, YOU'LL NEVER MAKE IT AS A LEADER.
I'LL BOW MY HEAD A *THOUSAND* TIMES IF NEED BE...
...BECAUSE ***NO ONE*** HAS MORE PRIDE THAN ME.

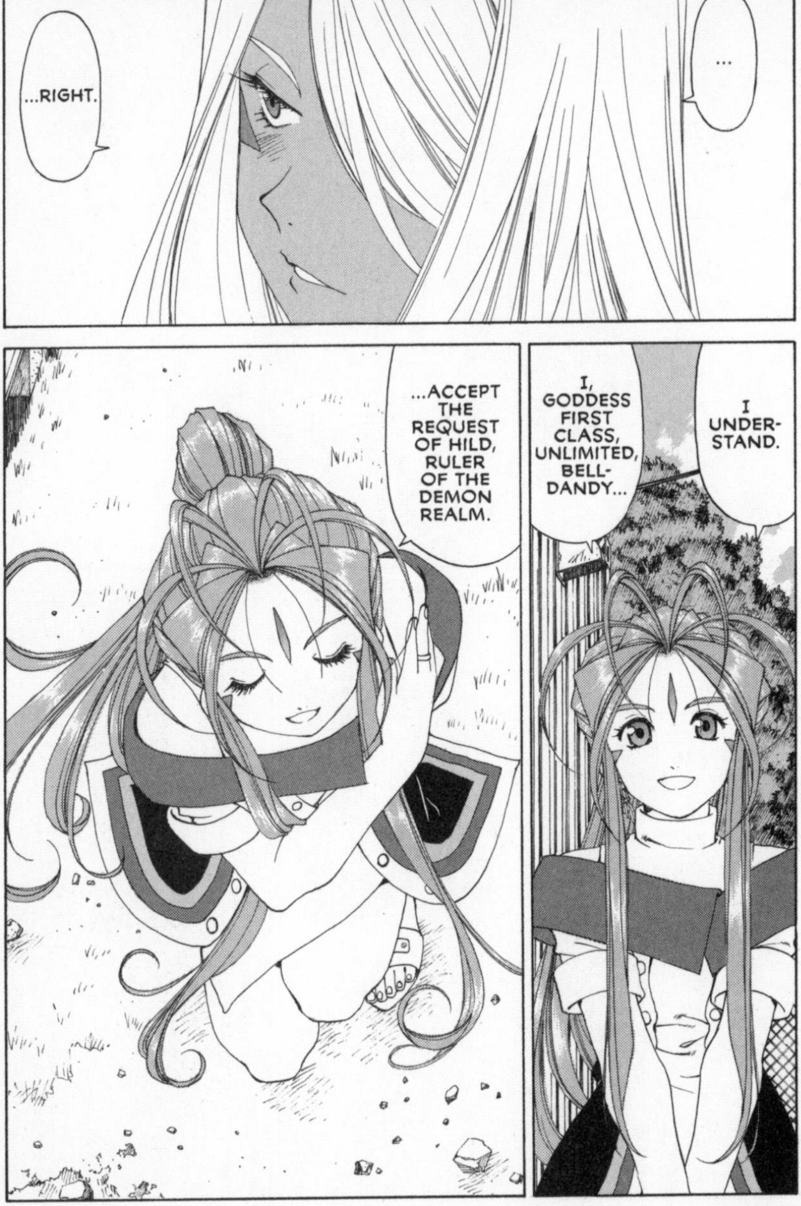
...
...RIGHT.
I UNDERSTAND.
I, GODDESS FIRST CLASS, UNLIMITED, BELLDANDY...
...ACCEPT THE REQUEST OF HILD, RULER OF THE DEMON REALM.

...EVEN IF I HAVE TO GO TO HELL...!

I'LL DO MY BEST...

EH?

CAN A *HUMAN BEING* ACCOMPANY YOU...?

HEY.

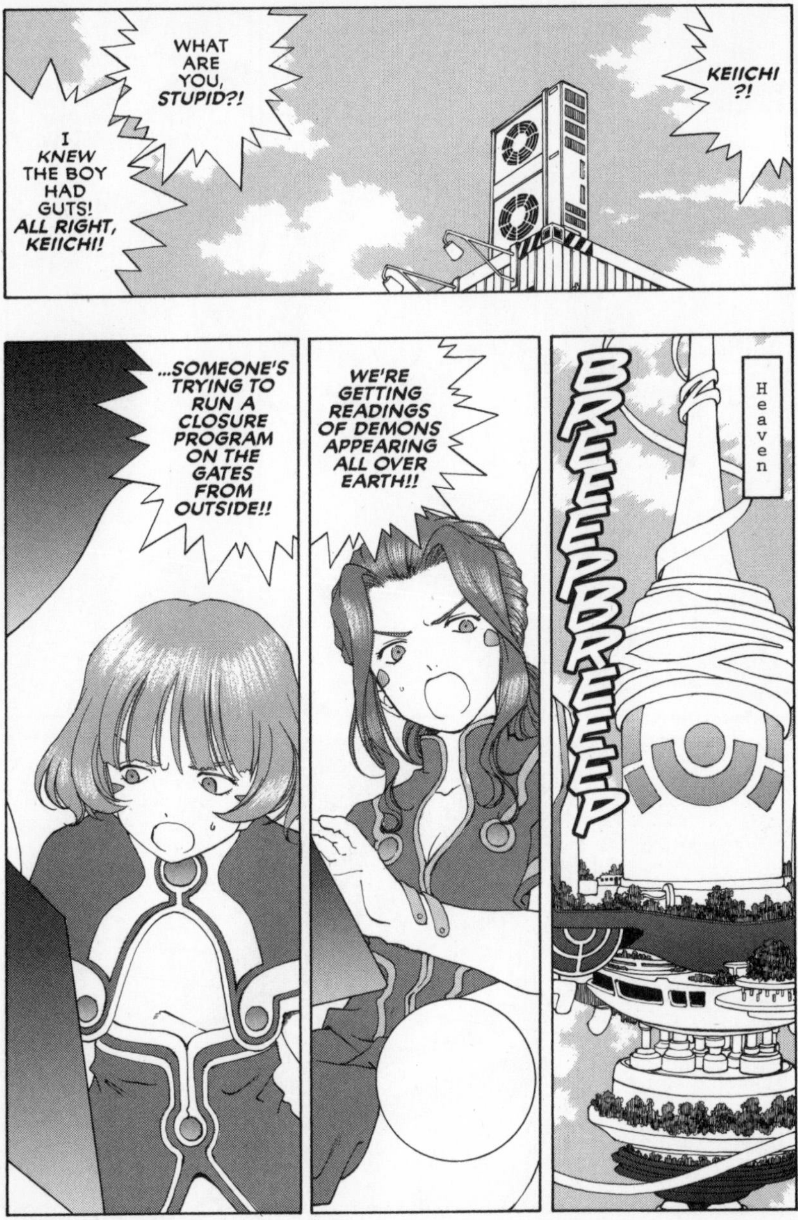
KEIICHI ?!
WHAT ARE YOU, STUPID?!
I KNEW THE BOY HAD GUTS! ALL RIGHT, KEIICHI!
Heaven
BREEEPBREEEP
WE'RE GETTING READINGS OF DEMONS APPEARING ALL OVER EARTH!!
...SOMEONE'S TRYING TO RUN A CLOSURE PROGRAM ON THE GATES FROM OUTSIDE!!

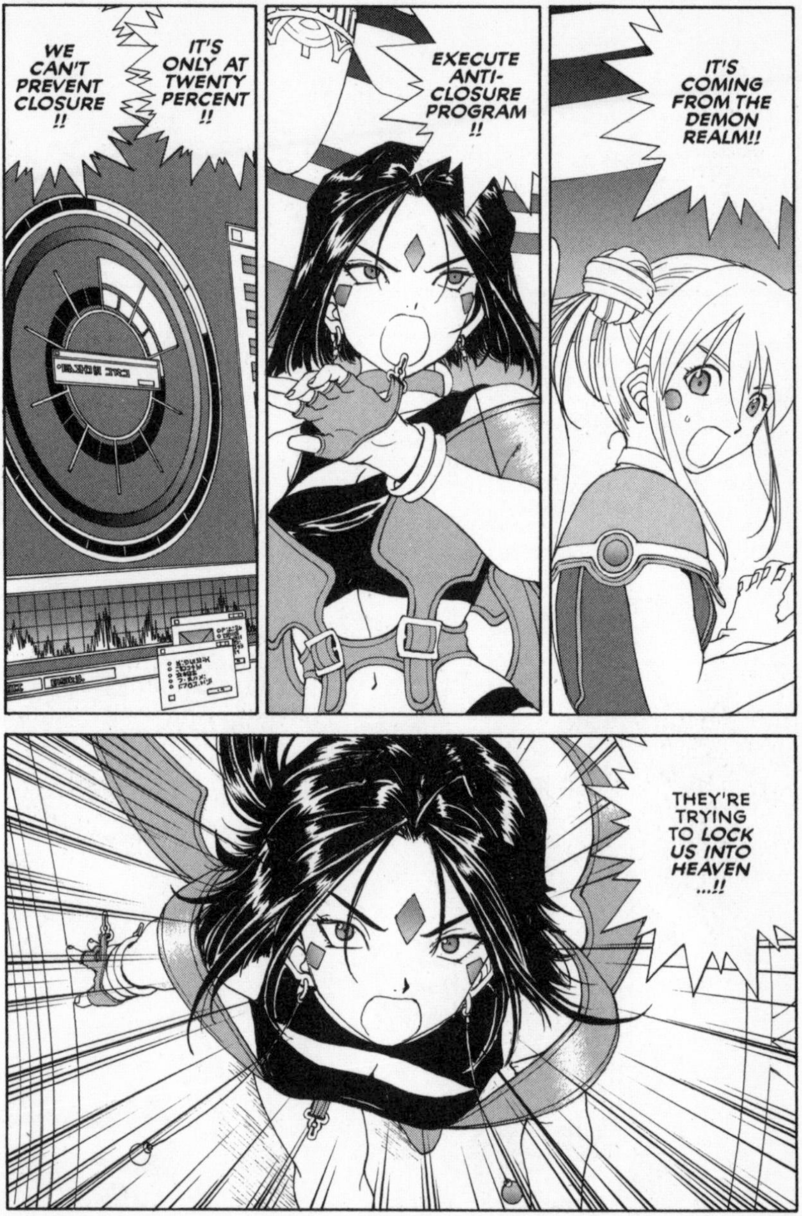
IT'S COMING FROM THE DEMON REALM!!
EXECUTE ANTI-CLOSURE PROGRAM!!
IT'S ONLY AT TWENTY PERCENT!!
WE CAN'T PREVENT CLOSURE!!
THEY'RE TRYING TO LOCK US INTO HEAVEN ...!!

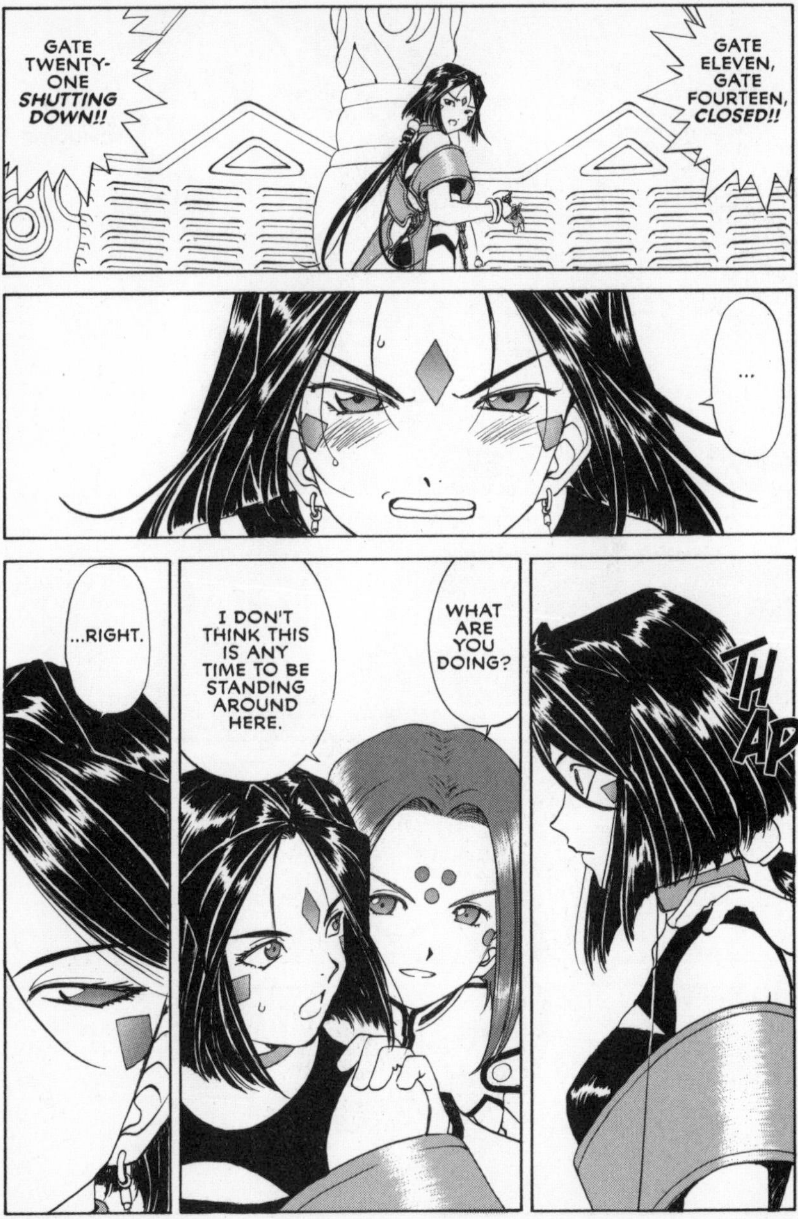
GATE ELEVEN, GATE FOURTEEN, CLOSED!!
GATE TWENTY-ONE SHUTTING DOWN!!
...
THAP
WHAT ARE YOU DOING?
I DON'T THINK THIS IS ANY TIME TO BE STANDING AROUND HERE.
...RIGHT.

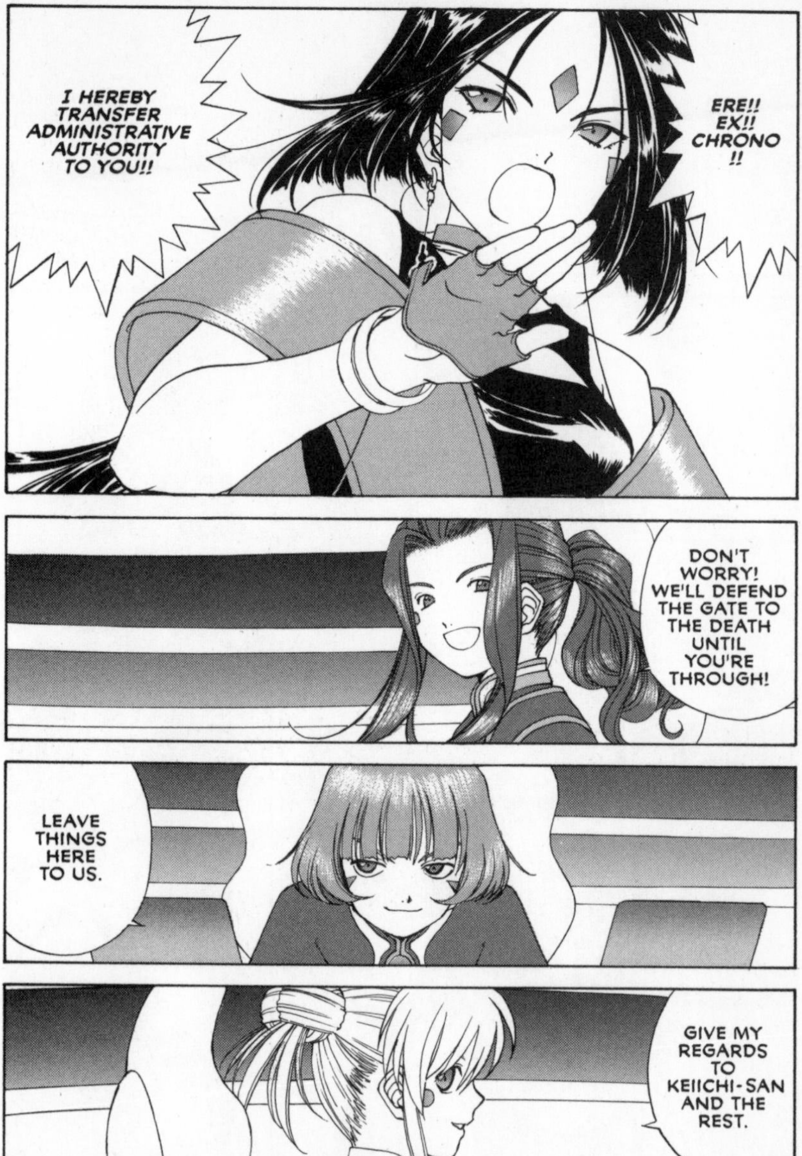
ERE!! EX!! CHRONO !!
I HEREBY TRANSFER ADMINISTRATIVE AUTHORITY TO YOU!!
DON'T WORRY! WE'LL DEFEND THE GATE TO THE DEATH UNTIL YOU'RE THROUGH!
LEAVE THINGS HERE TO US.
GIVE MY REGARDS TO KEIICHI-SAN AND THE REST.

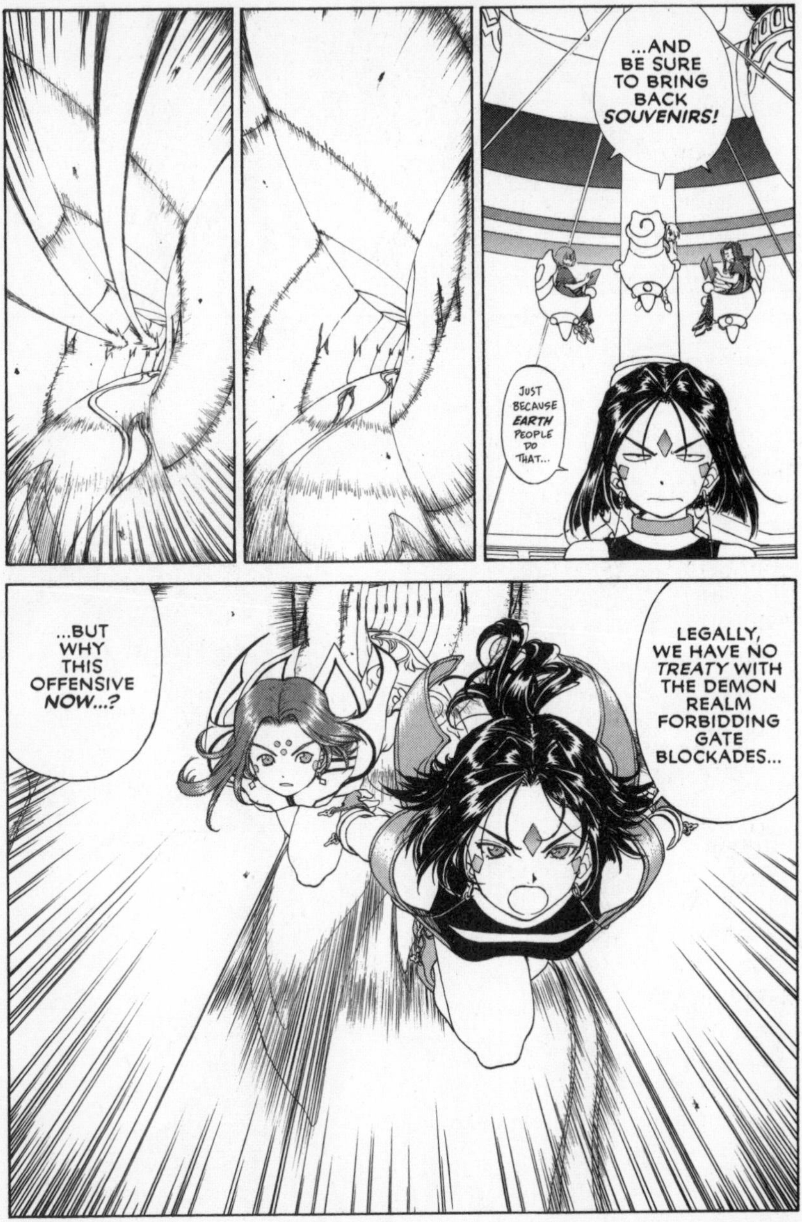
...AND BE SURE TO BRING BACK SOUVENIRS!
JUST BECAUSE EARTH PEOPLE DO THAT...
LEGALLY, WE HAVE NO TREATY WITH THE DEMON REALM FORBIDDING GATE BLOCKADES...
...BUT WHY THIS OFFENSIVE NOW...?

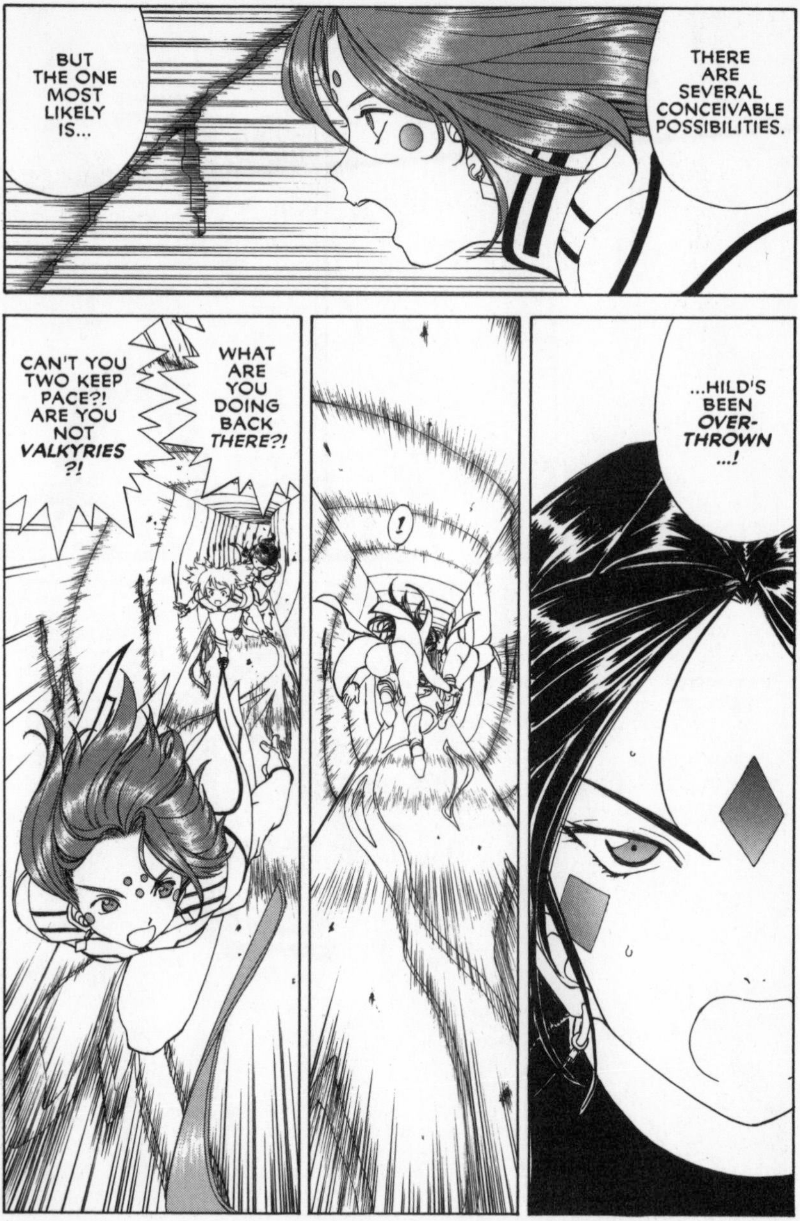
THERE ARE SEVERAL CONCEIVABLE POSSIBILITIES.
BUT THE ONE MOST LIKELY IS...
...HILD'S BEEN *OVER-THROWN* ...!
!
WHAT ARE YOU DOING BACK *THERE?!*
CAN'T YOU TWO KEEP PACE?! ARE YOU NOT *VALKYRIES ?!*

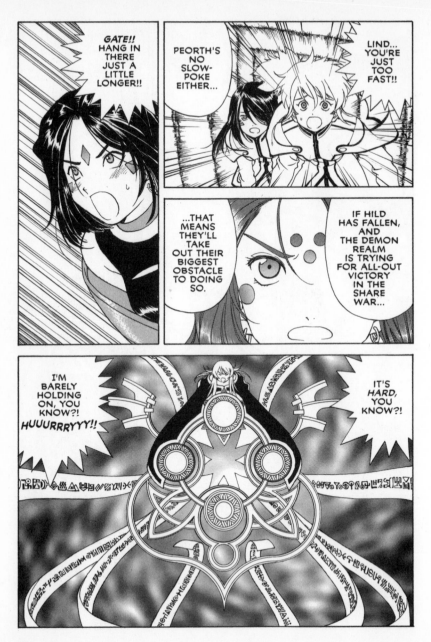

LIND... YOU'RE JUST TOO FAST!!
PEORTH'S NO SLOW-POKE EITHER...
IF HILD HAS FALLEN, AND THE DEMON REALM IS TRYING FOR ALL-OUT VICTORY IN THE SHARE WAR...
...THAT MEANS THEY'LL TAKE OUT THEIR BIGGEST OBSTACLE TO DOING SO.
GATE!! HANG IN THERE JUST A LITTLE LONGER!!
IT'S HARD, YOU KNOW?!
I'M BARELY HOLDING ON, YOU KNOW?! HUUURRRYYY!!

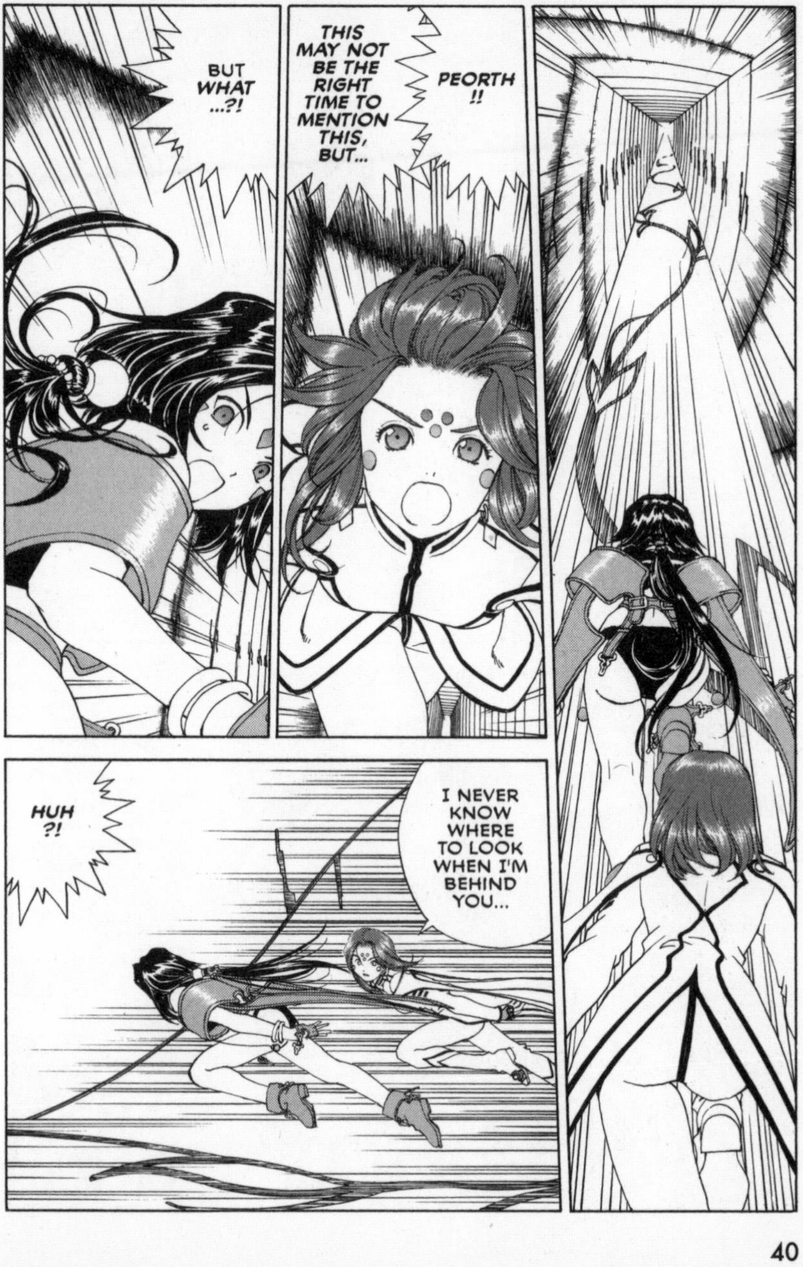
PEORTH !!
THIS MAY NOT BE THE RIGHT TIME TO MENTION THIS, BUT...
BUT WHAT ...?!
I NEVER KNOW WHERE TO LOOK WHEN I'M BEHIND YOU...
HUH ?!

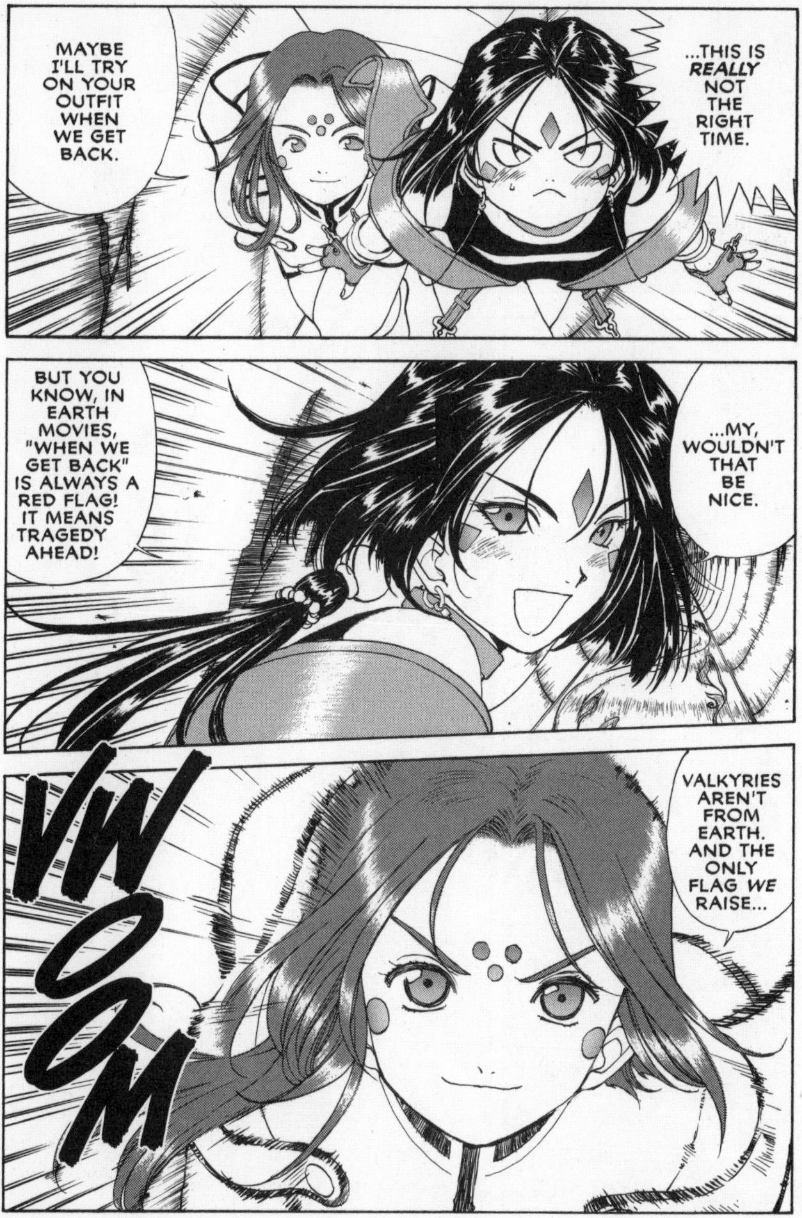
...THIS IS REALLY NOT THE RIGHT TIME.
MAYBE I'LL TRY ON YOUR OUTFIT WHEN WE GET BACK.
...MY, WOULDN'T THAT BE NICE.
BUT YOU KNOW, IN EARTH MOVIES, "WHEN WE GET BACK" IS ALWAYS A RED FLAG! IT MEANS TRAGEDY AHEAD!
VALKYRIES AREN'T FROM EARTH. AND THE ONLY FLAG WE RAISE...
VWOOM

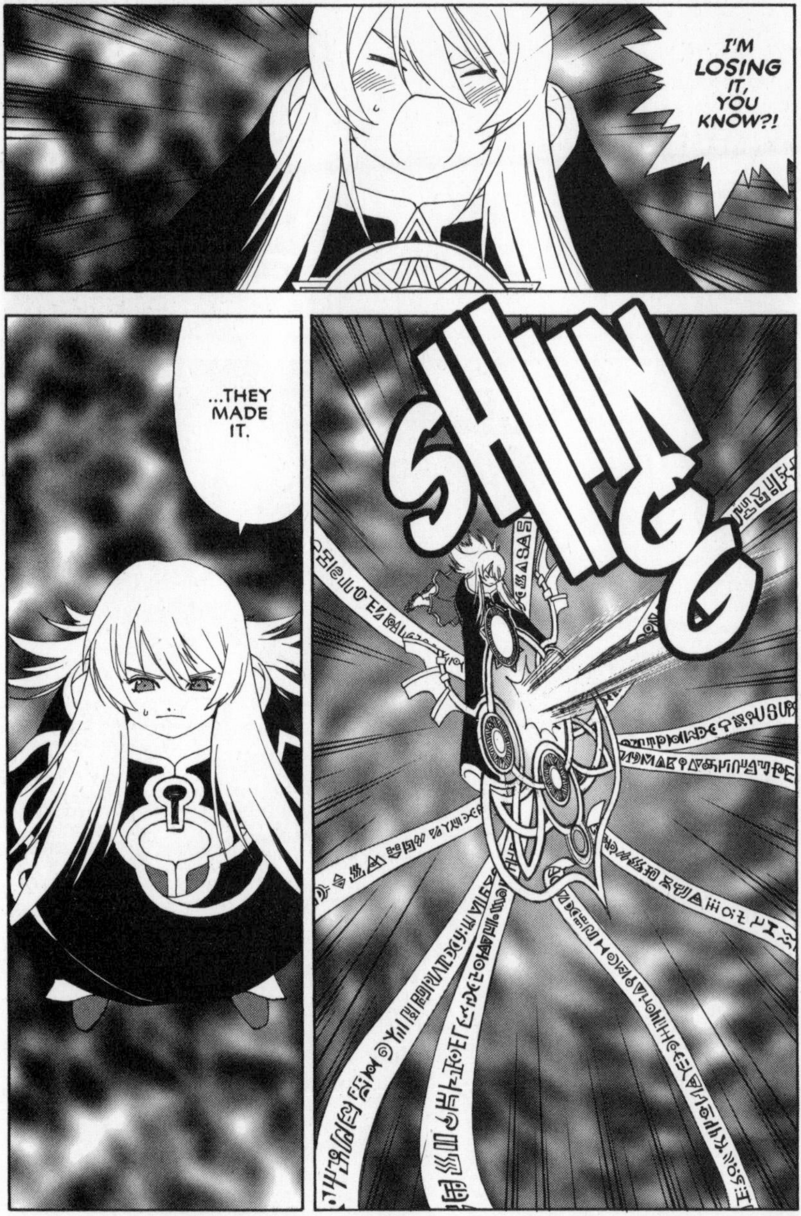
I'M LOSING IT, YOU KNOW?!
SHIIIN GG
...THEY MADE IT.

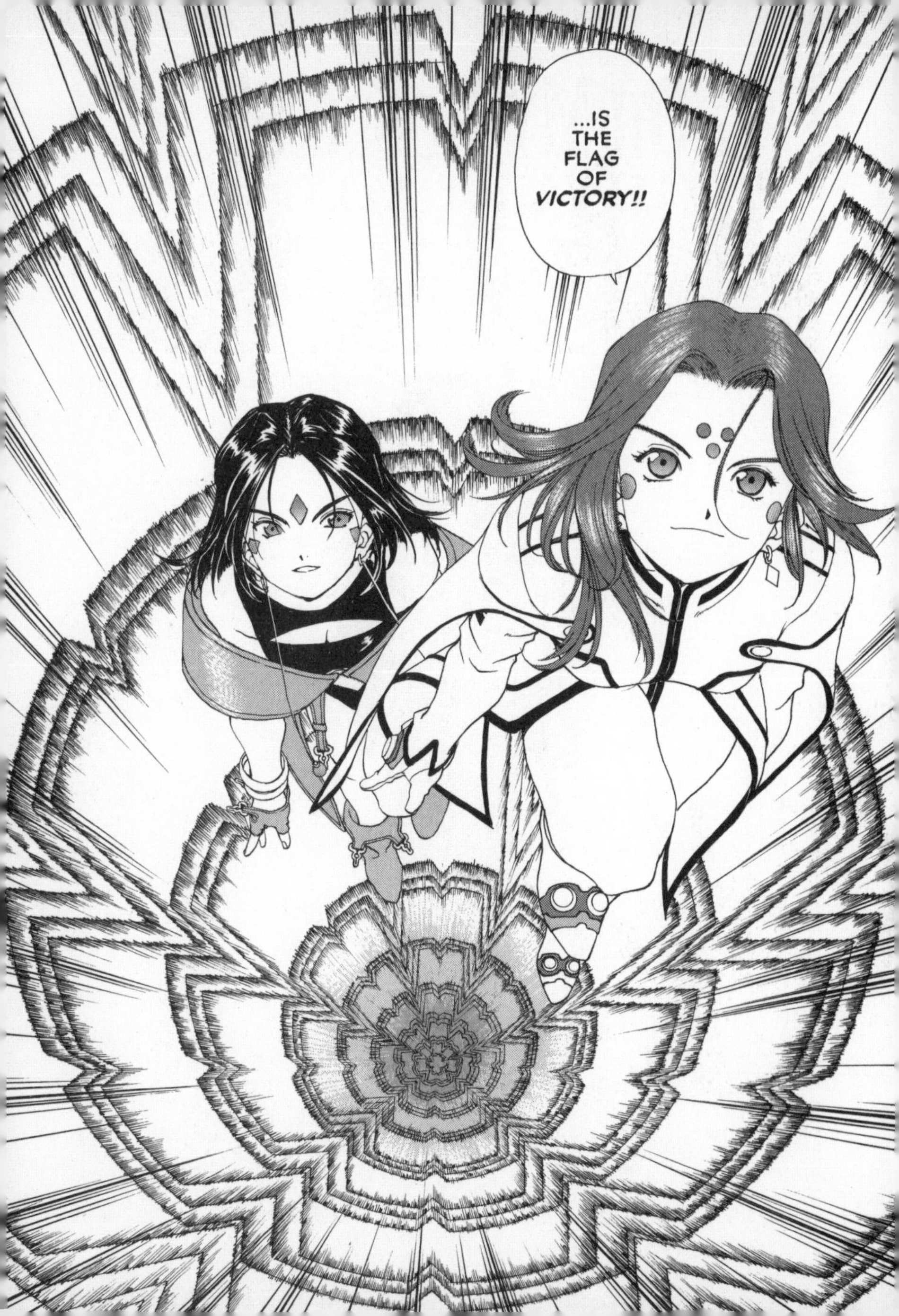
...IS THE FLAG OF VICTORY!!

OH MY GODDESS!
TOSHIYUKI AOSHIMA

CHAPTER 245

Risking All

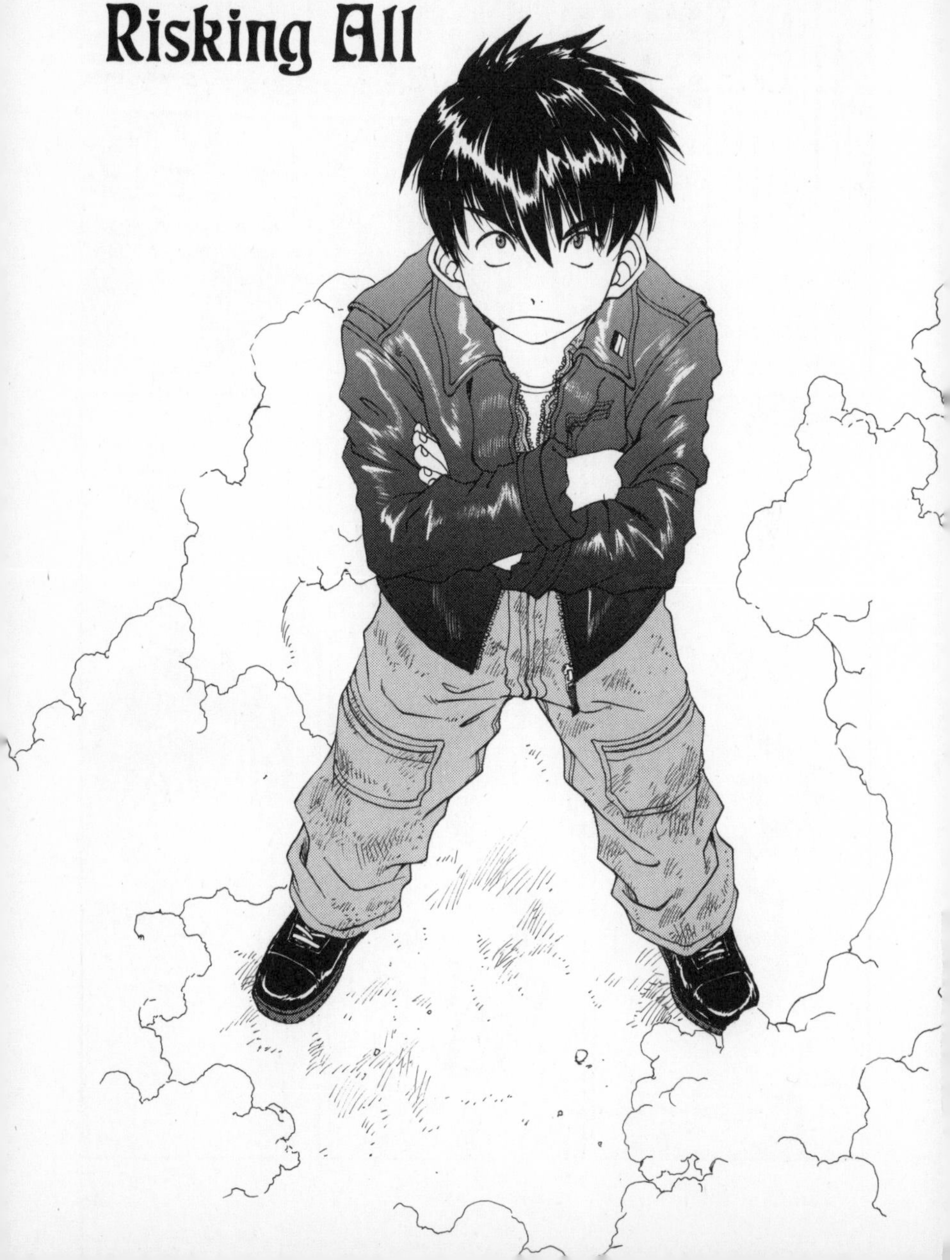

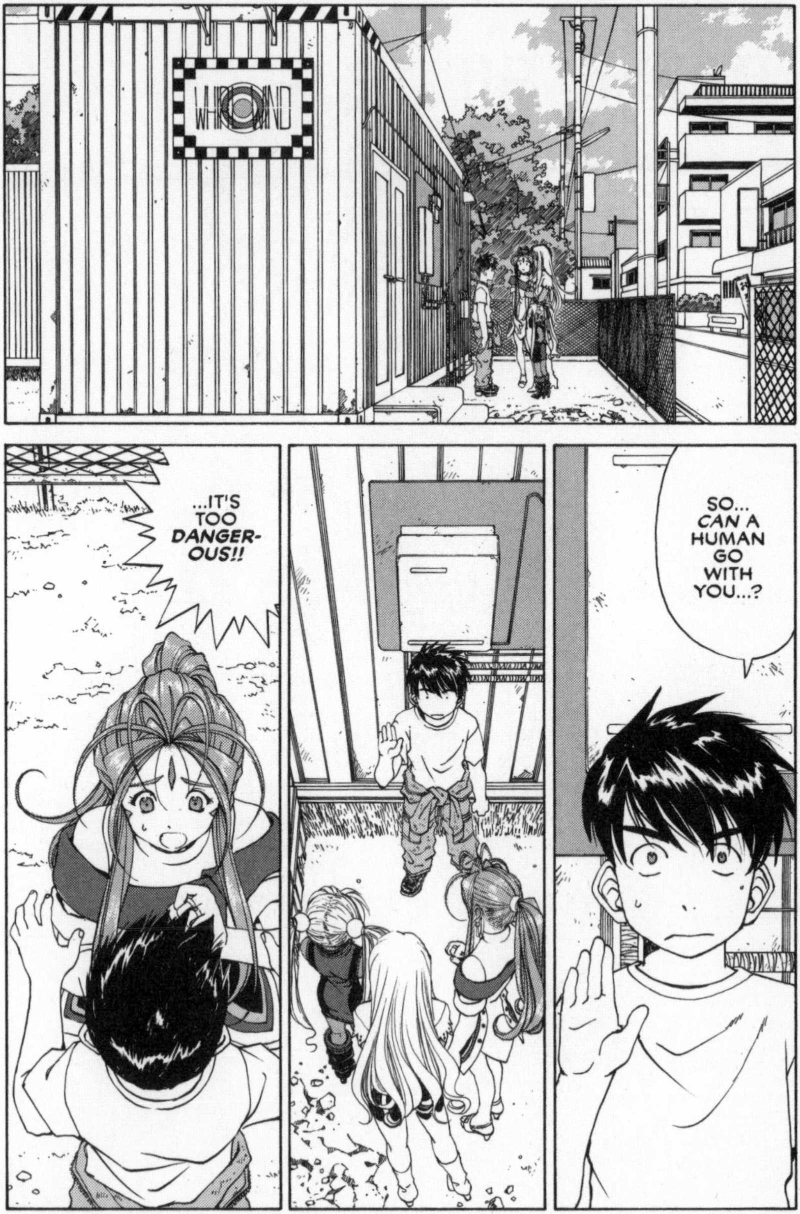
SO... CAN A HUMAN GO WITH YOU...?
...IT'S TOO DANGER-OUS!!

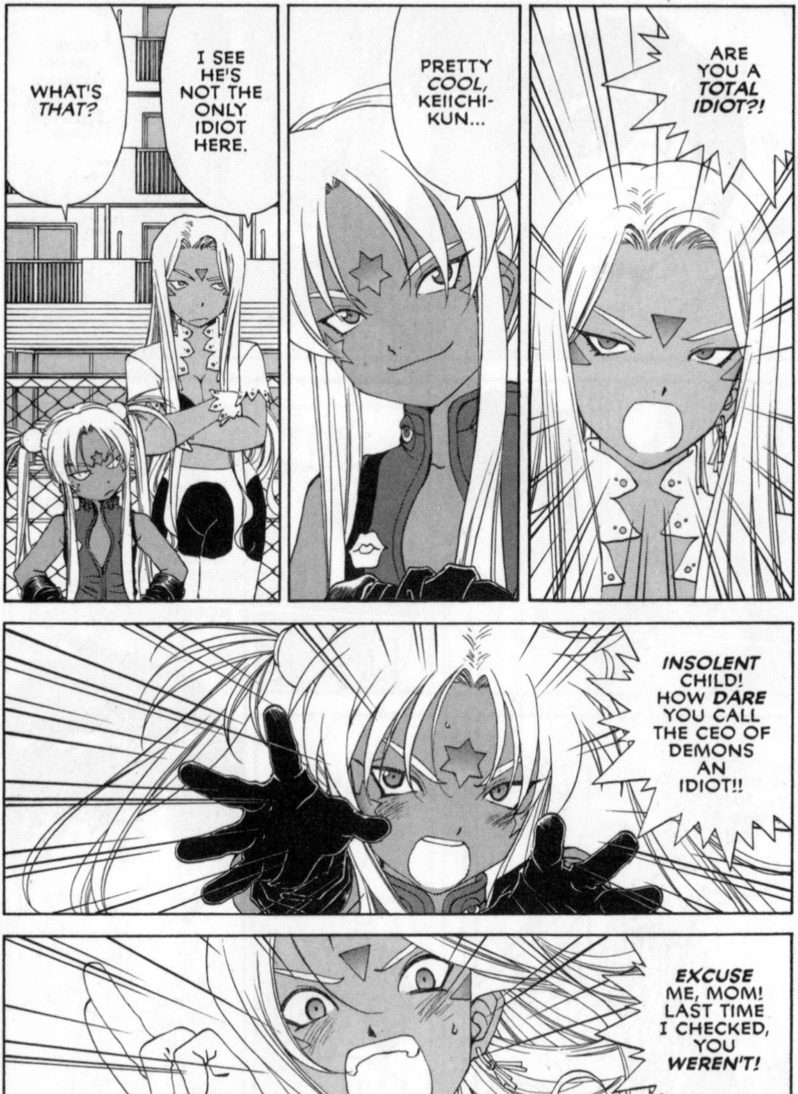
ARE YOU A *TOTAL IDIOT?!*
PRETTY *COOL,* KEIICHI-KUN...
I SEE HE'S NOT THE ONLY IDIOT HERE.
WHAT'S *THAT?*
INSOLENT CHILD! HOW ***DARE*** YOU CALL THE CEO OF DEMONS AN IDIOT!!
EXCUSE ME, MOM! LAST TIME I CHECKED, YOU ***WEREN'T!***

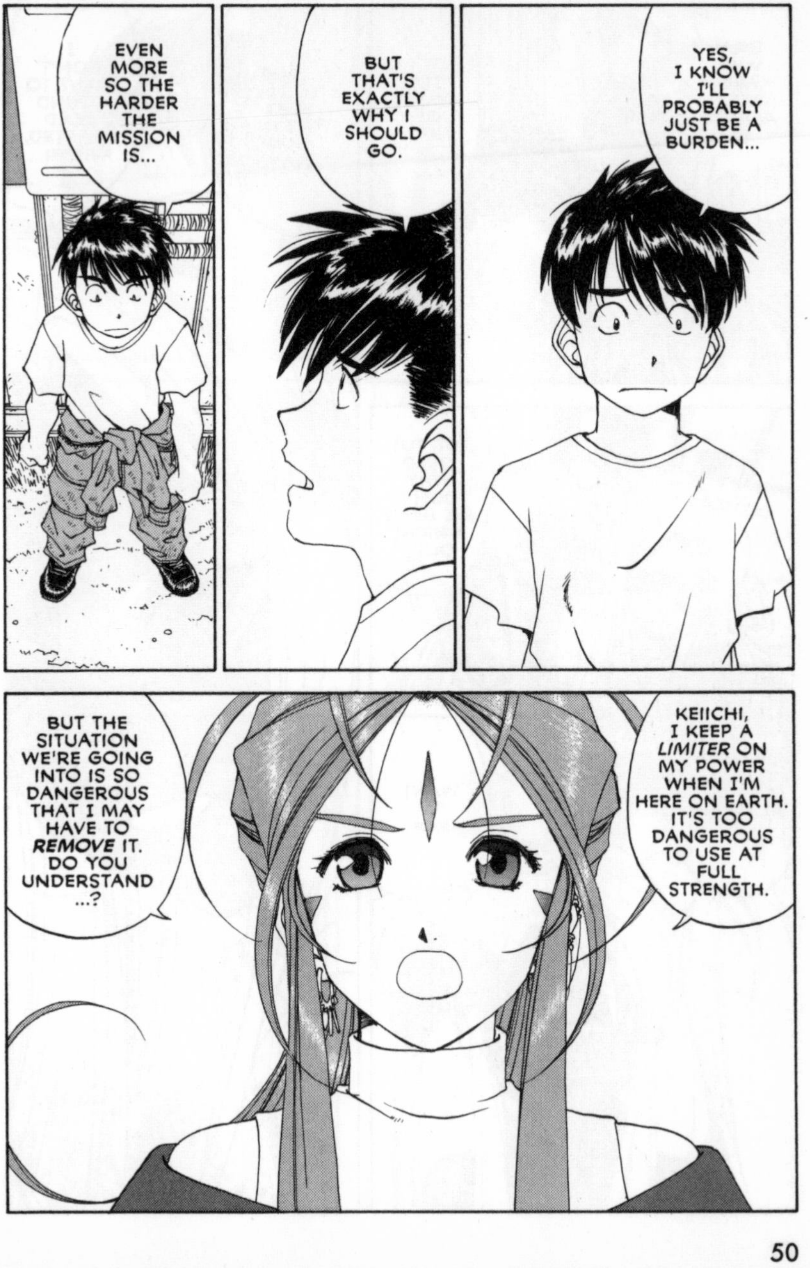
YES, I KNOW I'LL PROBABLY JUST BE A BURDEN...
BUT THAT'S EXACTLY WHY I SHOULD GO.
EVEN MORE SO THE HARDER THE MISSION IS...
KEIICHI, I KEEP A *LIMITER* ON MY POWER WHEN I'M HERE ON EARTH. IT'S TOO DANGEROUS TO USE AT FULL STRENGTH.
BUT THE SITUATION WE'RE GOING INTO IS SO DANGEROUS THAT I MAY HAVE TO ***REMOVE*** IT. DO YOU UNDERSTAND ...?

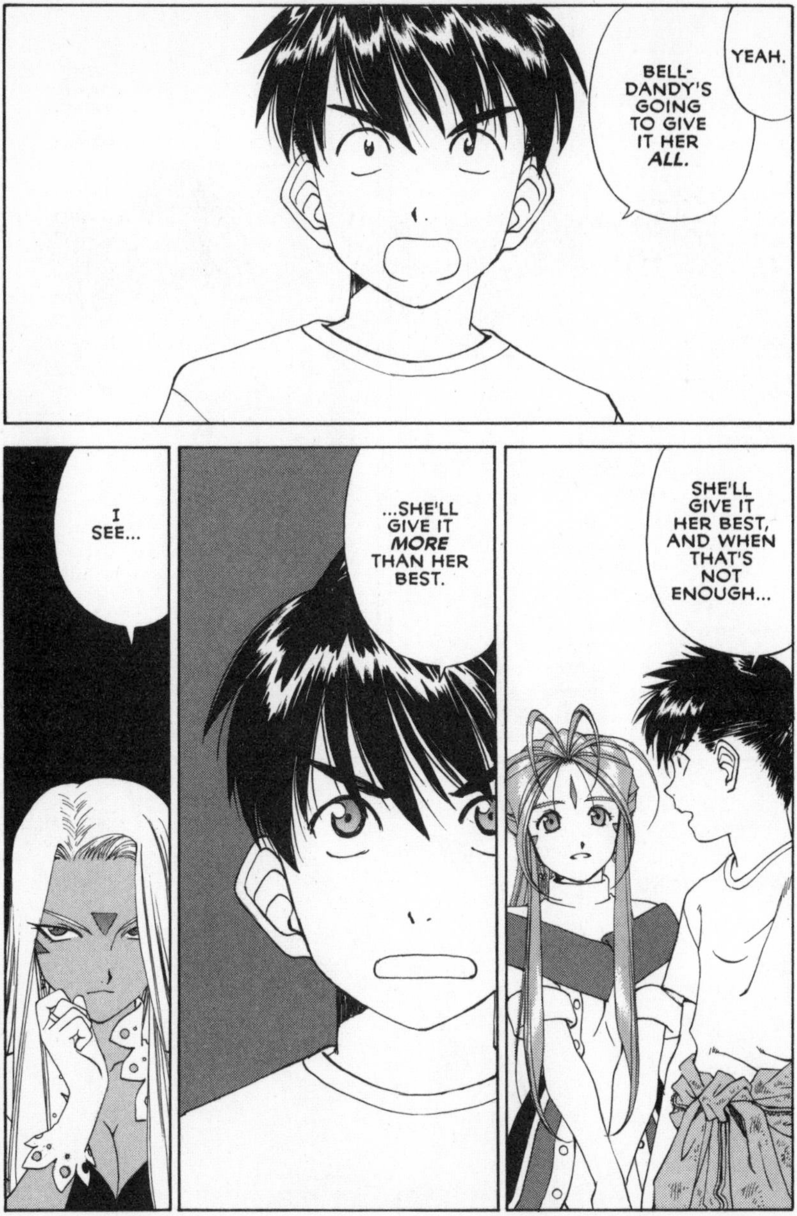
YEAH.
BELL-DANDY'S GOING TO GIVE IT HER ALL.
SHE'LL GIVE IT HER BEST, AND WHEN THAT'S NOT ENOUGH...
...SHE'LL GIVE IT MORE THAN HER BEST.
I SEE...

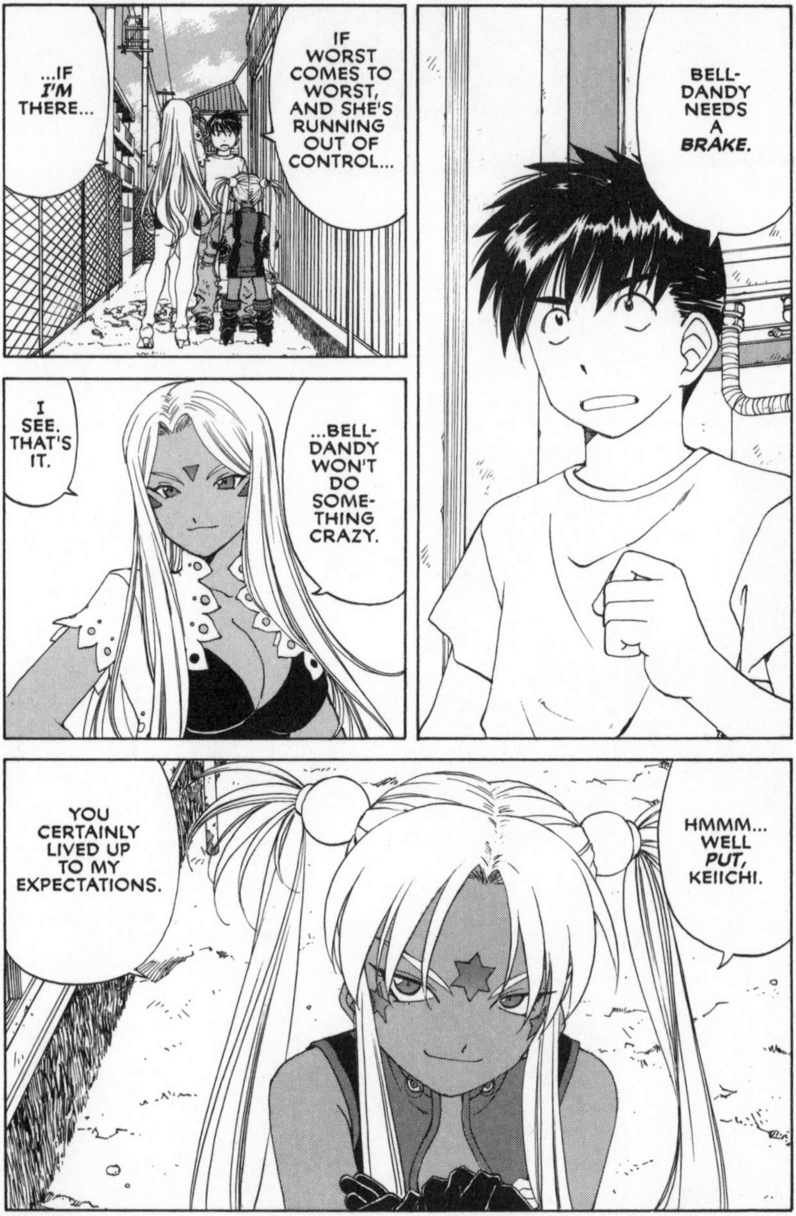
BELL-DANDY NEEDS A *BRAKE.*
IF WORST COMES TO WORST, AND SHE'S RUNNING OUT OF CONTROL...
...IF *I'M* THERE...
...BELL-DANDY WON'T DO SOME-THING CRAZY.
I SEE. THAT'S IT.
HMMM... WELL *PUT,* KEIICHI.
YOU CERTAINLY LIVED UP TO MY EXPECTATIONS.

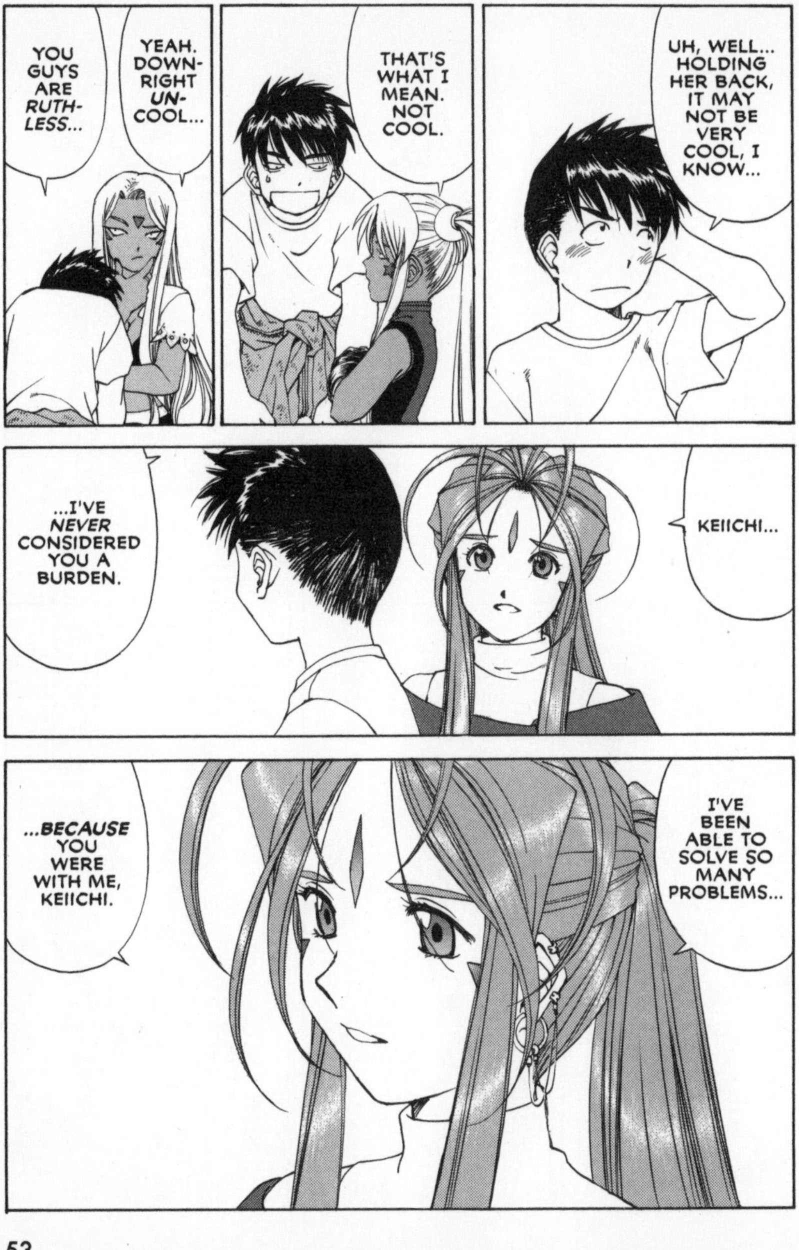
UH, WELL... HOLDING HER BACK, IT MAY NOT BE VERY COOL, I KNOW...
THAT'S WHAT I MEAN. NOT COOL.
YEAH. DOWN-RIGHT *UN-*COOL...
YOU GUYS ARE *RUTHLESS*...
KEIICHI...
...I'VE *NEVER* CONSIDERED YOU A BURDEN.
I'VE BEEN ABLE TO SOLVE SO MANY PROBLEMS...
...***BECAUSE*** YOU WERE WITH ME, KEIICHI.

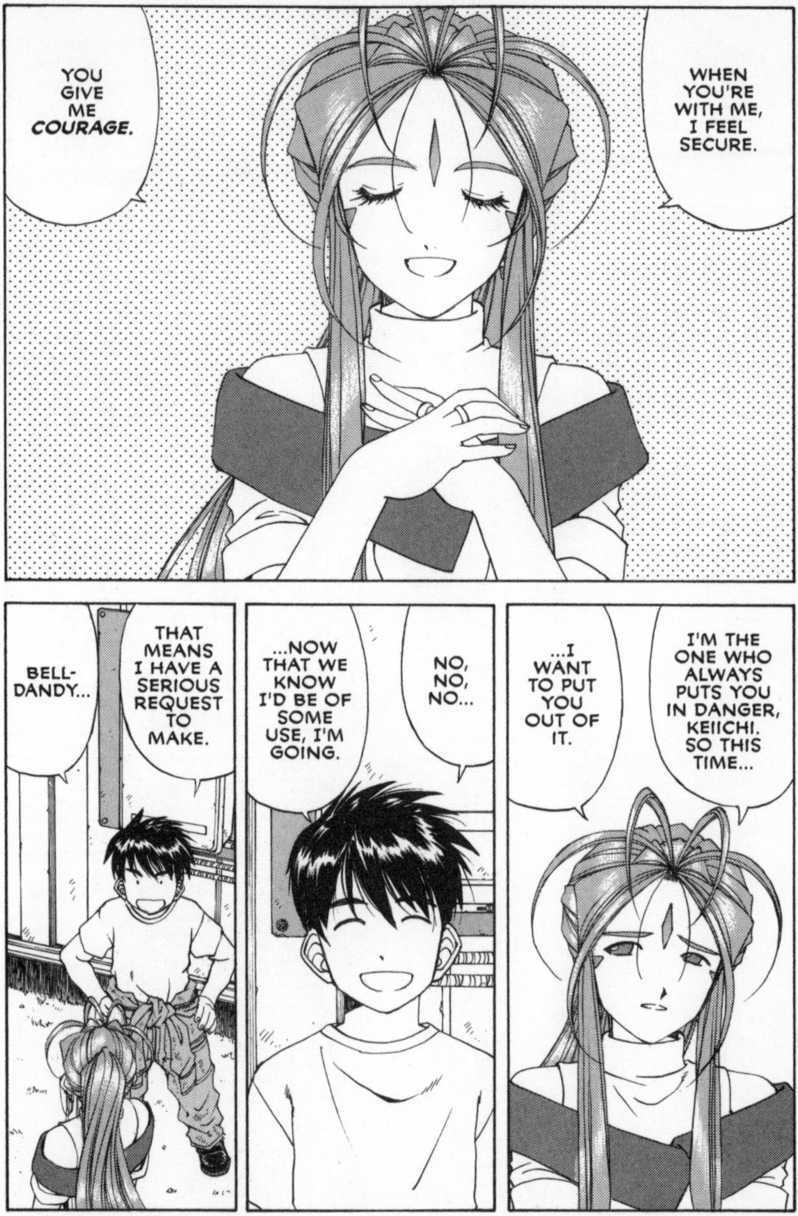
WHEN YOU'RE WITH ME, I FEEL SECURE.
YOU GIVE ME *COURAGE.*
I'M THE ONE WHO ALWAYS PUTS YOU IN DANGER, KEIICHI. SO THIS TIME...
...I WANT TO PUT YOU OUT OF IT.
NO, NO, NO...
...NOW THAT WE KNOW I'D BE OF SOME USE, I'M GOING.
THAT MEANS I HAVE A SERIOUS REQUEST TO MAKE.
BELL-DANDY...

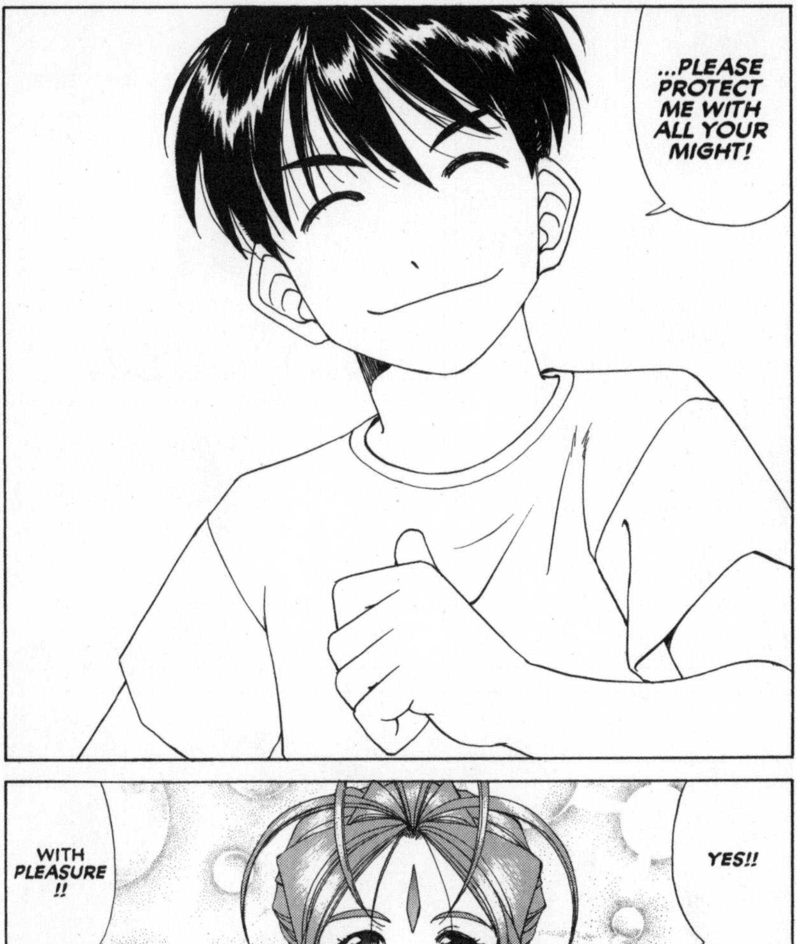
...PLEASE PROTECT ME WITH ALL YOUR MIGHT!

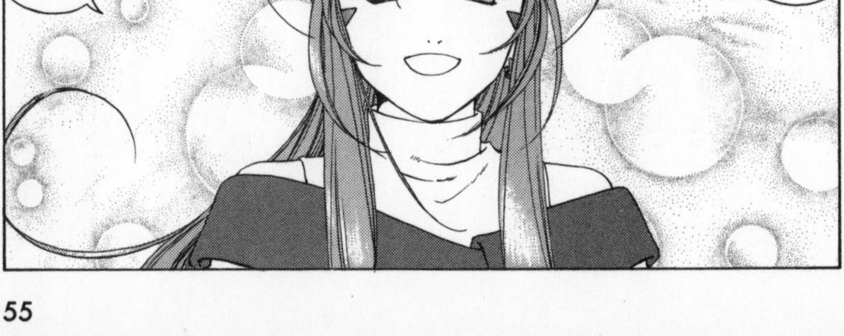
YES!!
WITH PLEASURE !!

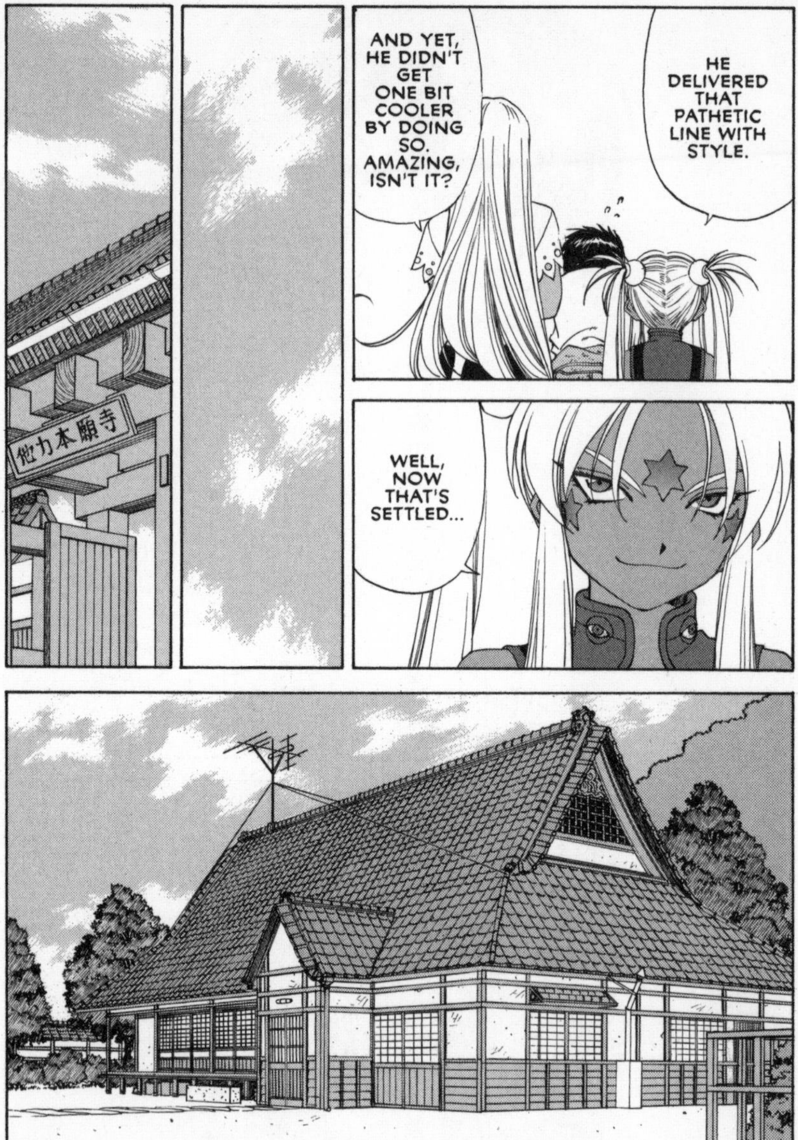
HE DELIVERED THAT PATHETIC LINE WITH STYLE.
AND YET, HE DIDN'T GET ONE BIT COOLER BY DOING SO. AMAZING, ISN'T IT?
WELL, NOW THAT'S SETTLED...
他力本願寺

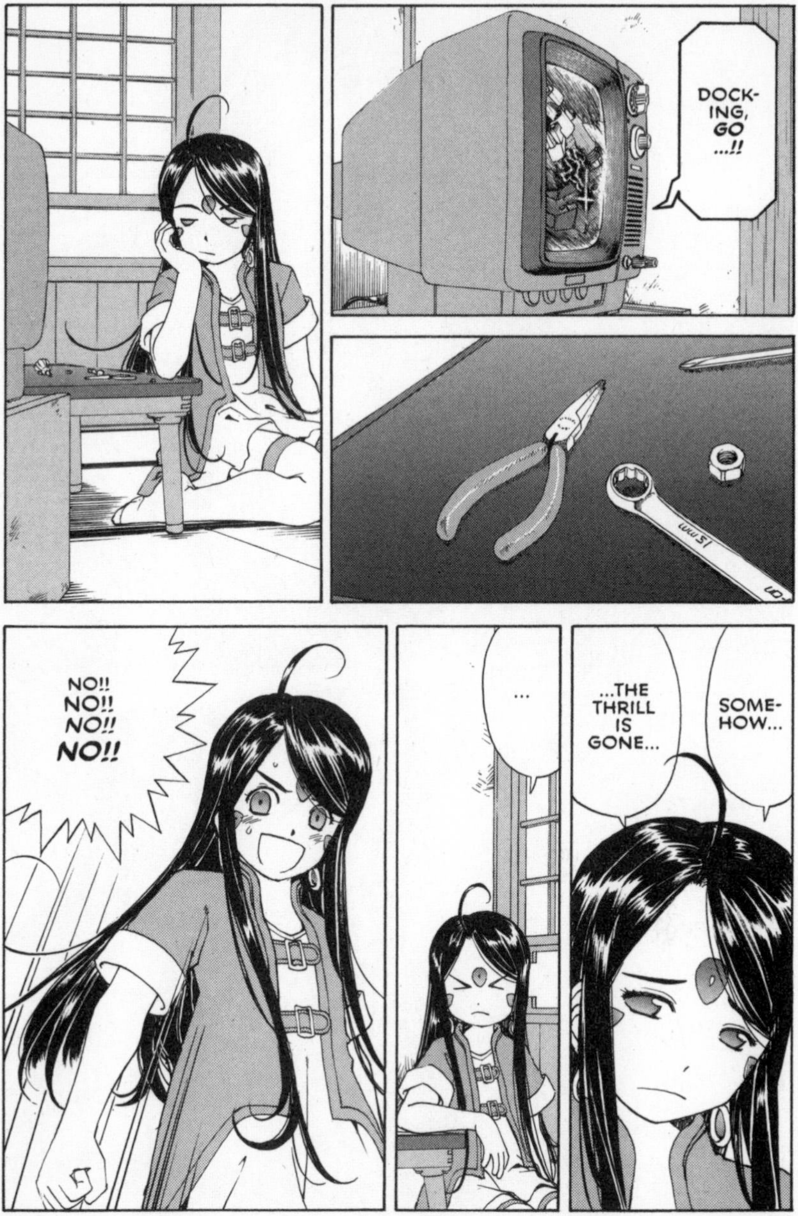
DOCK-ING, GO ...!!
SOME-HOW...
...THE THRILL IS GONE...
...
NO!! NO!! NO!! NO!!

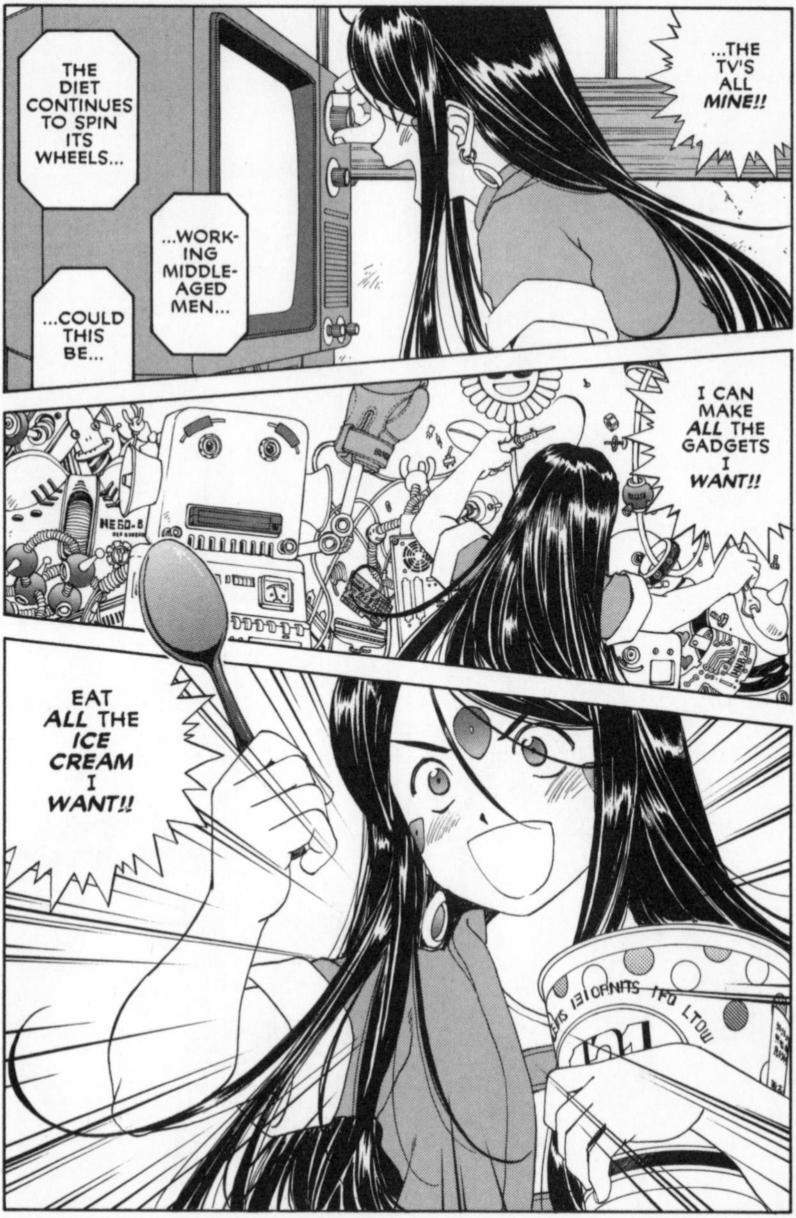
...THE TV'S ALL MINE!!
THE DIET CONTINUES TO SPIN ITS WHEELS...
...WORKING MIDDLE-AGED MEN...
...COULD THIS BE...
I CAN MAKE ALL THE GADGETS I WANT!!
EAT ALL THE ICE CREAM I WANT!!

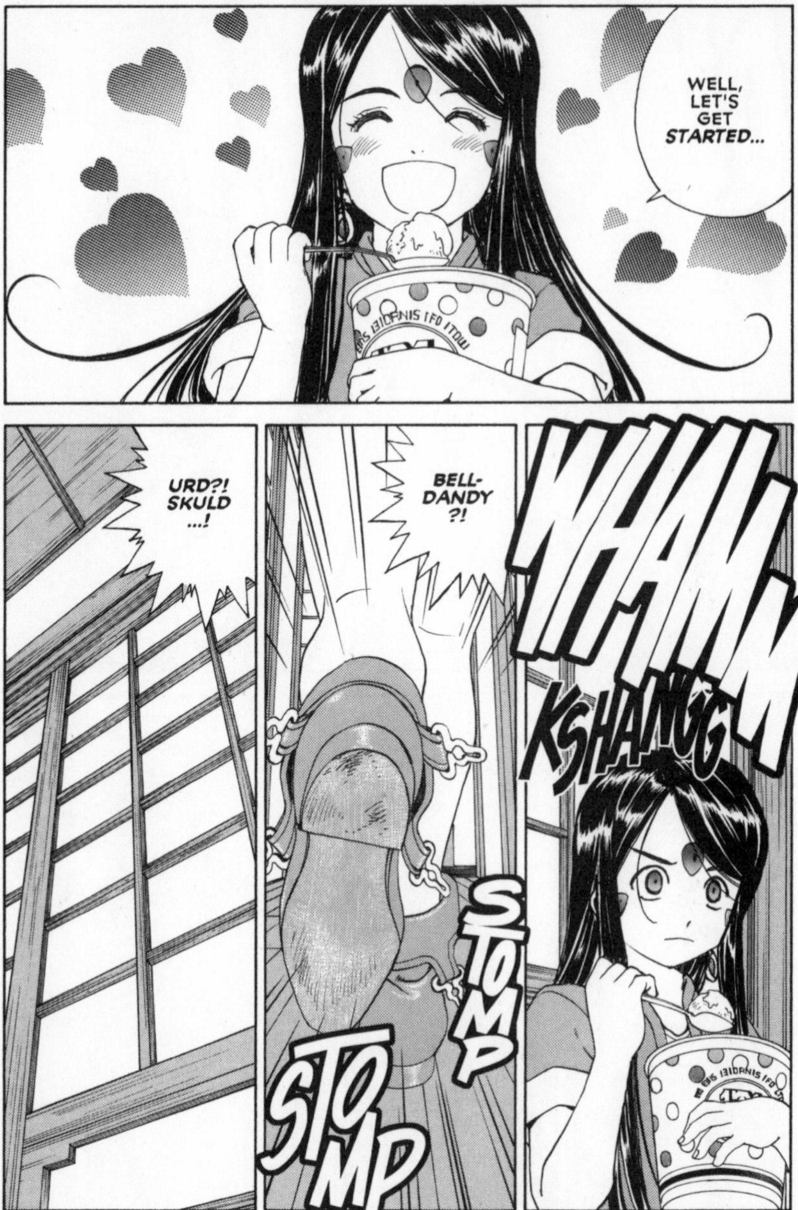
WELL, LET'S GET STARTED...
WHAMM
KSHANGG
BELL-DANDY ?!
STOMP
STOMP
URD?! SKULD ...!

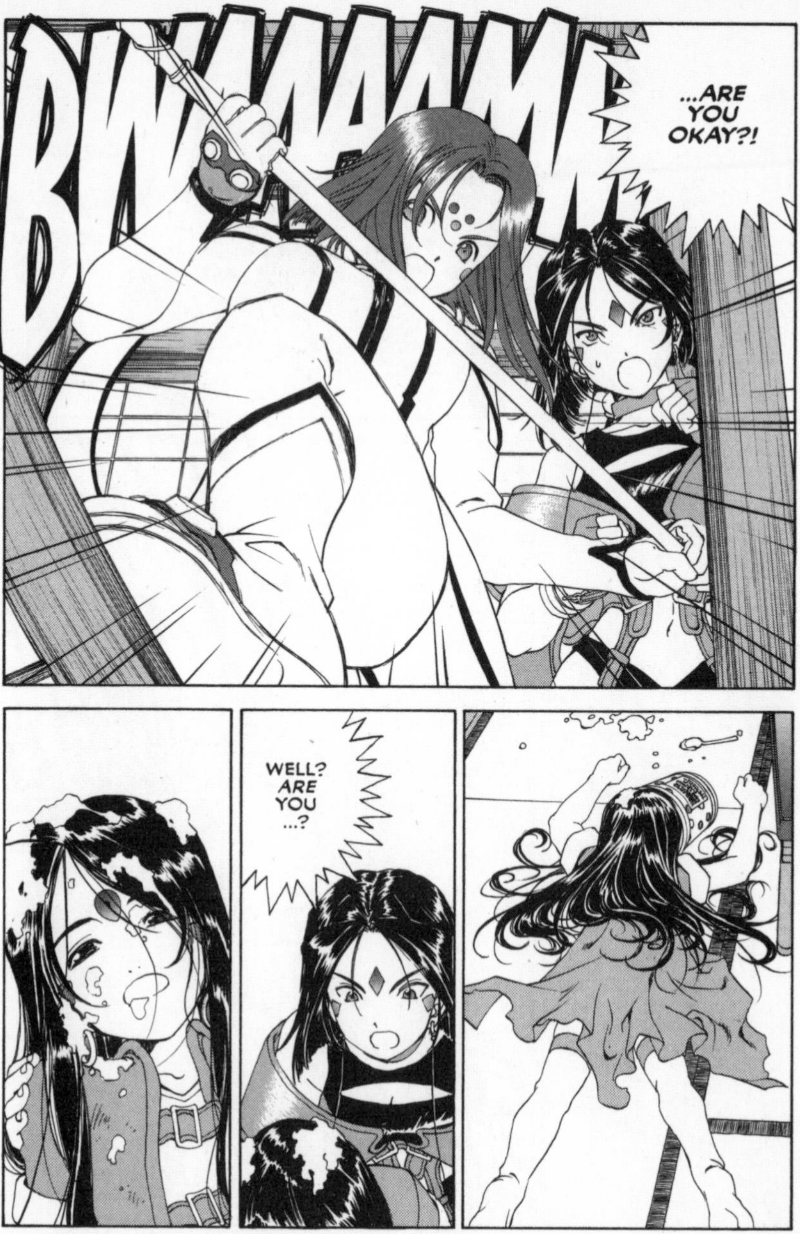
BWAAAM!
...ARE YOU OKAY?!
WELL? ARE YOU ...?

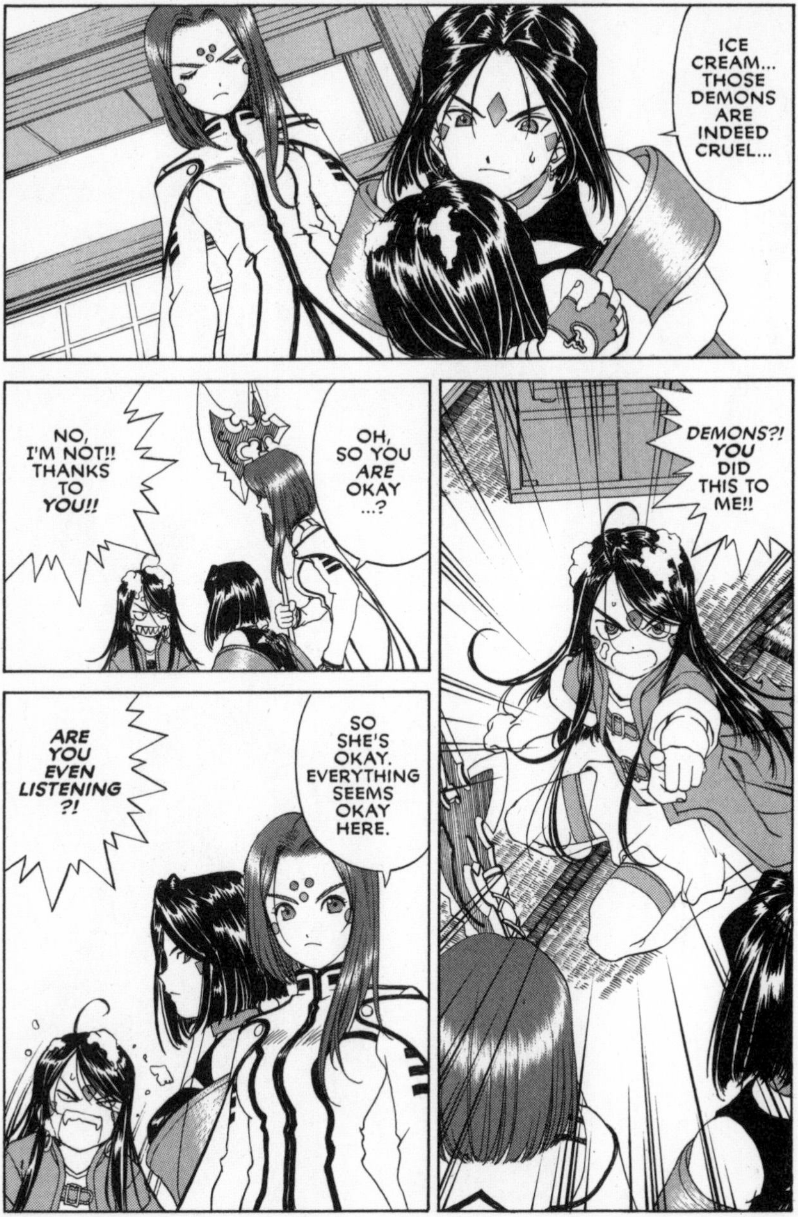
ICE CREAM... THOSE DEMONS ARE INDEED CRUEL...
DEMONS?! YOU DID THIS TO ME!!
OH, SO YOU ARE OKAY ...?
NO, I'M NOT!! THANKS TO YOU!!
SO SHE'S OKAY. EVERYTHING SEEMS OKAY HERE.
ARE YOU EVEN LISTENING ?!

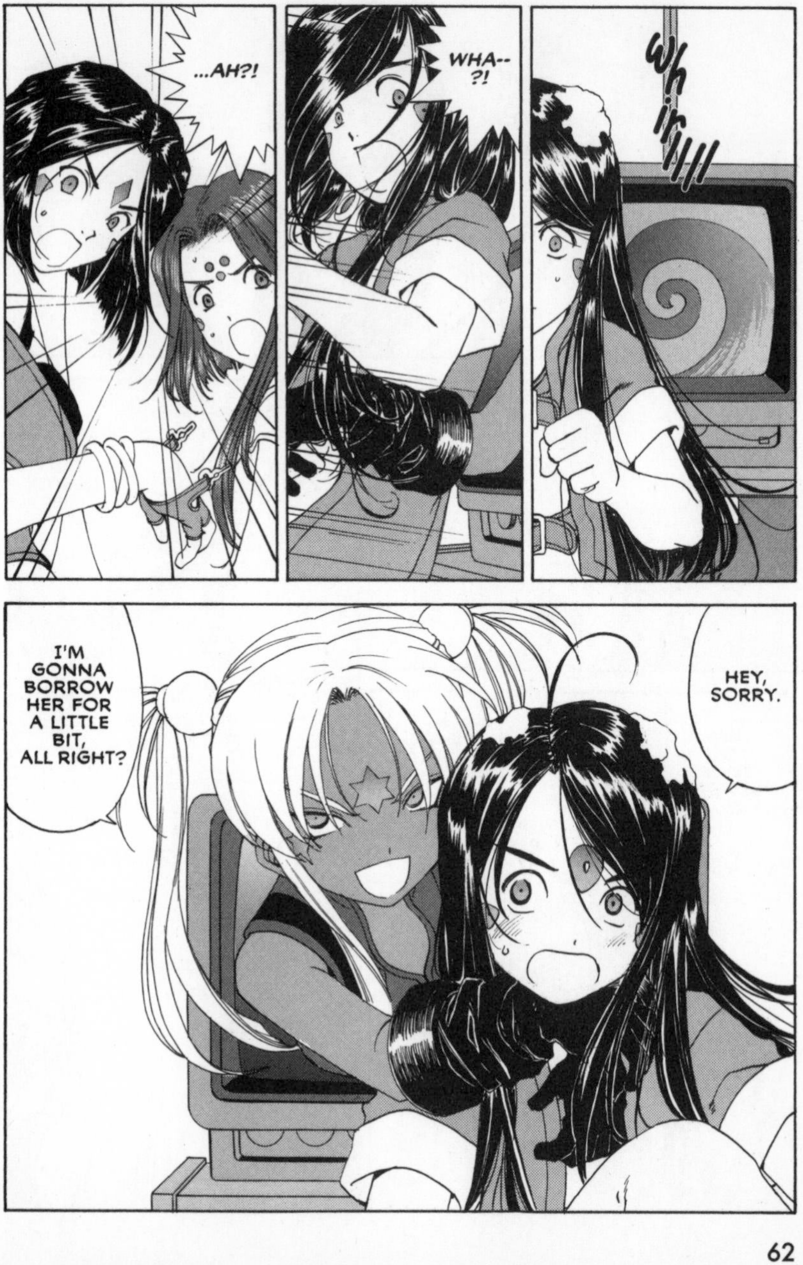
whirl!!!
WHA-- ?!
...AH?!
HEY, SORRY.
I'M GONNA BORROW HER FOR A LITTLE BIT, ALL RIGHT?

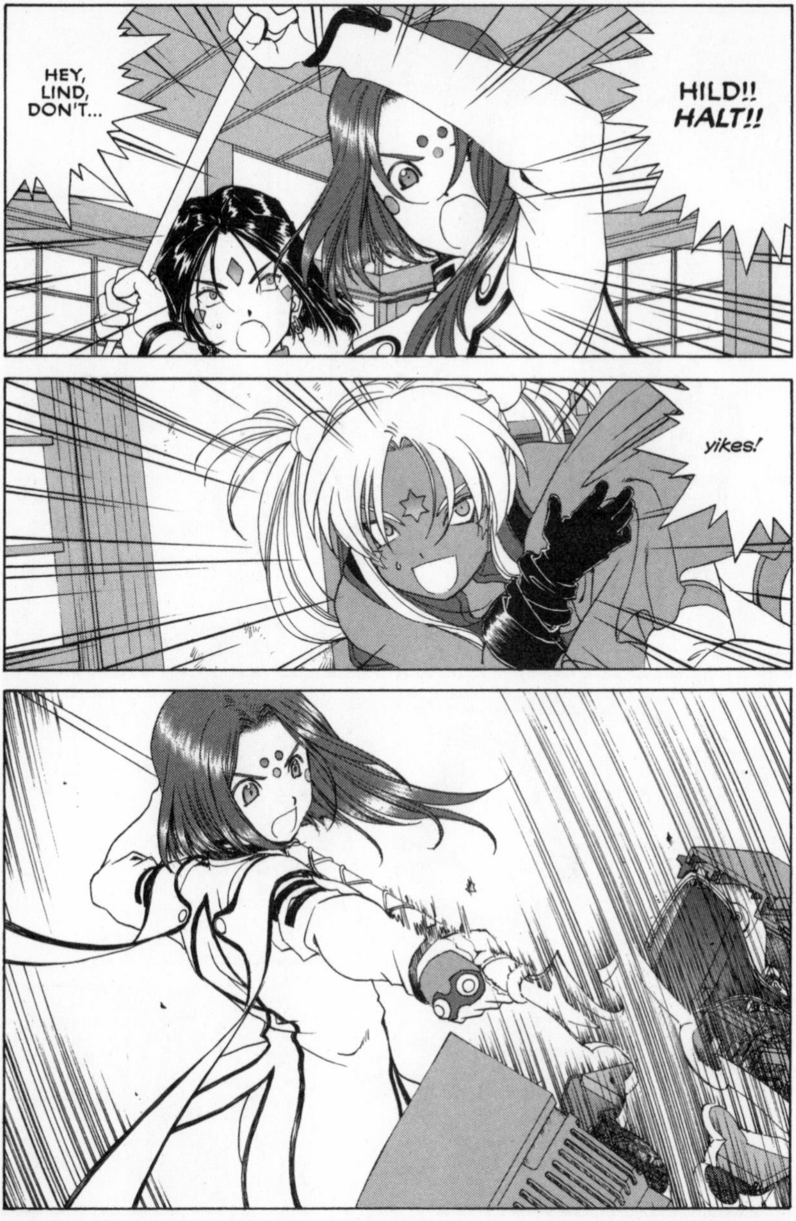
HILD!! *HALT!!*
HEY, LIND, DON'T...
yikes!

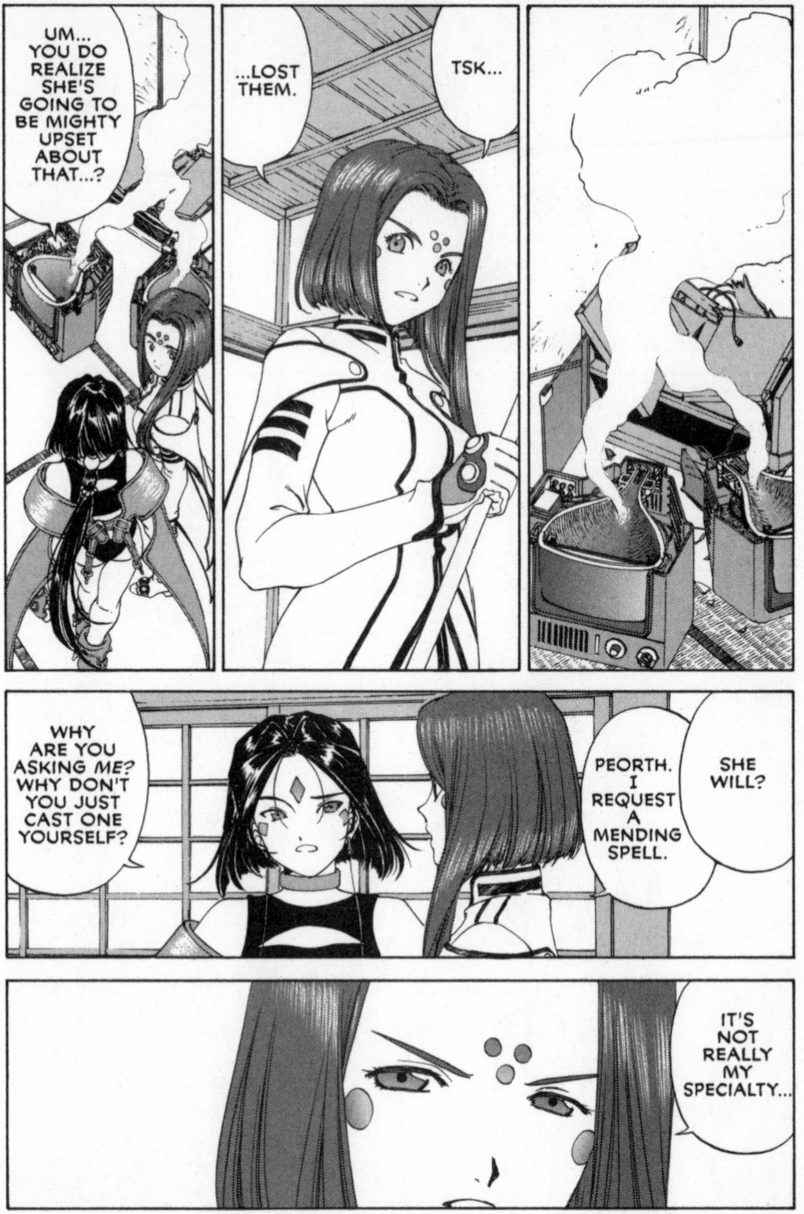
TSK...
...LOST THEM.
UM... YOU DO REALIZE SHE'S GOING TO BE MIGHTY UPSET ABOUT THAT...?
SHE WILL?
PEORTH. I REQUEST A MENDING SPELL.
WHY ARE YOU ASKING *ME?* WHY DON'T YOU JUST CAST ONE YOURSELF?
IT'S NOT REALLY MY SPECIALTY...

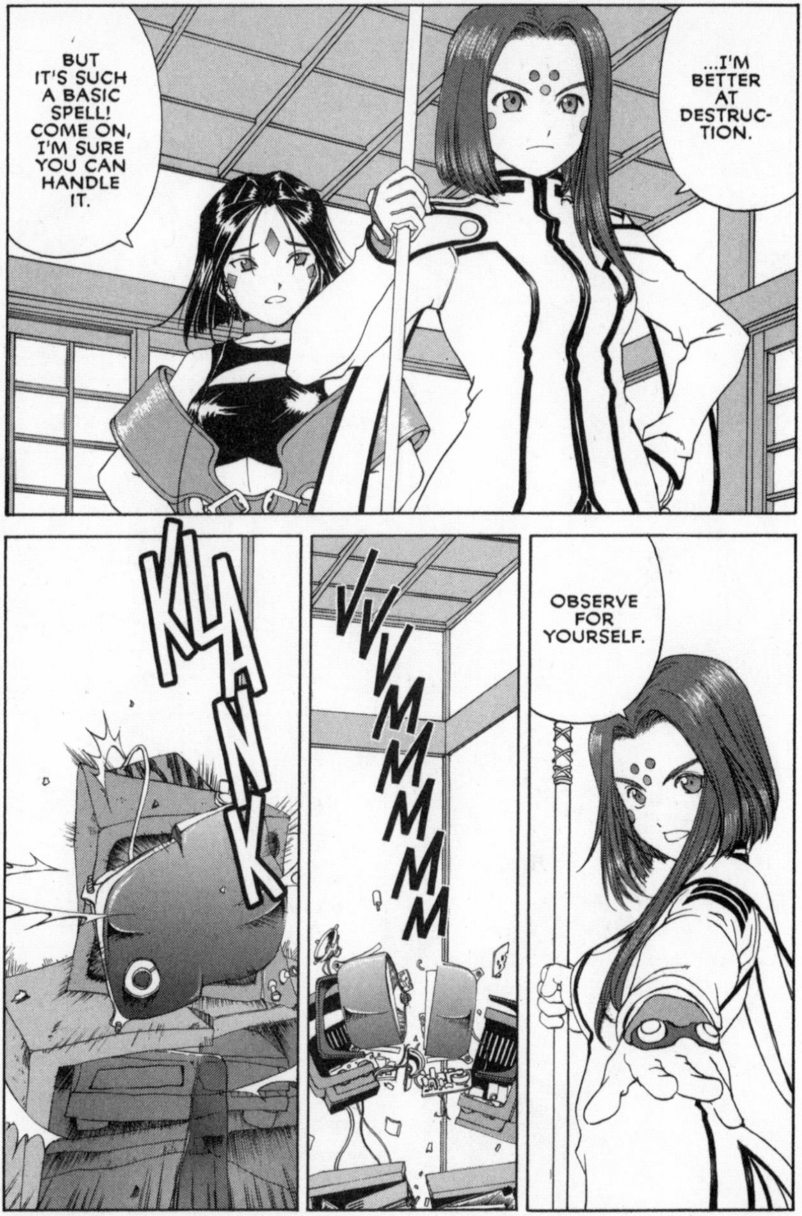
...I'M BETTER AT DESTRUCTION.
BUT IT'S SUCH A BASIC SPELL! COME ON, I'M SURE YOU CAN HANDLE IT.
OBSERVE FOR YOURSELF.
VVVMMMMMMM
KLANK

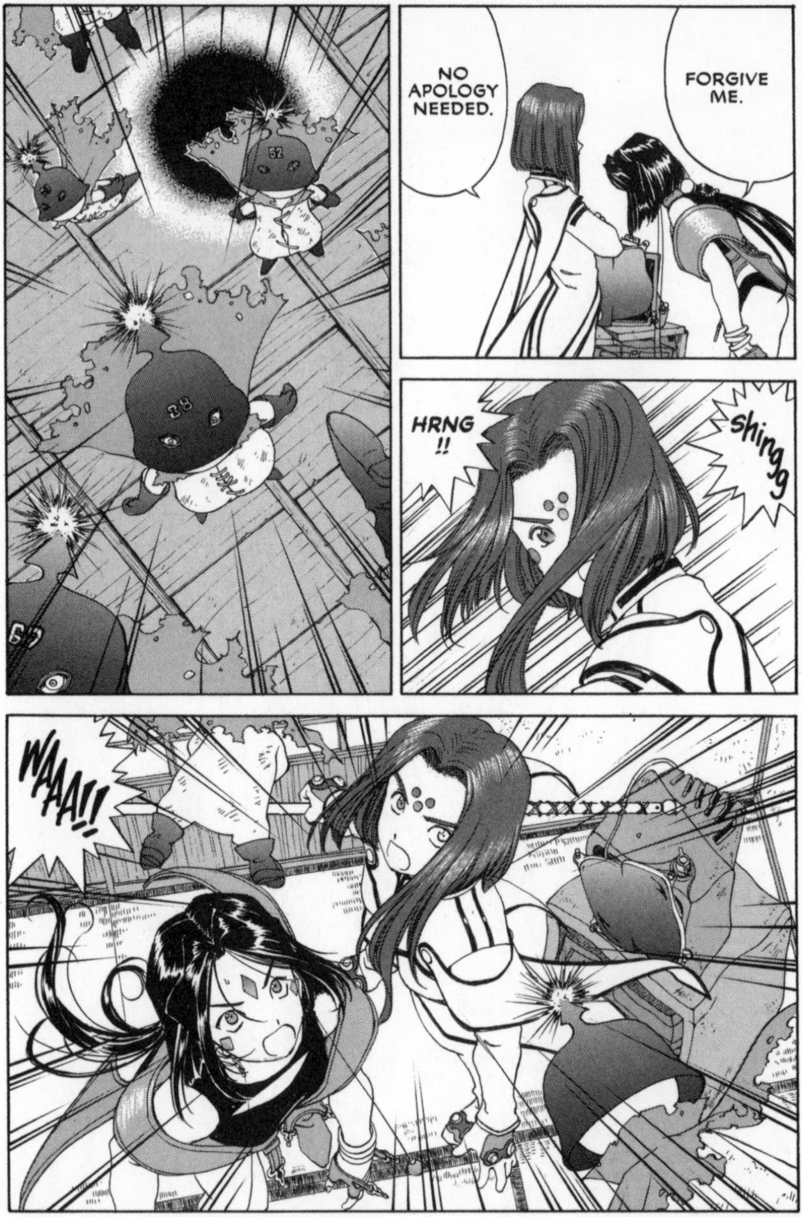
FORGIVE ME.
NO APOLOGY NEEDED.
shingg
HRNG !!
WAAAA!!

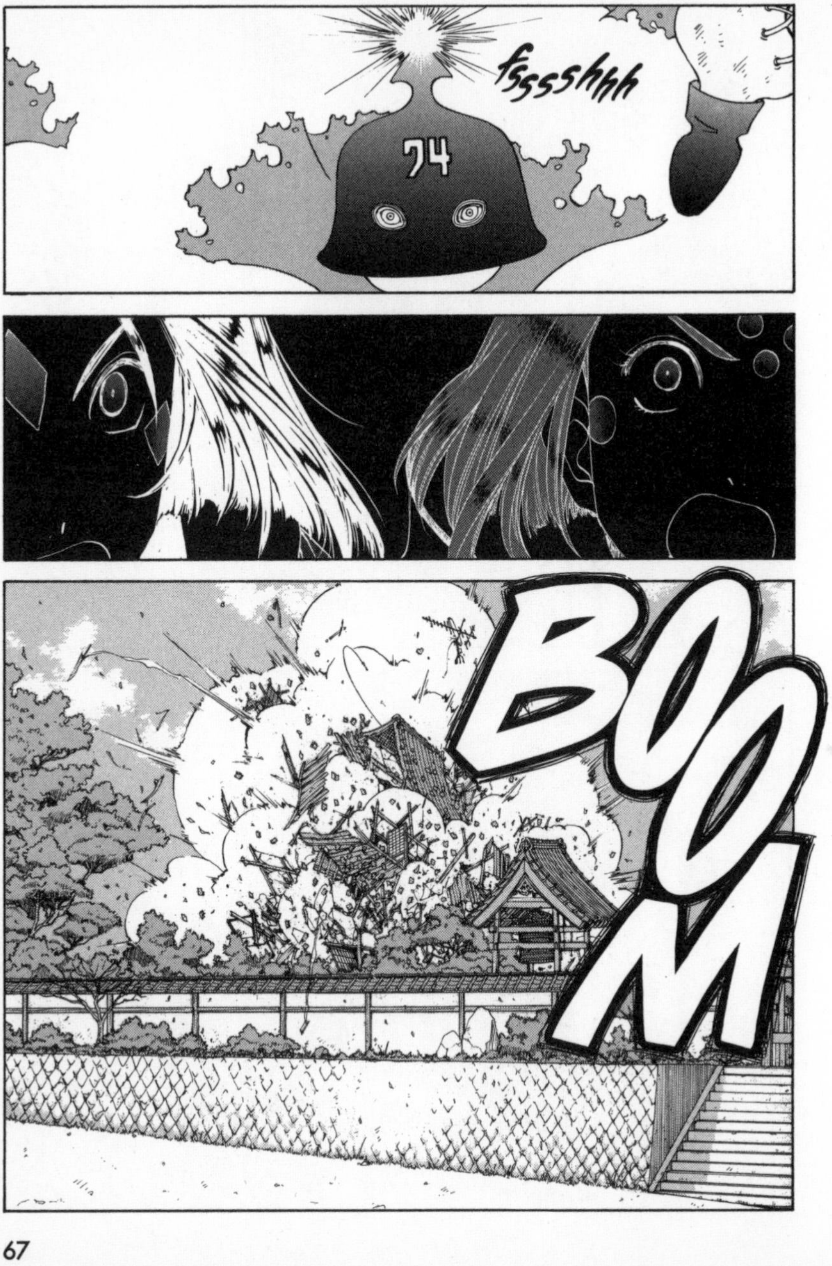
fsssshhh
74
BOOOM

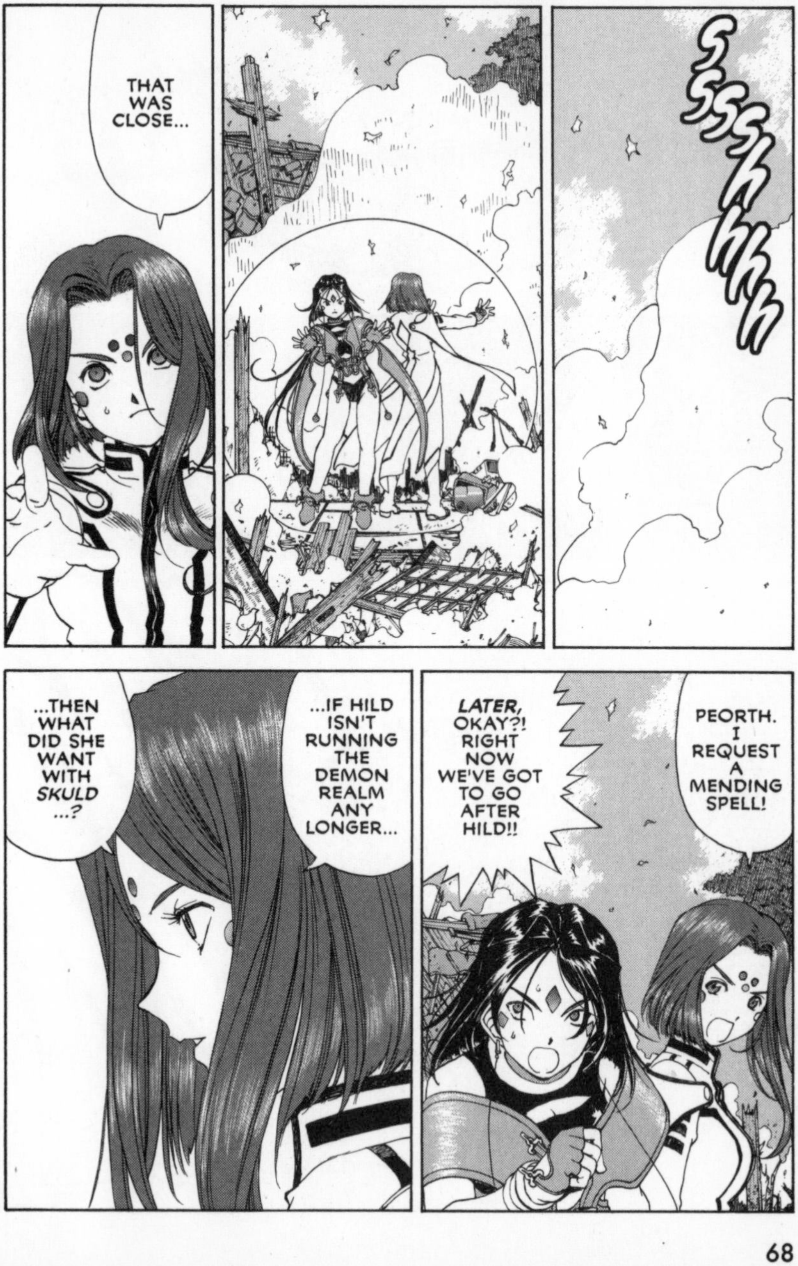
SSShhhh
THAT WAS CLOSE...
PEORTH. I REQUEST A MENDING SPELL!
LATER, OKAY?! RIGHT NOW WE'VE GOT TO GO AFTER HILD!!
...IF HILD ISN'T RUNNING THE DEMON REALM ANY LONGER...
...THEN WHAT DID SHE WANT WITH SKULD ...?

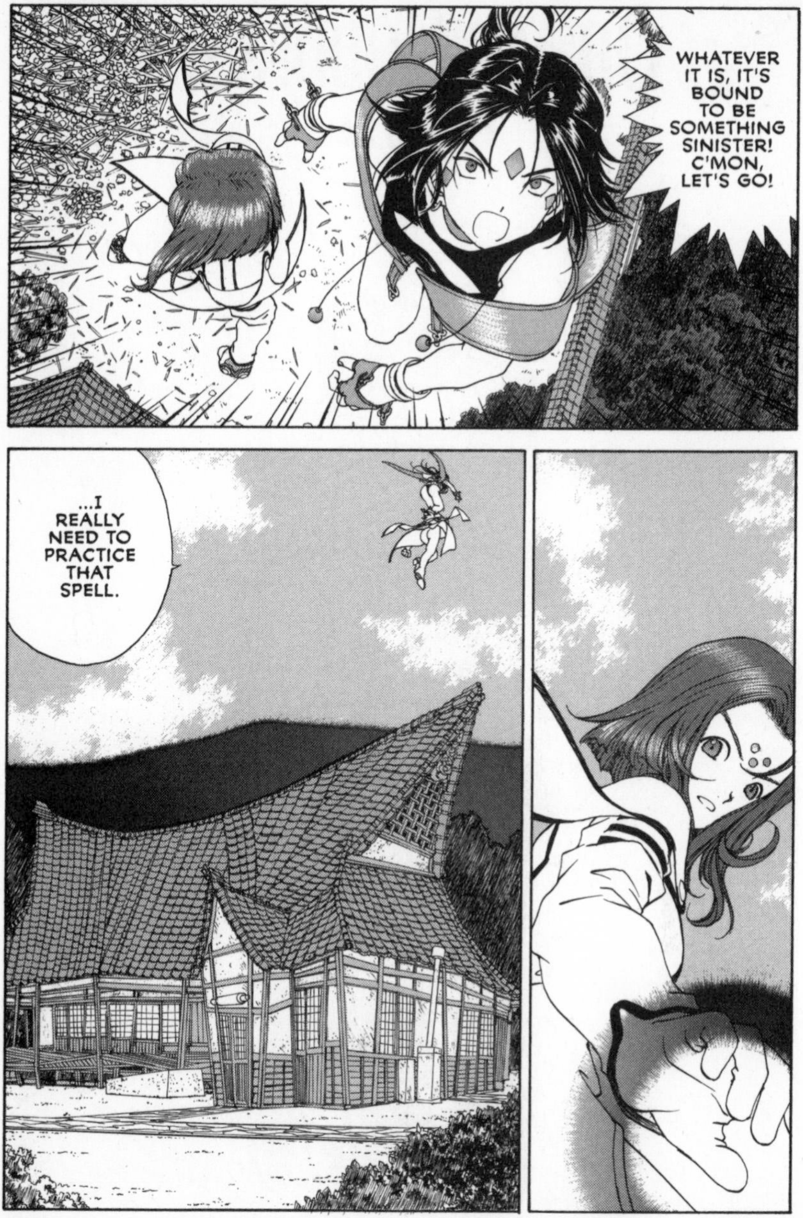
WHATEVER IT IS, IT'S BOUND TO BE SOMETHING SINISTER! C'MON, LET'S GO!
...I REALLY NEED TO PRACTICE THAT SPELL.

OH MY GODDESS!
HILD

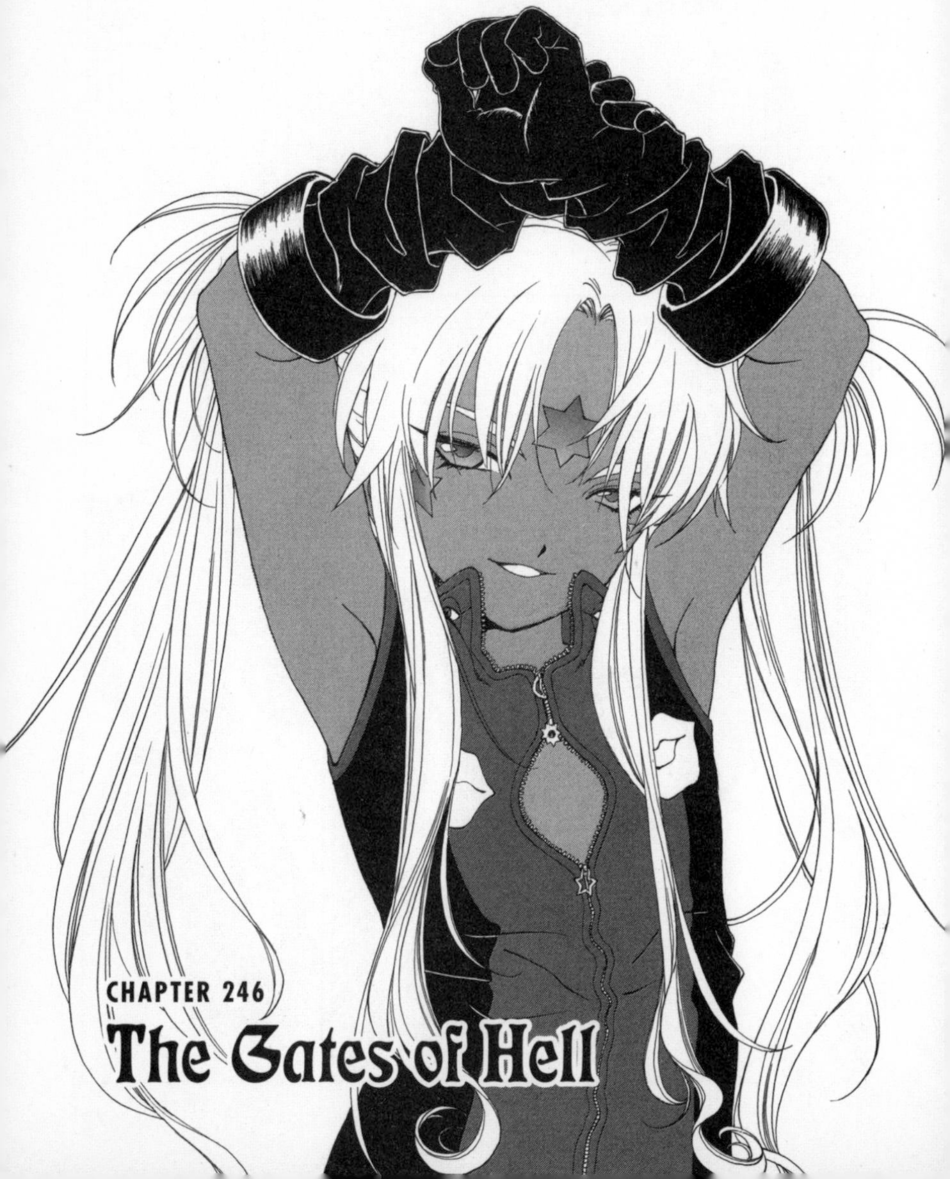
CHAPTER 246
The Gates of Hell

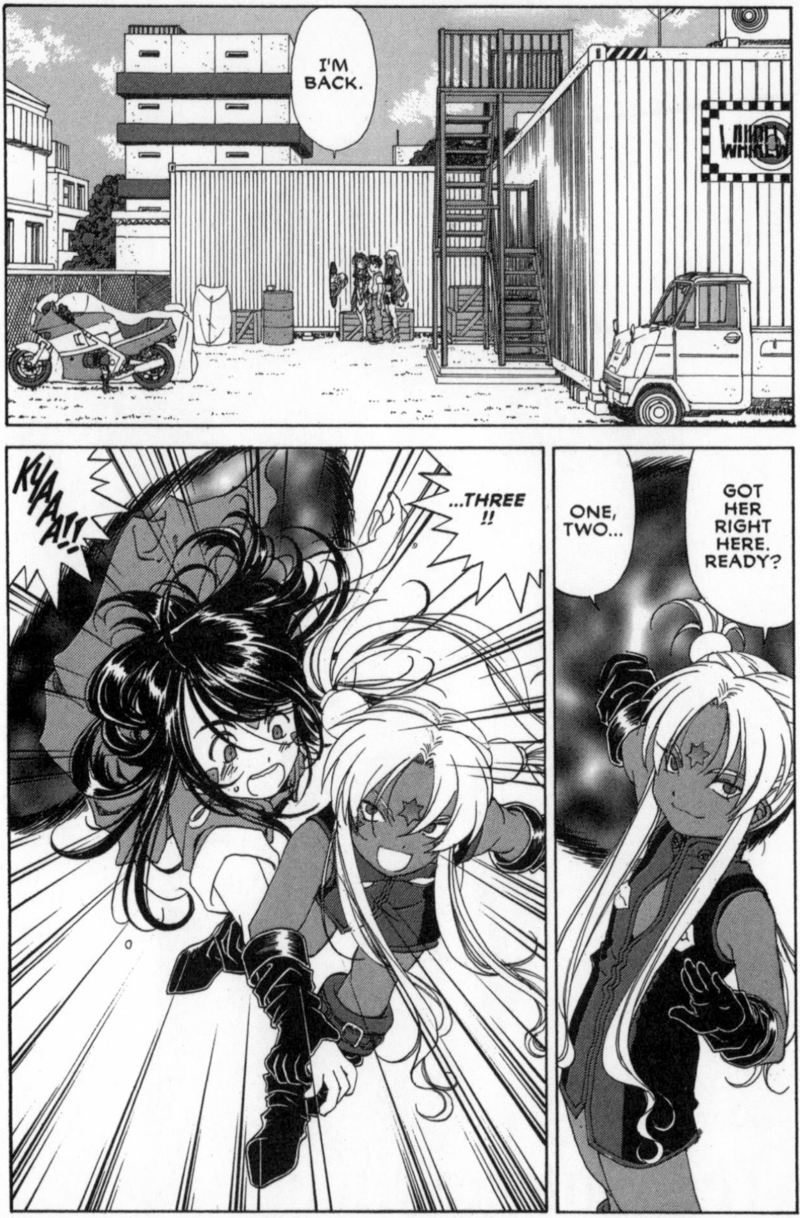
I'M BACK.
GOT HER RIGHT HERE. READY?
ONE, TWO...
...THREE !!
KYAAAA!!!

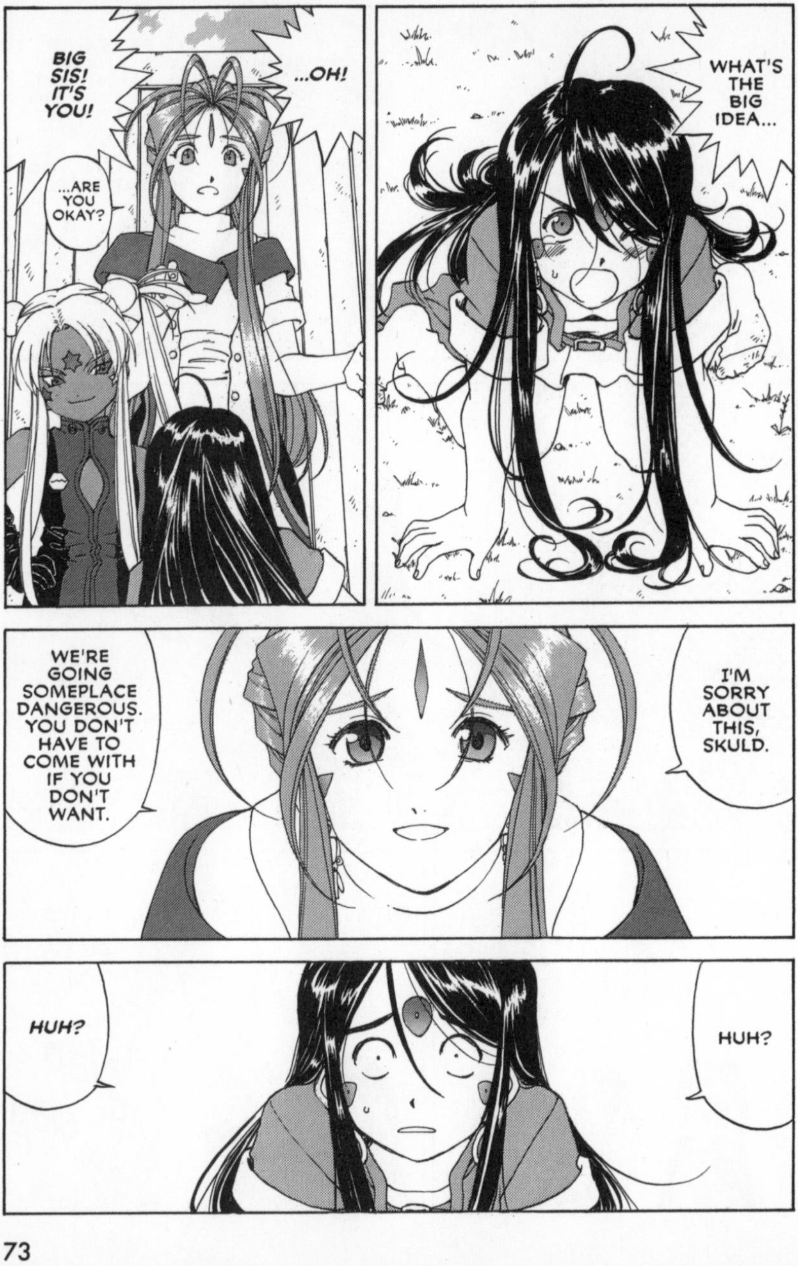
WHAT'S THE BIG IDEA...
...OH!
BIG SIS! IT'S YOU!
...ARE YOU OKAY?
I'M SORRY ABOUT THIS, SKULD.
WE'RE GOING SOMEPLACE DANGEROUS. YOU DON'T HAVE TO COME WITH IF YOU DON'T WANT.
HUH?
HUH?

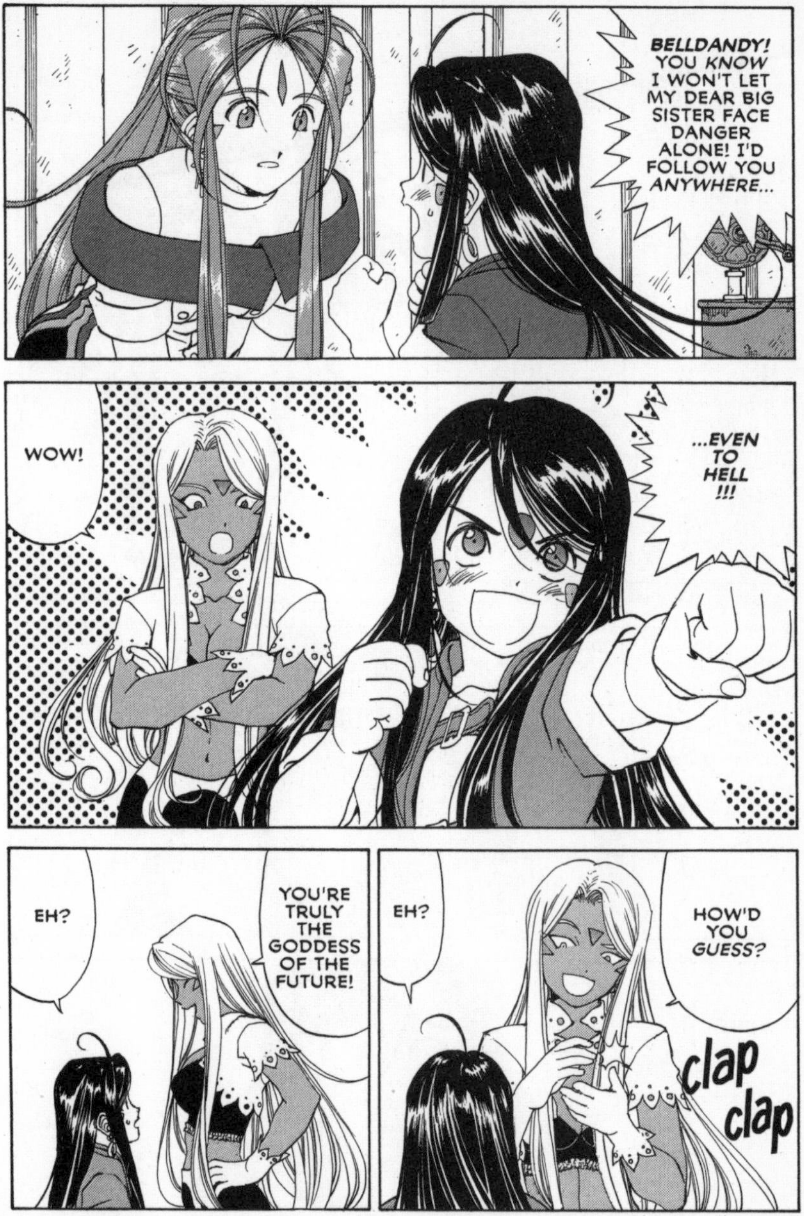
BELLDANDY! YOU KNOW I WON'T LET MY DEAR BIG SISTER FACE DANGER ALONE! I'D FOLLOW YOU ANYWHERE...
...EVEN TO HELL !!!
WOW!
HOW'D YOU GUESS?
EH?
clap clap
YOU'RE TRULY THE GODDESS OF THE FUTURE!
EH?

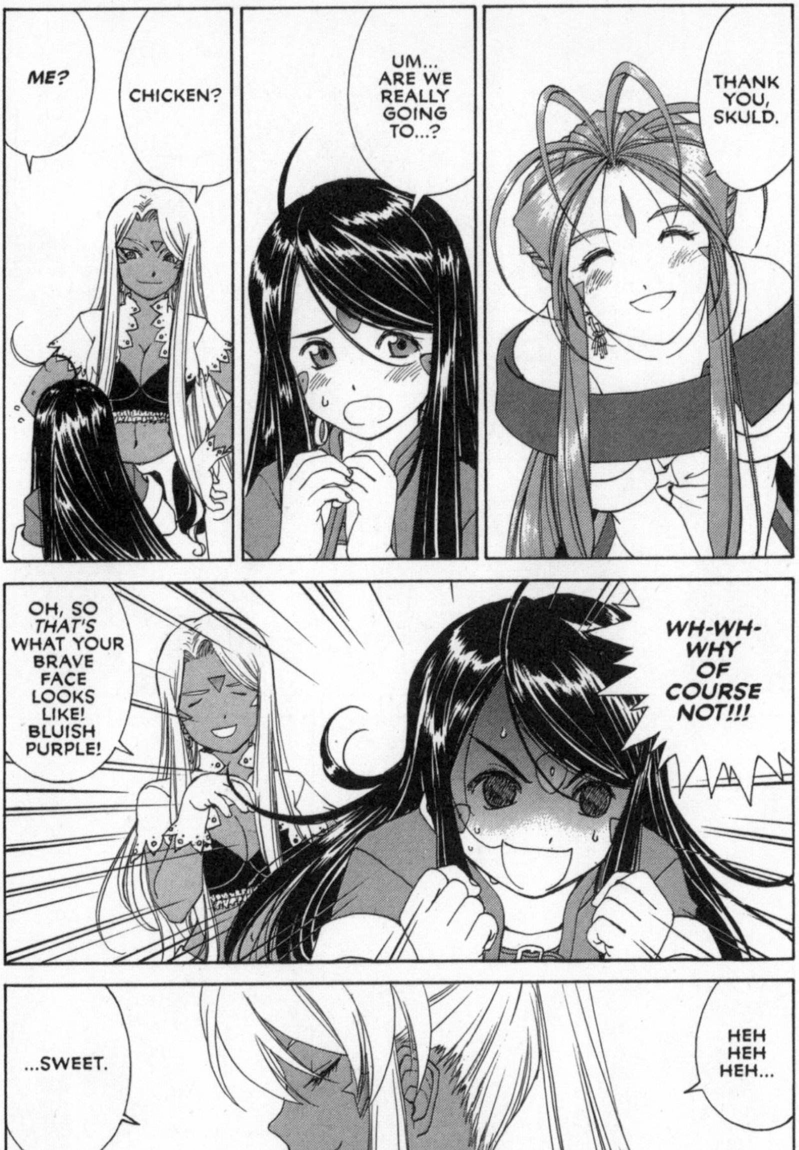
THANK YOU, SKULD.
UM... ARE WE REALLY GOING TO...?
CHICKEN?
ME?
WH-WH-WHY OF COURSE NOT!!!
OH, SO *THAT'S* WHAT YOUR BRAVE FACE LOOKS LIKE! BLUISH PURPLE!
HEH HEH HEH...
...SWEET.

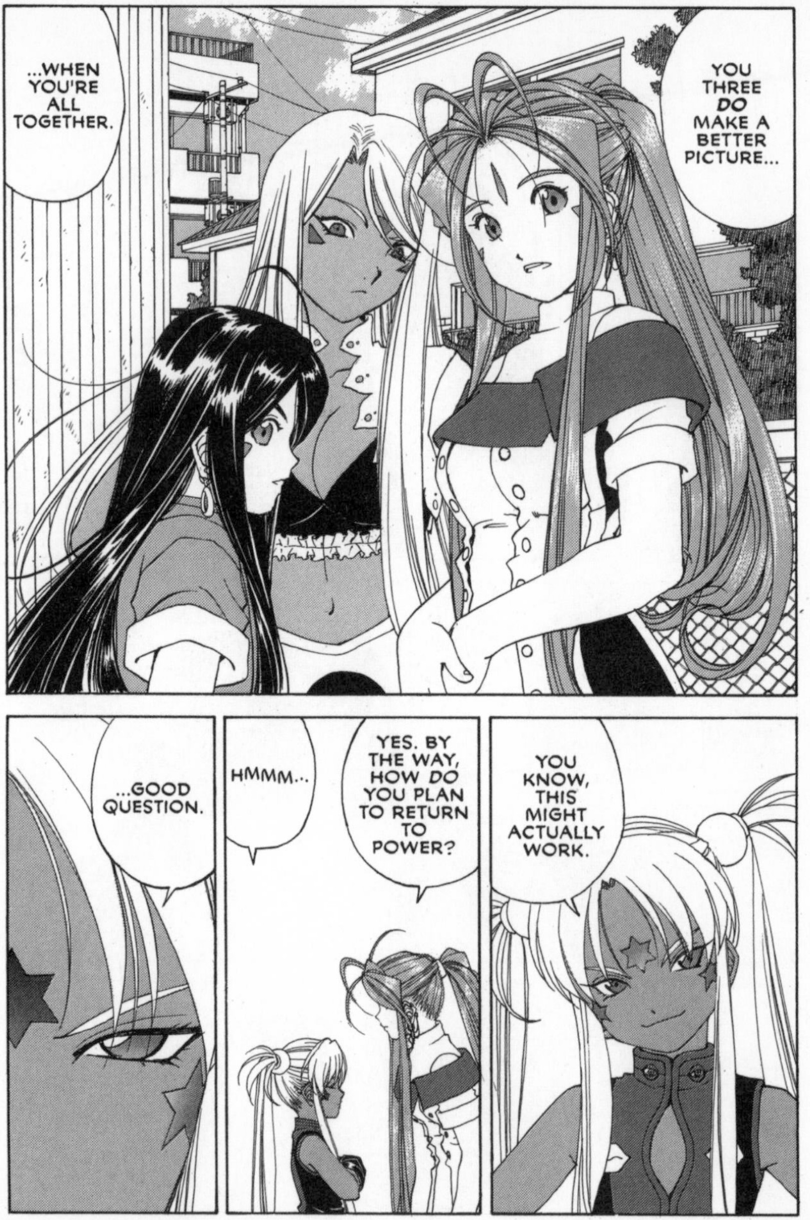
YOU THREE *DO* MAKE A BETTER PICTURE...
...WHEN YOU'RE ALL TOGETHER.
YOU KNOW, THIS MIGHT ACTUALLY WORK.
YES. BY THE WAY, HOW *DO* YOU PLAN TO RETURN TO POWER?
HMMM...
...GOOD QUESTION.

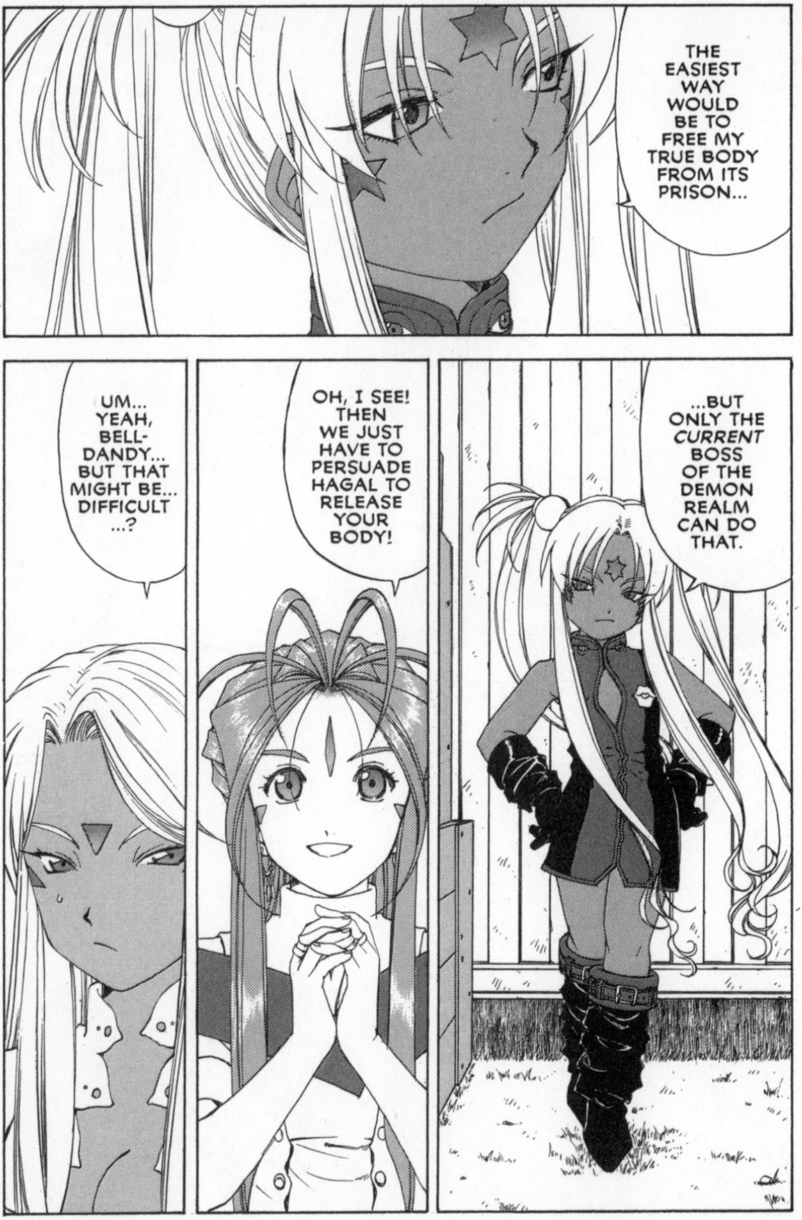
THE EASIEST WAY WOULD BE TO FREE MY TRUE BODY FROM ITS PRISON...
...BUT ONLY THE *CURRENT* BOSS OF THE DEMON REALM CAN DO THAT.
OH, I SEE! THEN WE JUST HAVE TO PERSUADE HAGAL TO RELEASE YOUR BODY!
UM... YEAH, BELL-DANDY... BUT THAT MIGHT BE... DIFFICULT ...?

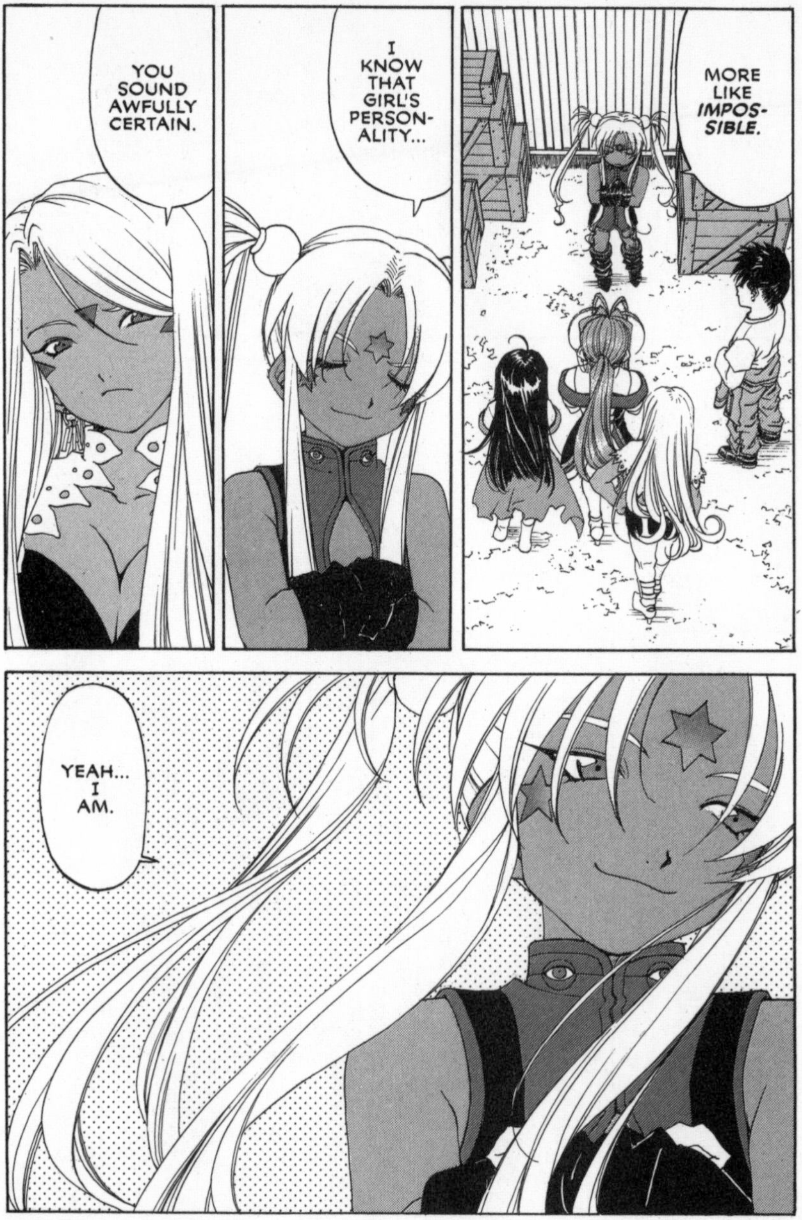
MORE LIKE IMPOSSIBLE.
I KNOW THAT GIRL'S PERSONALITY...
YOU SOUND AWFULLY CERTAIN.
YEAH... I AM.

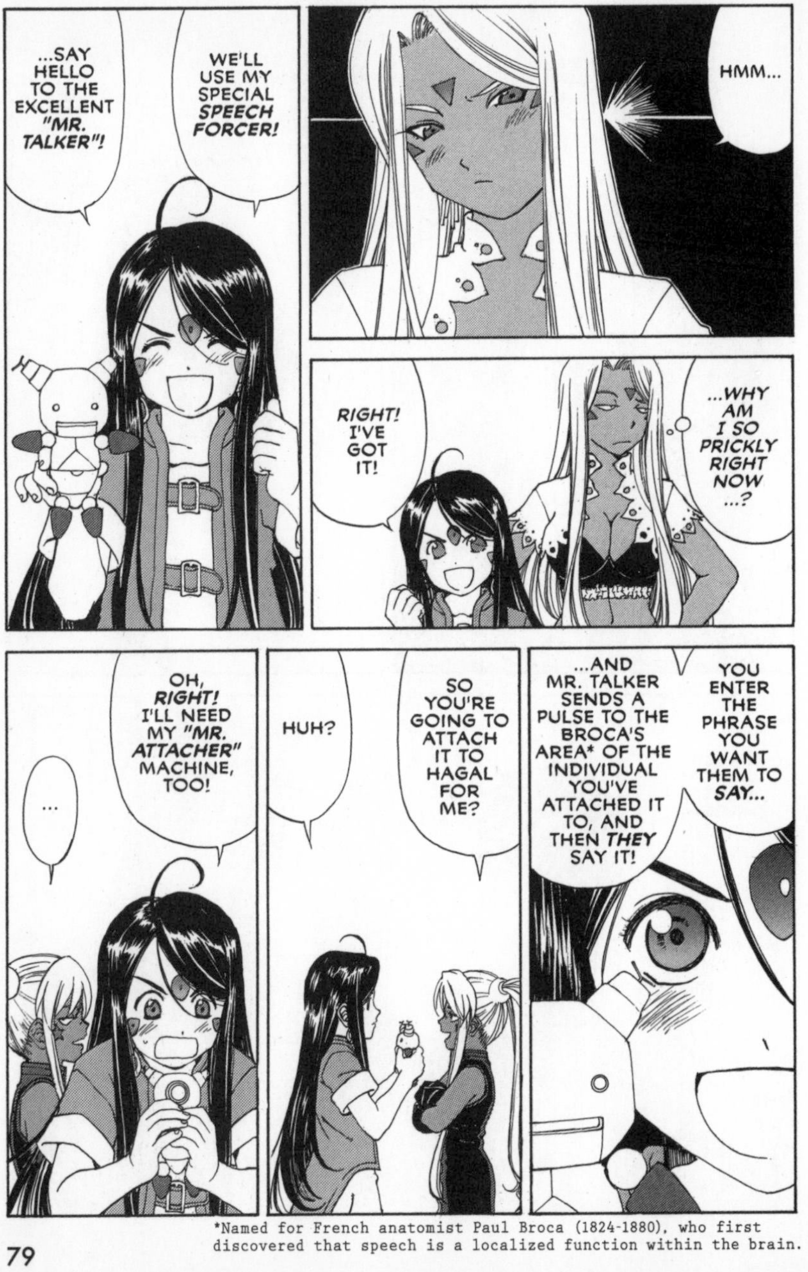
HMM...
...WHY AM I SO PRICKLY RIGHT NOW ...?
RIGHT! I'VE GOT IT!
WE'LL USE MY SPECIAL SPEECH FORCER!
...SAY HELLO TO THE EXCELLENT "MR. TALKER"!
YOU ENTER THE PHRASE YOU WANT THEM TO SAY...
...AND MR. TALKER SENDS A PULSE TO THE BROCA'S AREA* OF THE INDIVIDUAL YOU'VE ATTACHED IT TO, AND THEN THEY SAY IT!
SO YOU'RE GOING TO ATTACH IT TO HAGAL FOR ME?
HUH?
OH, RIGHT! I'LL NEED MY "MR. ATTACHER" MACHINE, TOO!
...

*Named for French anatomist Paul Broca (1824-1880), who first discovered that speech is a localized function within the brain.

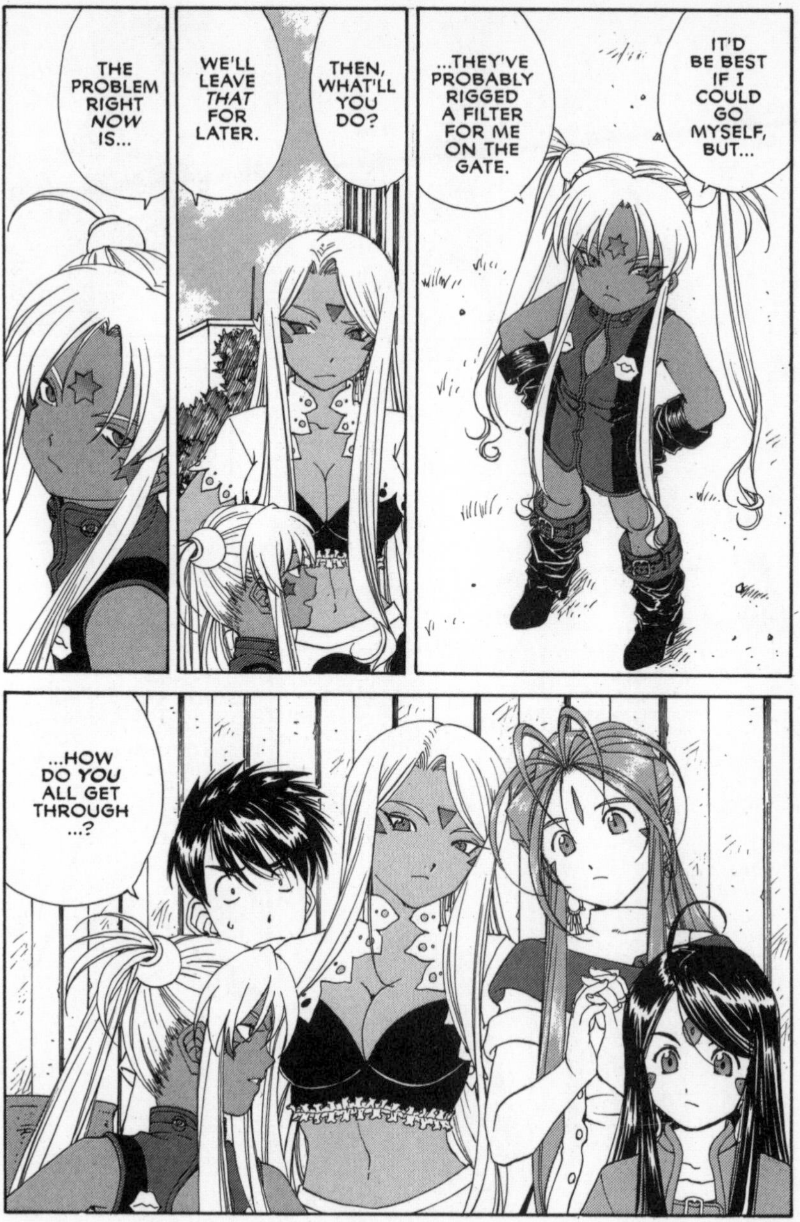
IT'D BE BEST IF I COULD GO MYSELF, BUT...
...THEY'VE PROBABLY RIGGED A FILTER FOR ME ON THE GATE.
THEN, WHAT'LL YOU DO?
WE'LL LEAVE *THAT* FOR LATER.
THE PROBLEM RIGHT *NOW* IS...
...HOW DO *YOU* ALL GET THROUGH ...?

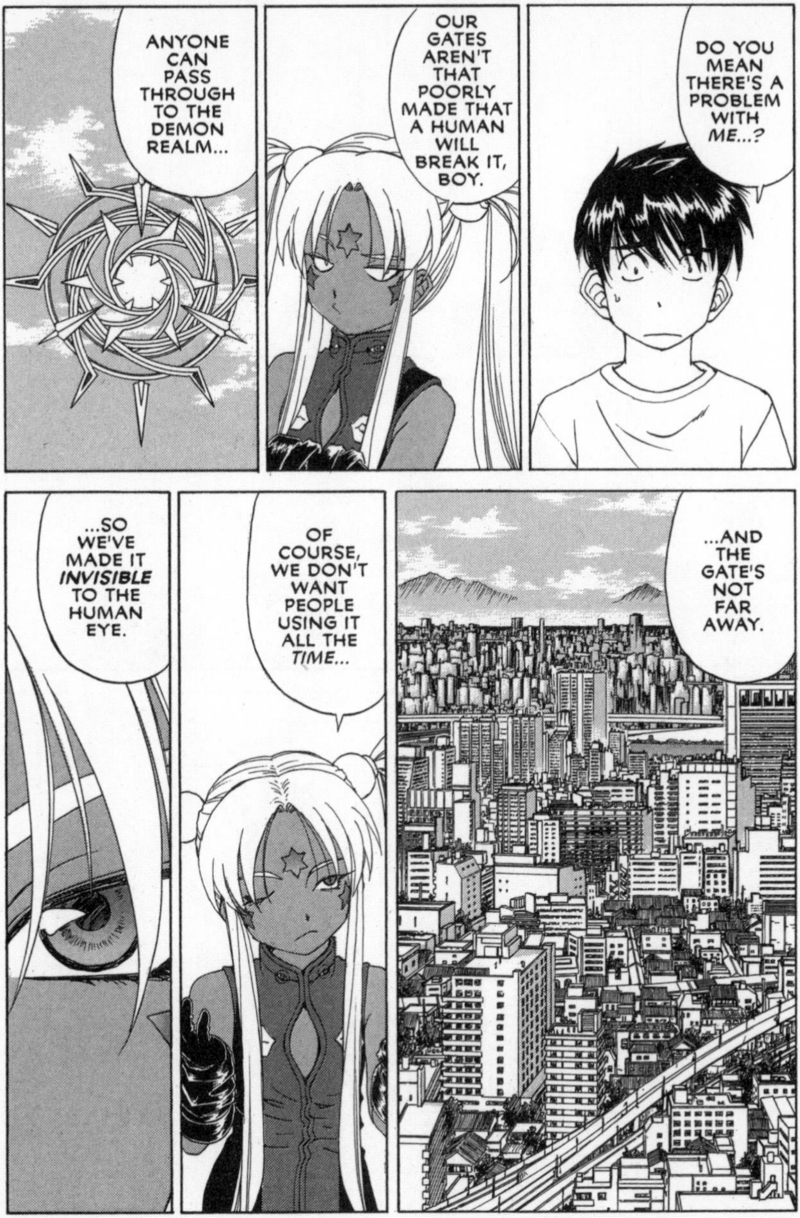
DO YOU MEAN THERE'S A PROBLEM WITH *ME...?*
OUR GATES AREN'T THAT POORLY MADE THAT A HUMAN WILL BREAK IT, BOY.
ANYONE CAN PASS THROUGH TO THE DEMON REALM...
...AND THE GATE'S NOT FAR AWAY.
OF COURSE, WE DON'T WANT PEOPLE USING IT ALL THE *TIME...*
...SO WE'VE MADE IT ***INVISIBLE*** TO THE HUMAN EYE.

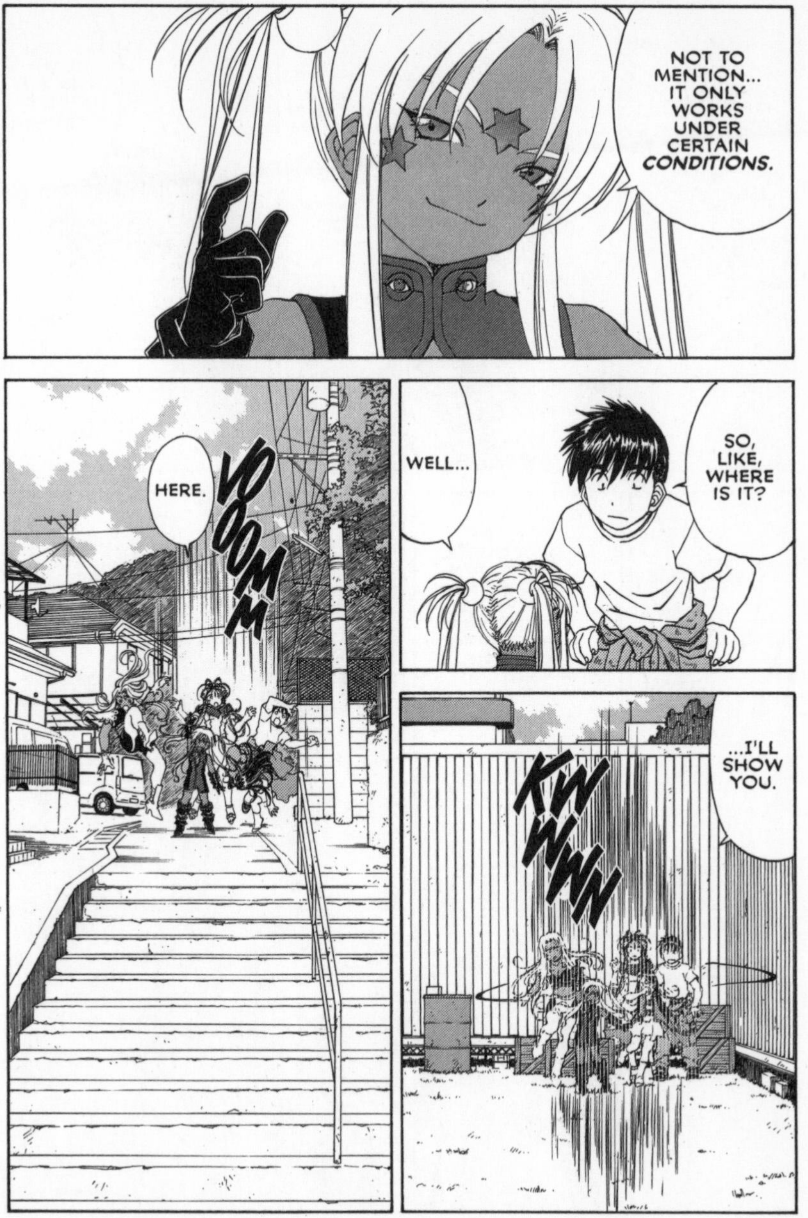
NOT TO MENTION... IT ONLY WORKS UNDER CERTAIN *CONDITIONS.*
SO, LIKE, WHERE IS IT?
WELL...
...I'LL SHOW YOU.
KWWWN
HERE.
VOOOMM

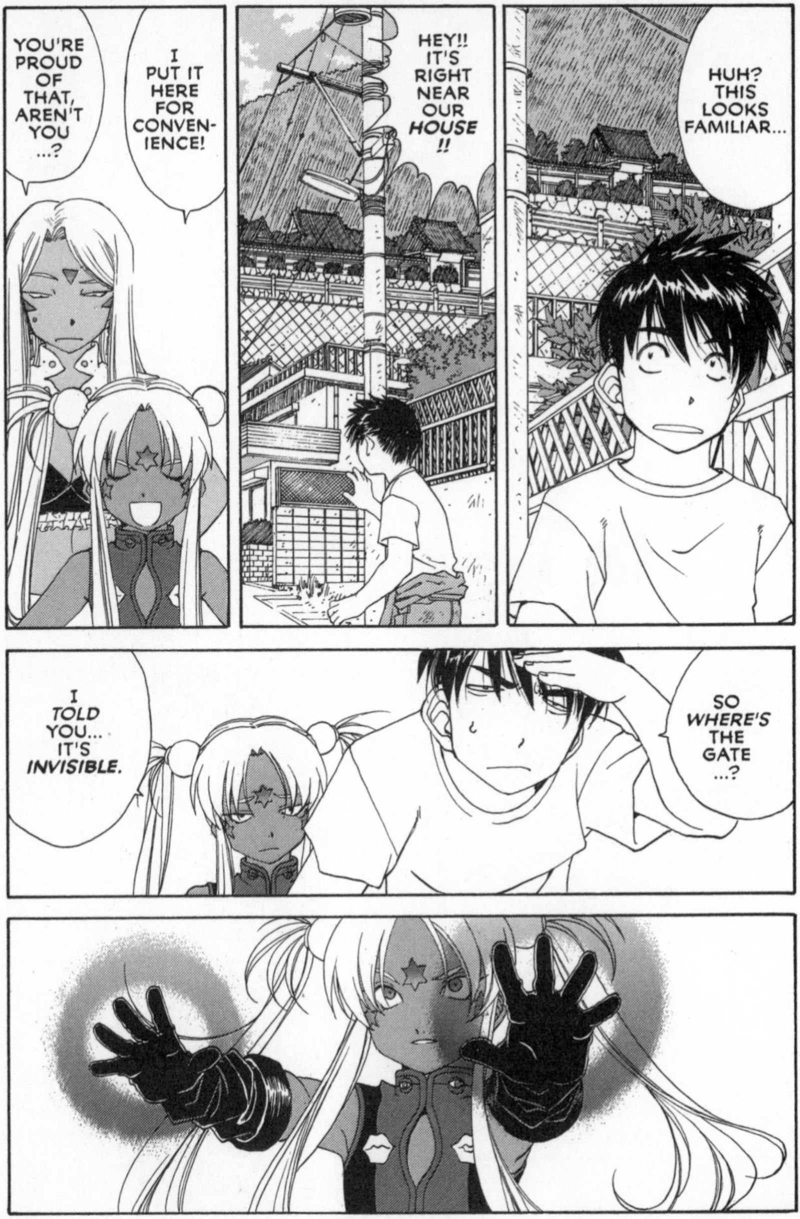
HUH? THIS LOOKS FAMILIAR...
HEY!! IT'S RIGHT NEAR OUR *HOUSE* !!
I PUT IT HERE FOR CONVENIENCE!
YOU'RE PROUD OF THAT, AREN'T YOU ...?
SO *WHERE'S* THE GATE ...?
I *TOLD* YOU... IT'S *INVISIBLE.*

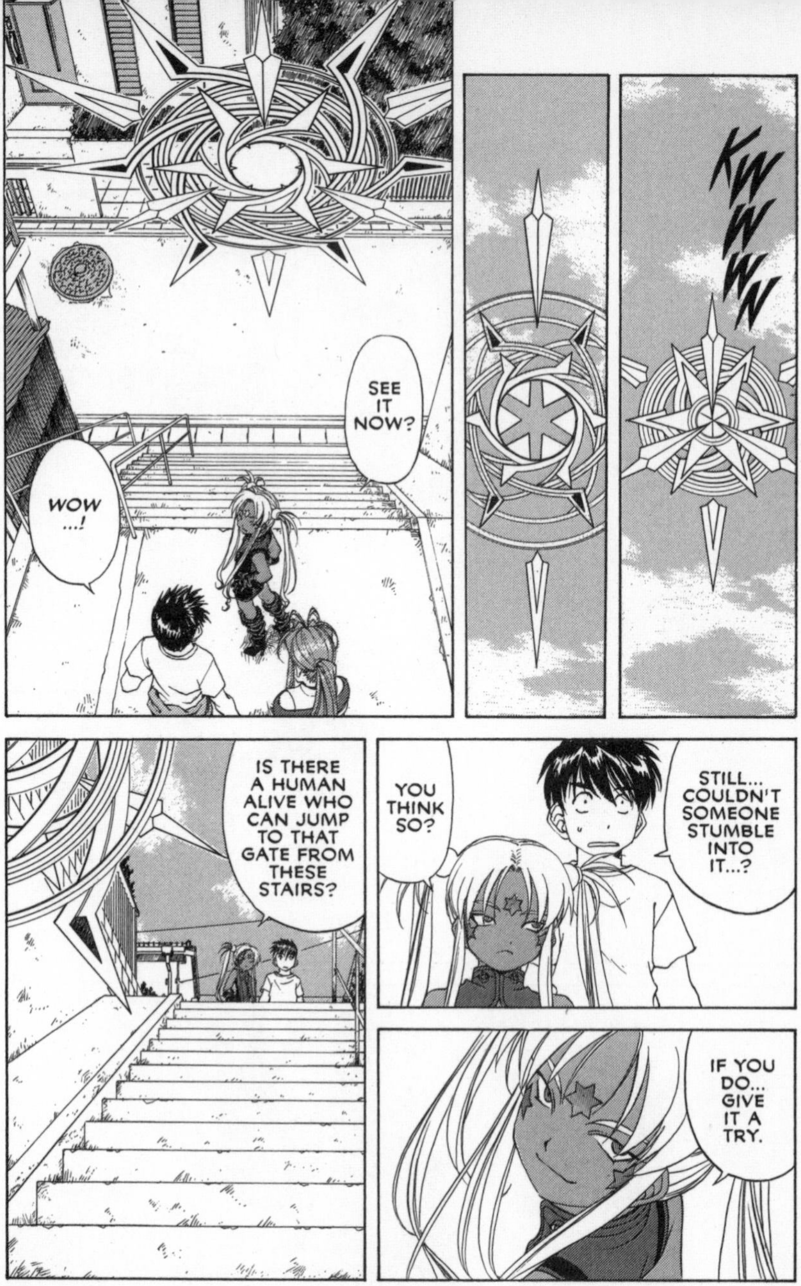
KWWWWN
SEE IT NOW?
WOW ...!
STILL... COULDN'T SOMEONE STUMBLE INTO IT...?
YOU THINK SO?
IF YOU DO... GIVE IT A TRY.
IS THERE A HUMAN ALIVE WHO CAN JUMP TO THAT GATE FROM THESE STAIRS?

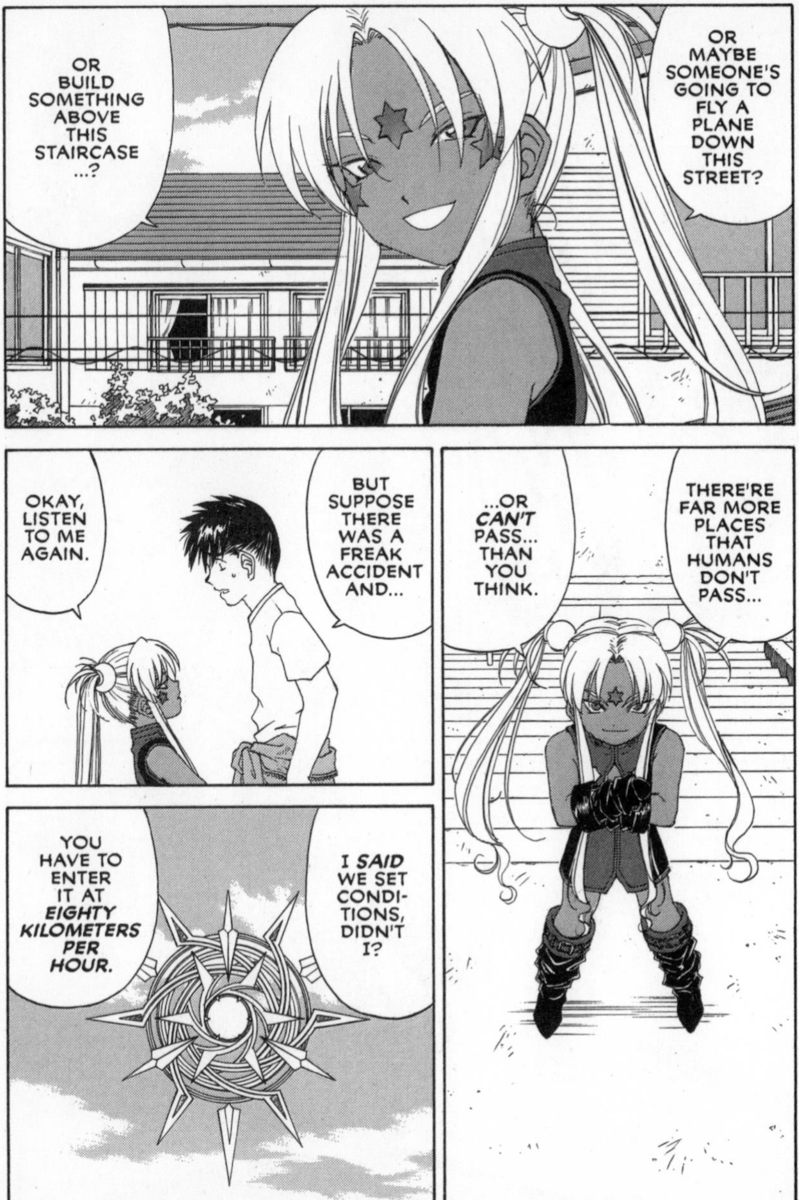
OR MAYBE SOMEONE'S GOING TO FLY A PLANE DOWN THIS STREET?
OR BUILD SOMETHING ABOVE THIS STAIRCASE ...?
THERE'RE FAR MORE PLACES THAT HUMANS DON'T PASS...
...OR *CAN'T* PASS... THAN YOU THINK.
BUT SUPPOSE THERE WAS A FREAK ACCIDENT AND...
OKAY, LISTEN TO ME AGAIN.
I *SAID* WE SET CONDITIONS, DIDN'T I?
YOU HAVE TO ENTER IT AT *EIGHTY KILOMETERS PER HOUR.*

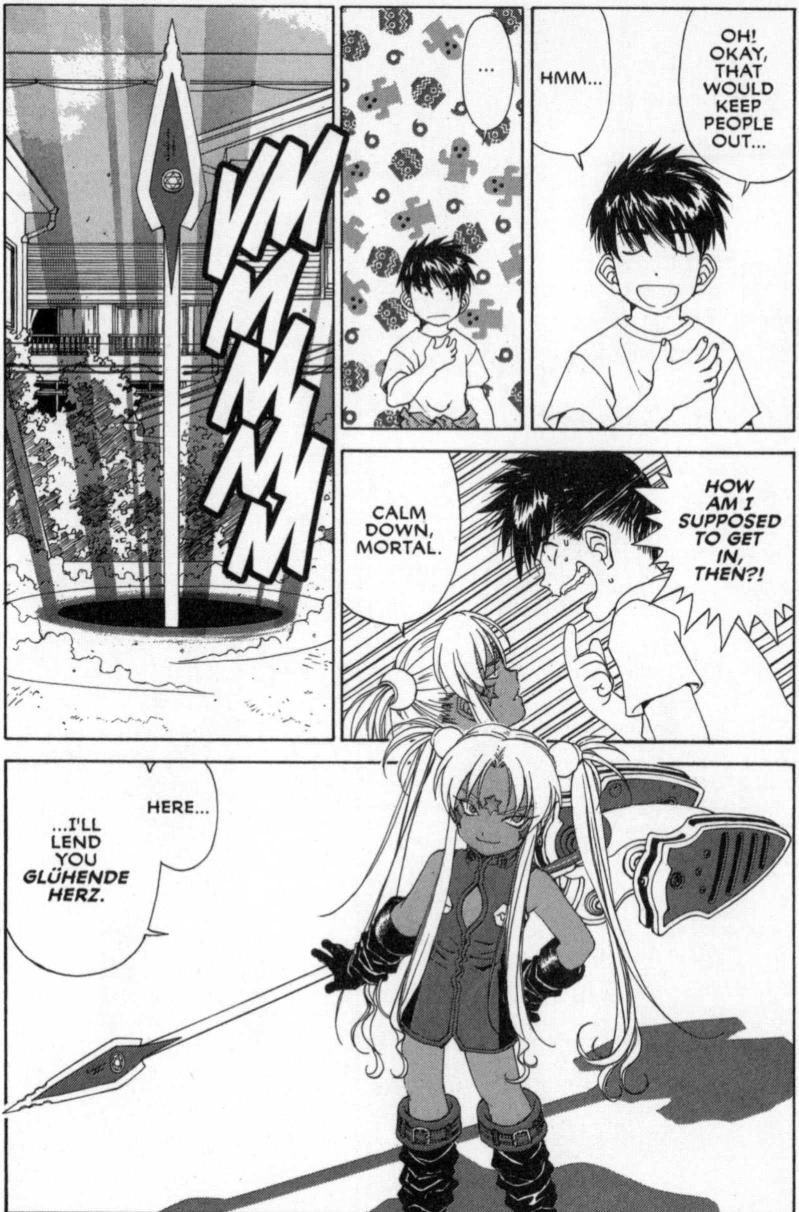
OH! OKAY, THAT WOULD KEEP PEOPLE OUT...
HMM...
...
HOW AM I SUPPOSED TO GET IN, THEN?!
CALM DOWN, MORTAL.
VMMMMM
HERE...
...I'LL LEND YOU GLÜHENDE HERZ.

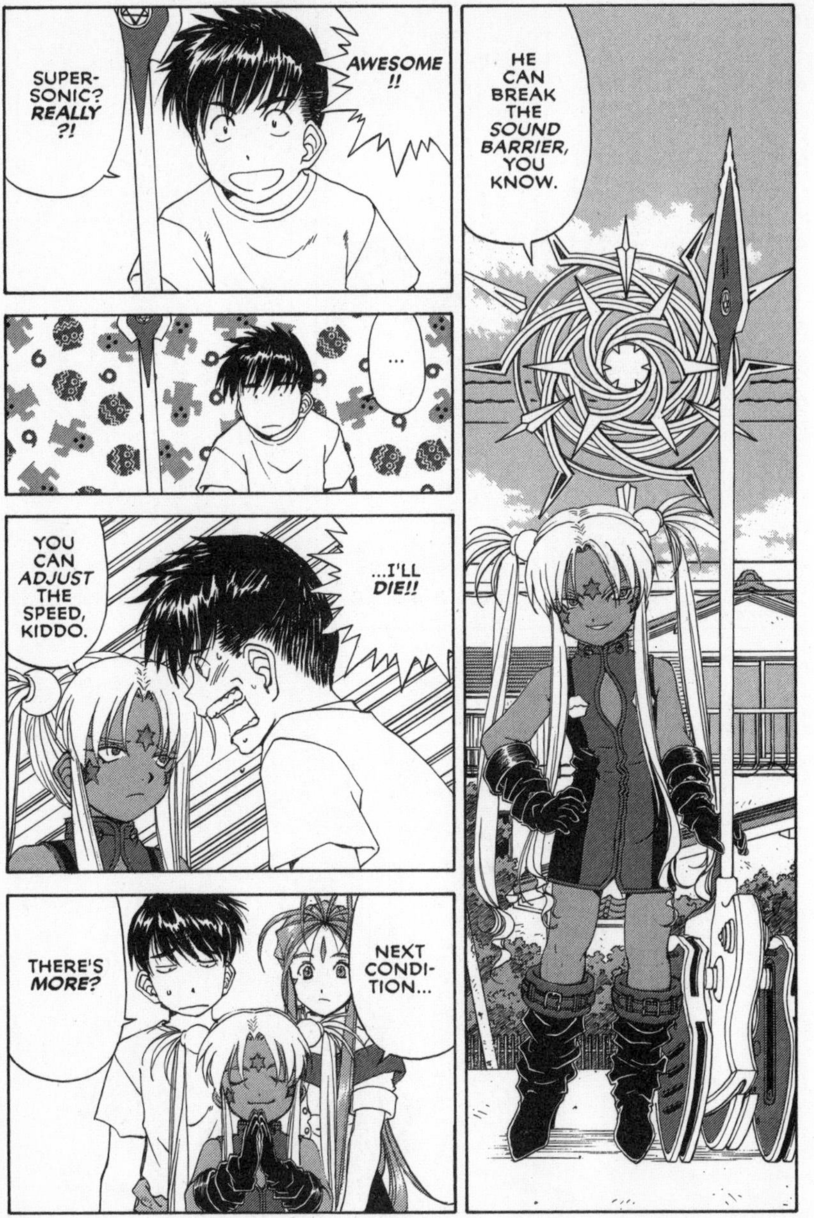
HE CAN BREAK THE SOUND BARRIER, YOU KNOW.
SUPER-SONIC? REALLY?!
AWESOME!!
...
...I'LL DIE!!
YOU CAN ADJUST THE SPEED, KIDDO.
NEXT CONDI-TION...
THERE'S MORE?

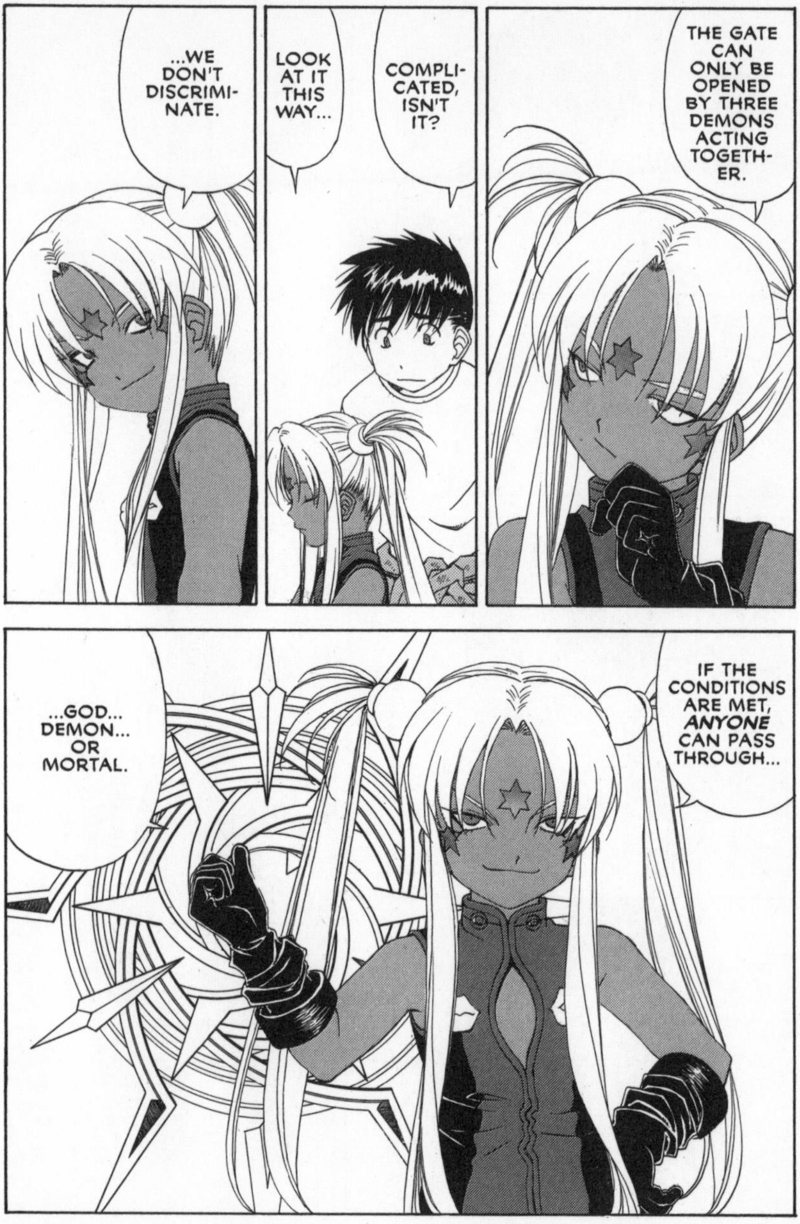
THE GATE CAN ONLY BE OPENED BY THREE DEMONS ACTING TOGETH-ER.
COMPLI-CATED, ISN'T IT?
LOOK AT IT THIS WAY...
...WE DON'T DISCRIMI-NATE.
IF THE CONDITIONS ARE MET, **ANYONE** CAN PASS THROUGH...
...GOD... DEMON... OR MORTAL.

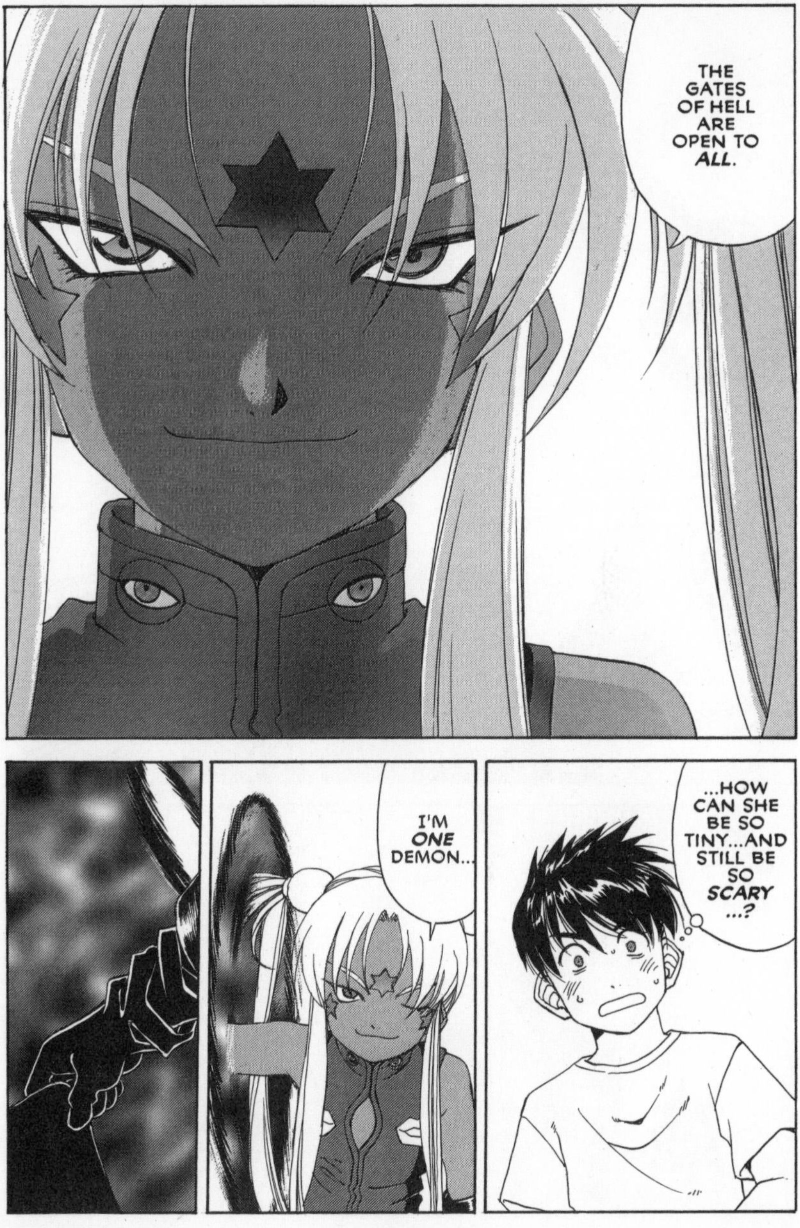
THE GATES OF HELL ARE OPEN TO ALL.
...HOW CAN SHE BE SO TINY...AND STILL BE SO SCARY ...?
I'M ONE DEMON...

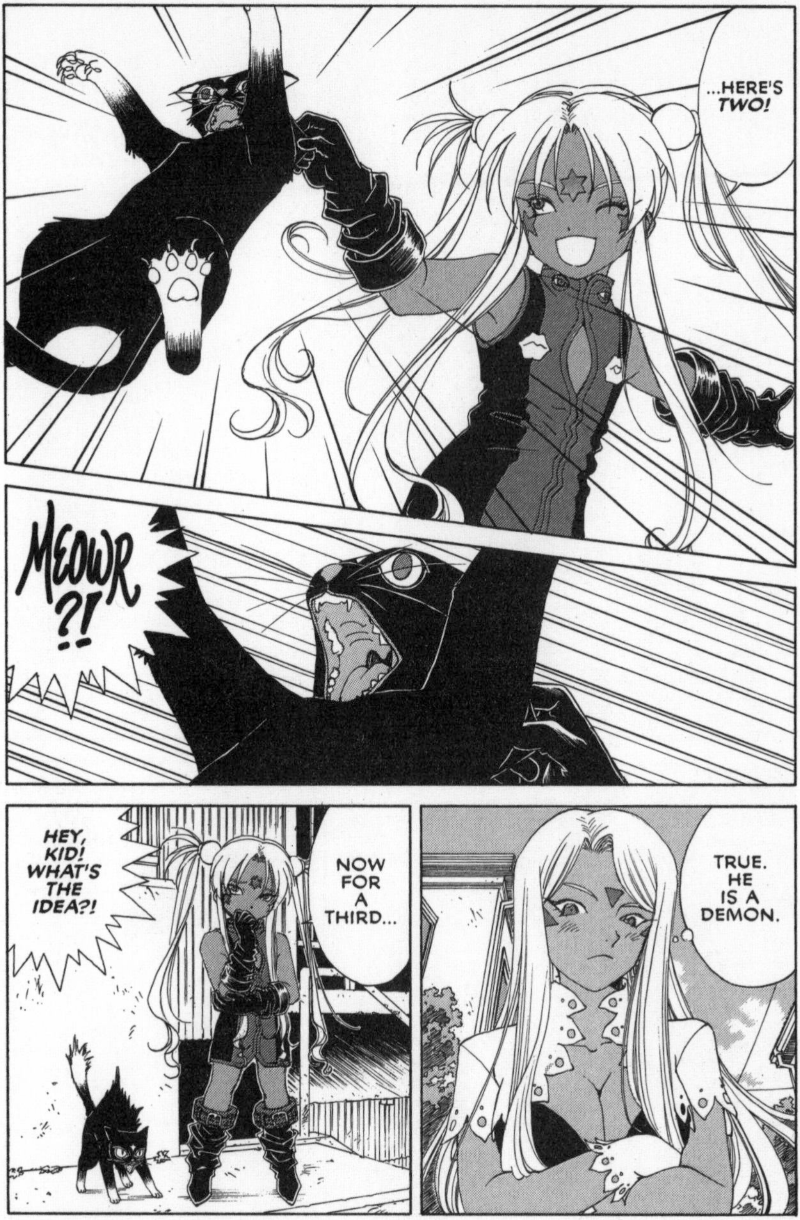
...HERE'S *TWO!*
MEOWR ?!
TRUE. HE IS A DEMON.
NOW FOR A THIRD...
HEY, KID! WHAT'S THE IDEA?!

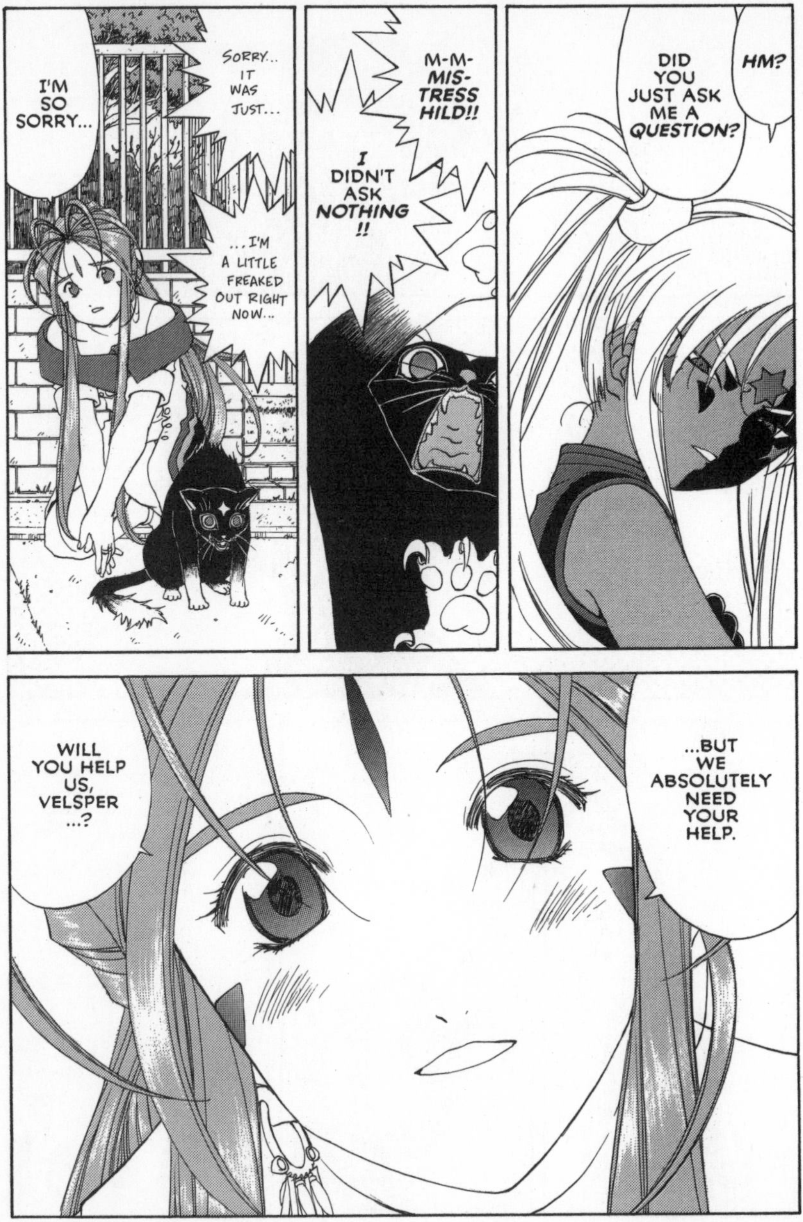
HM?
DID YOU JUST ASK ME A QUESTION?
M-M-MISTRESS HILD!!
I DIDN'T ASK NOTHING !!
SORRY... IT WAS JUST...
I'M SO SORRY...
...I'M A LITTLE FREAKED OUT RIGHT NOW...
...BUT WE ABSOLUTELY NEED YOUR HELP.
WILL YOU HELP US, VELSPER ...?

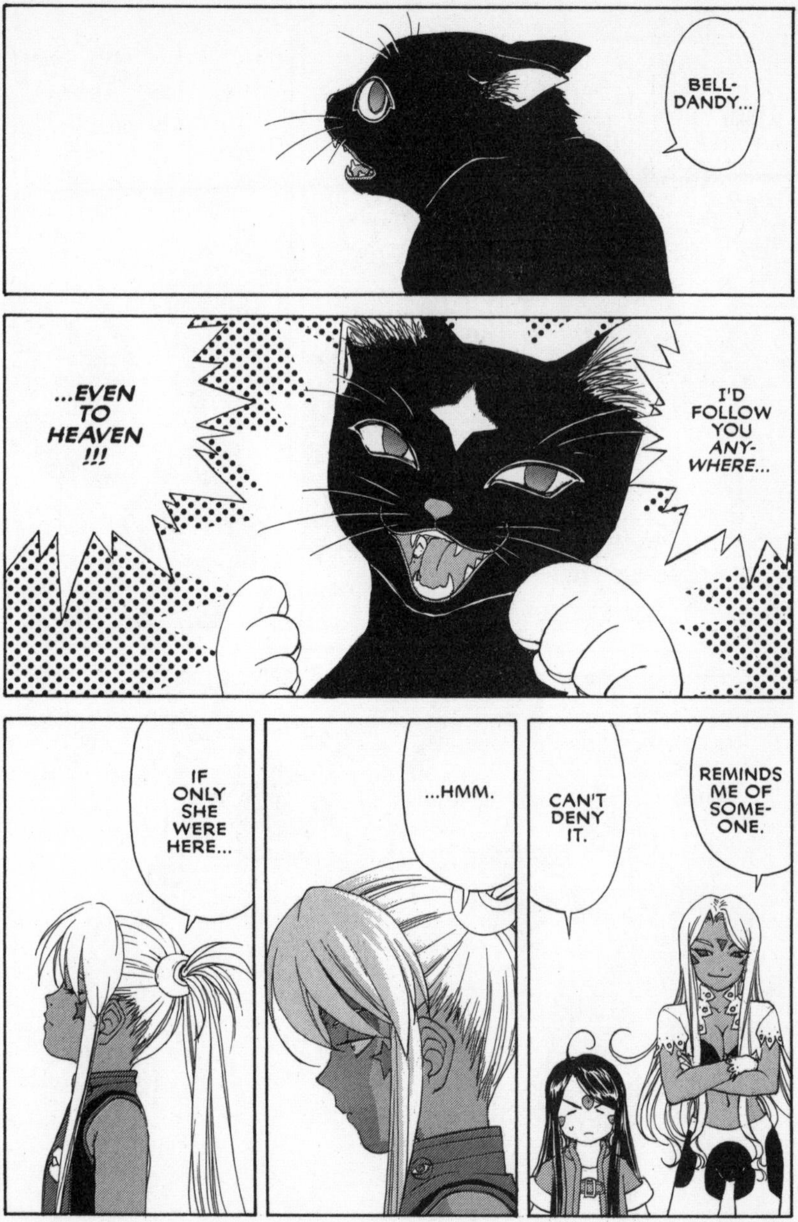
BELL-DANDY...
I'D FOLLOW YOU ANY-WHERE...
...EVEN TO HEAVEN!!!
REMINDS ME OF SOME-ONE.
CAN'T DENY IT.
...HMM.
IF ONLY SHE WERE HERE...

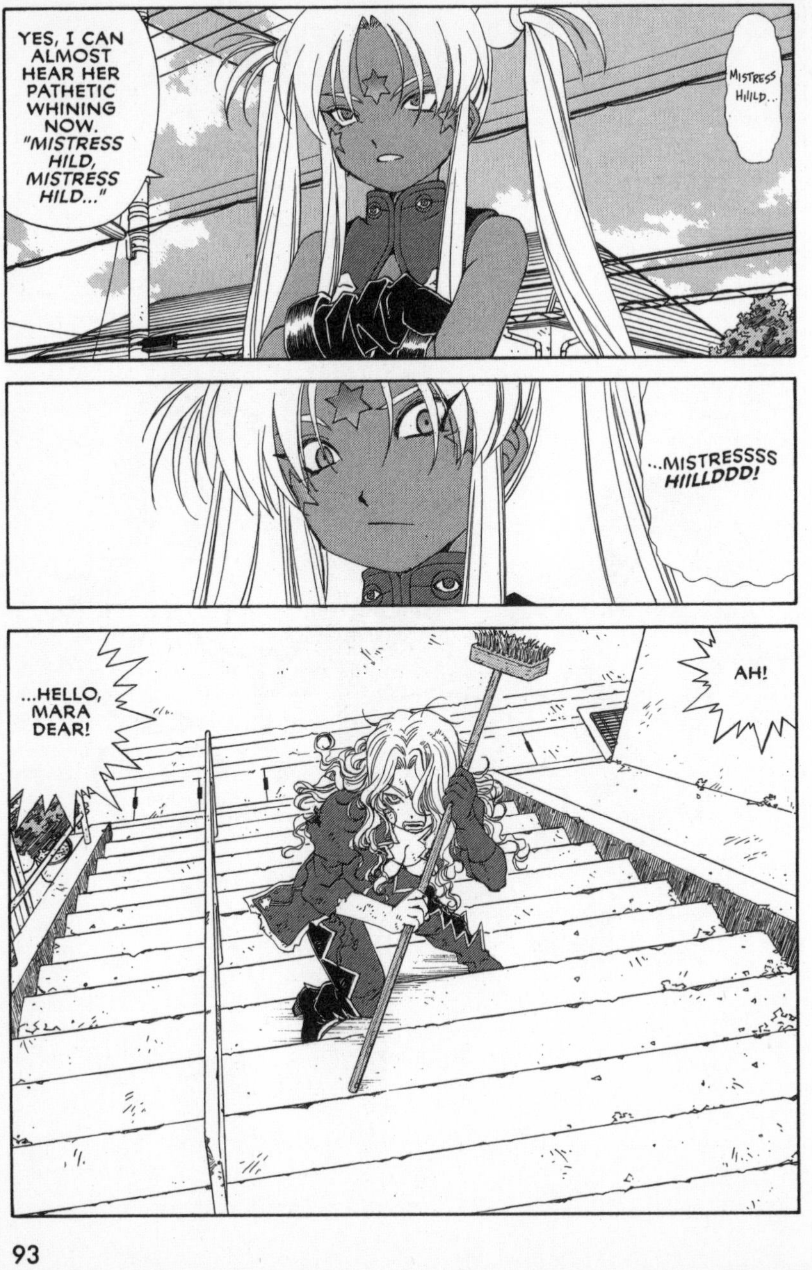
Mistress Hiiild...
YES, I CAN ALMOST HEAR HER PATHETIC WHINING NOW. "MISTRESS HILD, MISTRESS HILD..."
...MISTRESSSS HIILLDDD!
AH!
...HELLO, MARA DEAR!

OH MY GODDESS!
PEORTH & LIND

CHAPTER 247

Three Goddesses, Three Demons

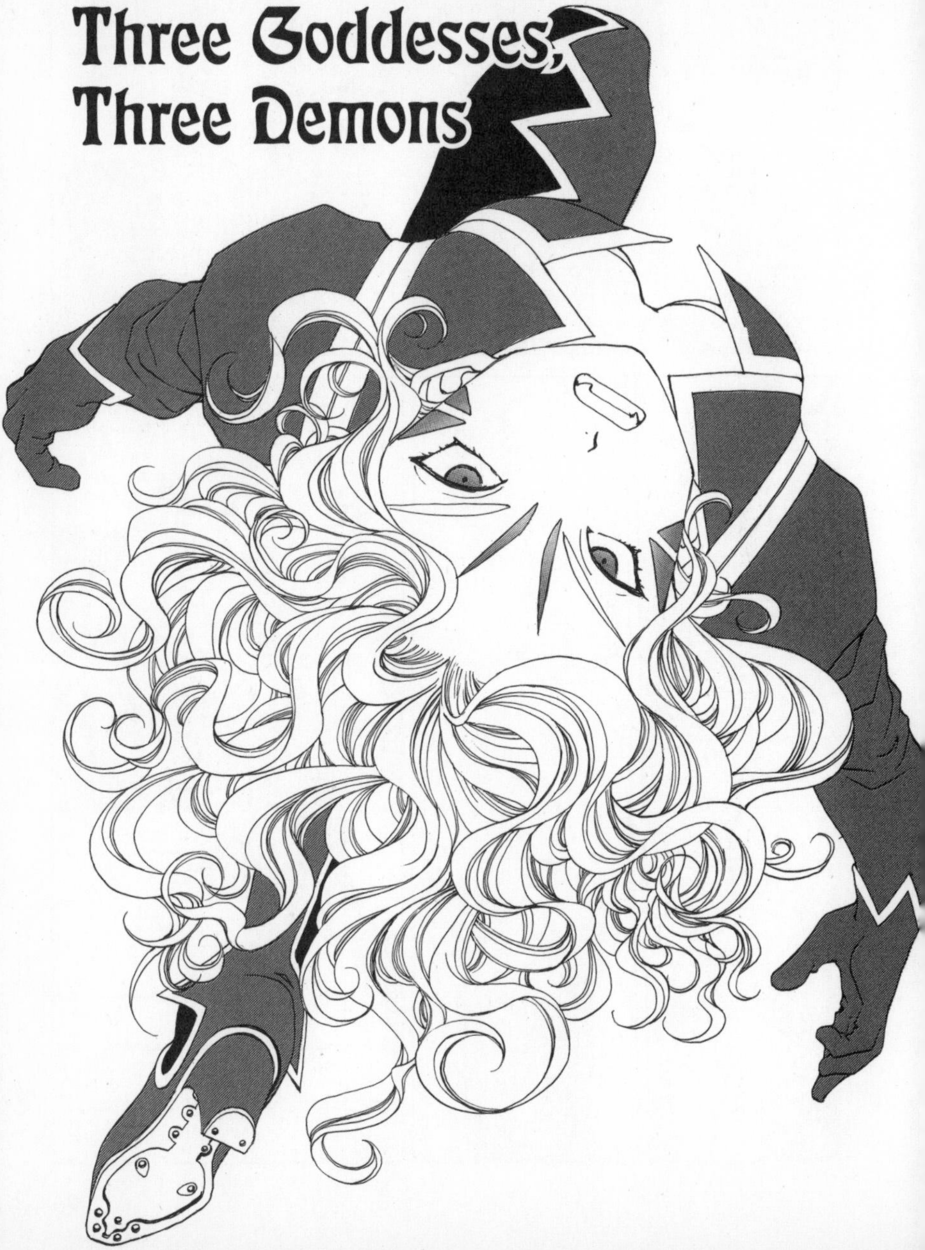

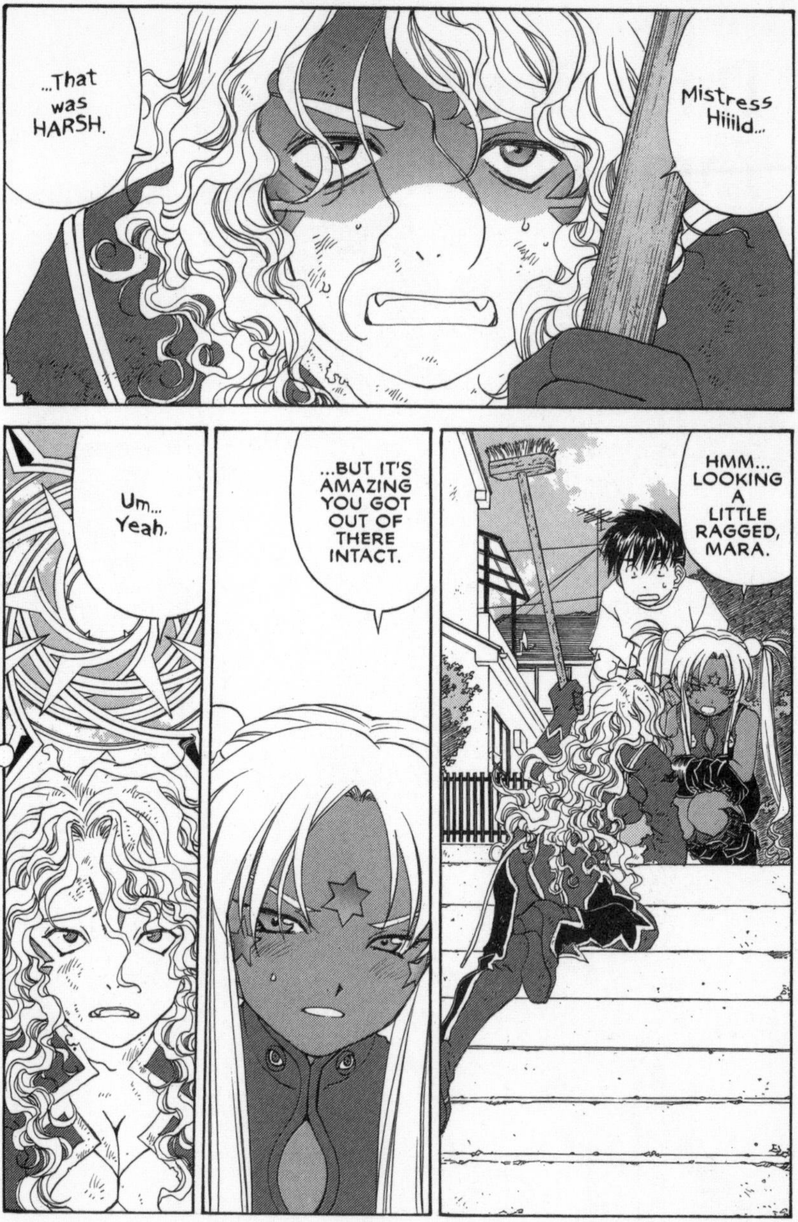
Mistress Hiiild...
...That was HARSH.
HMM... LOOKING A LITTLE RAGGED, MARA.
...BUT IT'S AMAZING YOU GOT OUT OF THERE INTACT.
Um... Yeah.

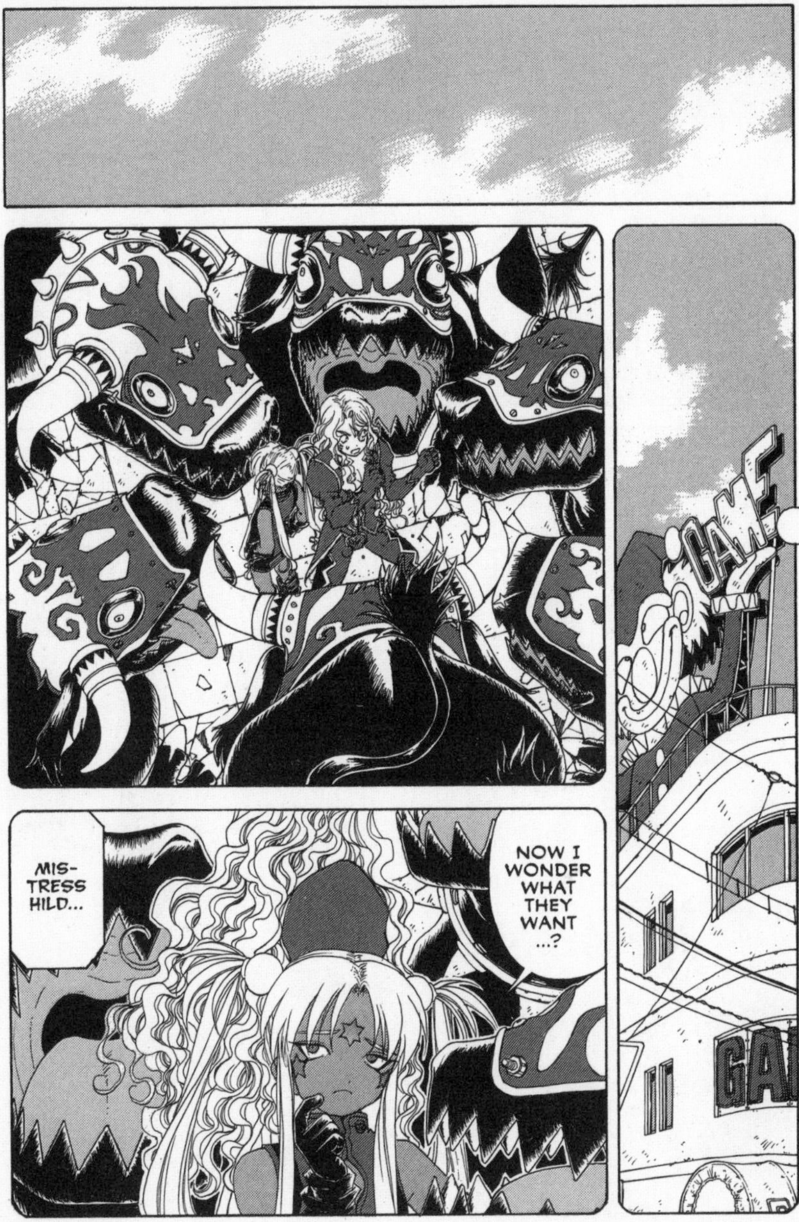
GAME
NOW I WONDER WHAT THEY WANT ...?
MIS-TRESS HILD...

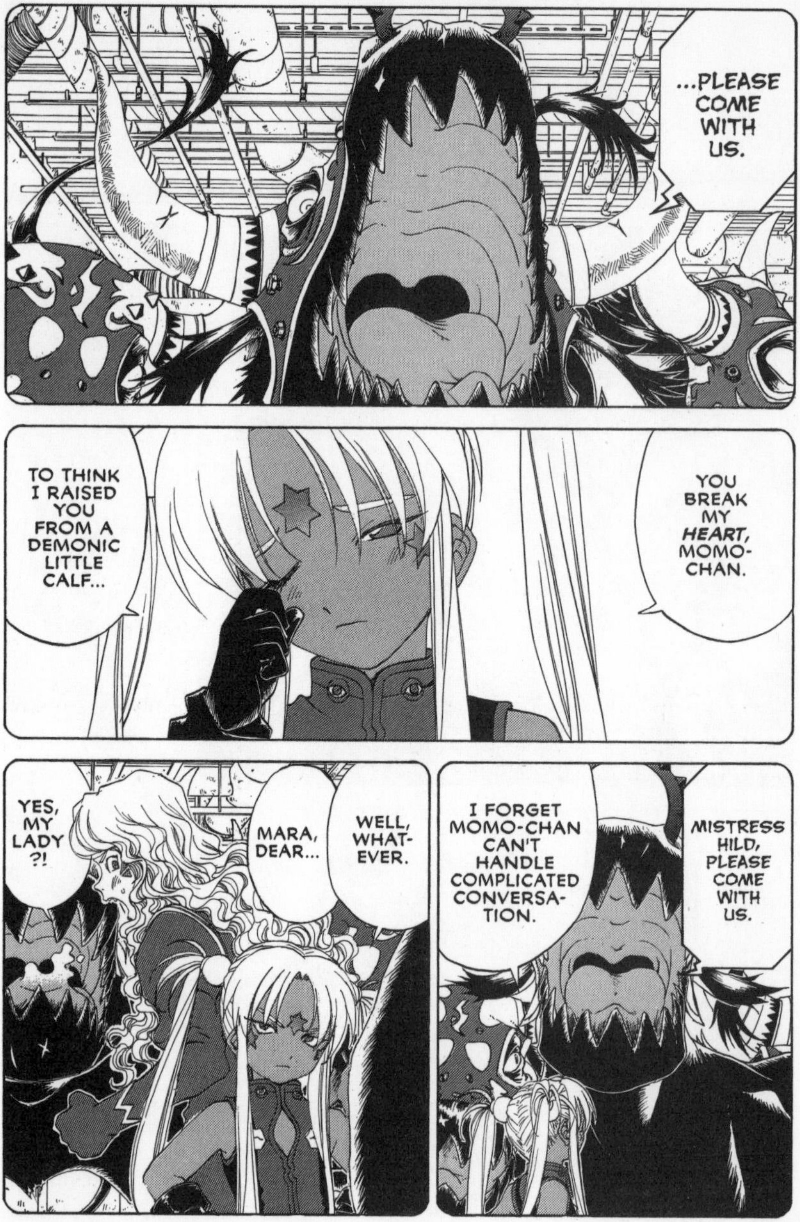
...PLEASE COME WITH US.
YOU BREAK MY *HEART,* MOMO-CHAN.
TO THINK I RAISED YOU FROM A DEMONIC LITTLE CALF...
MISTRESS HILD, PLEASE COME WITH US.
I FORGET MOMO-CHAN CAN'T HANDLE COMPLICATED CONVERSATION.
WELL, WHATEVER.
MARA, DEAR...
YES, MY LADY ?!

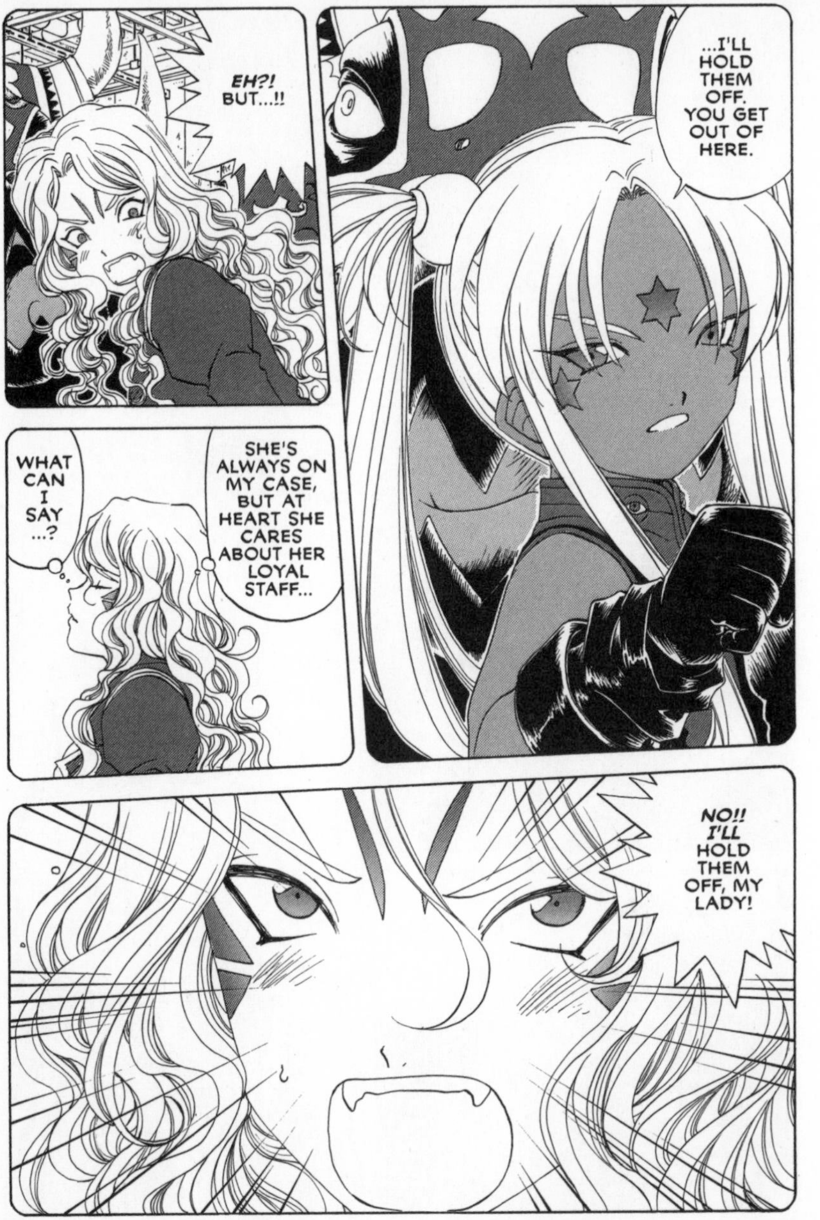
...I'LL HOLD THEM OFF. YOU GET OUT OF HERE.
EH?! BUT...!!
SHE'S ALWAYS ON MY CASE, BUT AT HEART SHE CARES ABOUT HER LOYAL STAFF...
WHAT CAN I SAY ...?
NO!! I'LL HOLD THEM OFF, MY LADY!

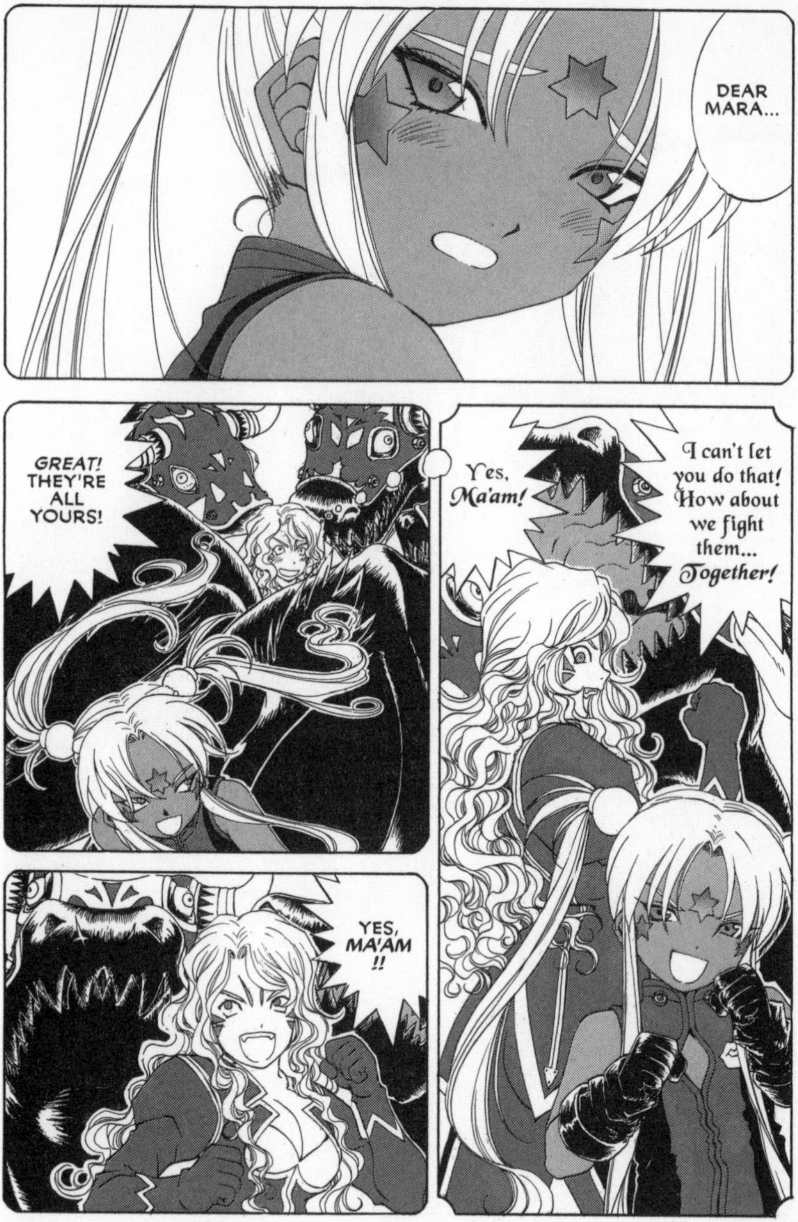
DEAR MARA...
I can't let you do that! How about we fight them... Together!
Yes, Ma'am!
GREAT! THEY'RE ALL YOURS!
YES, MA'AM !!

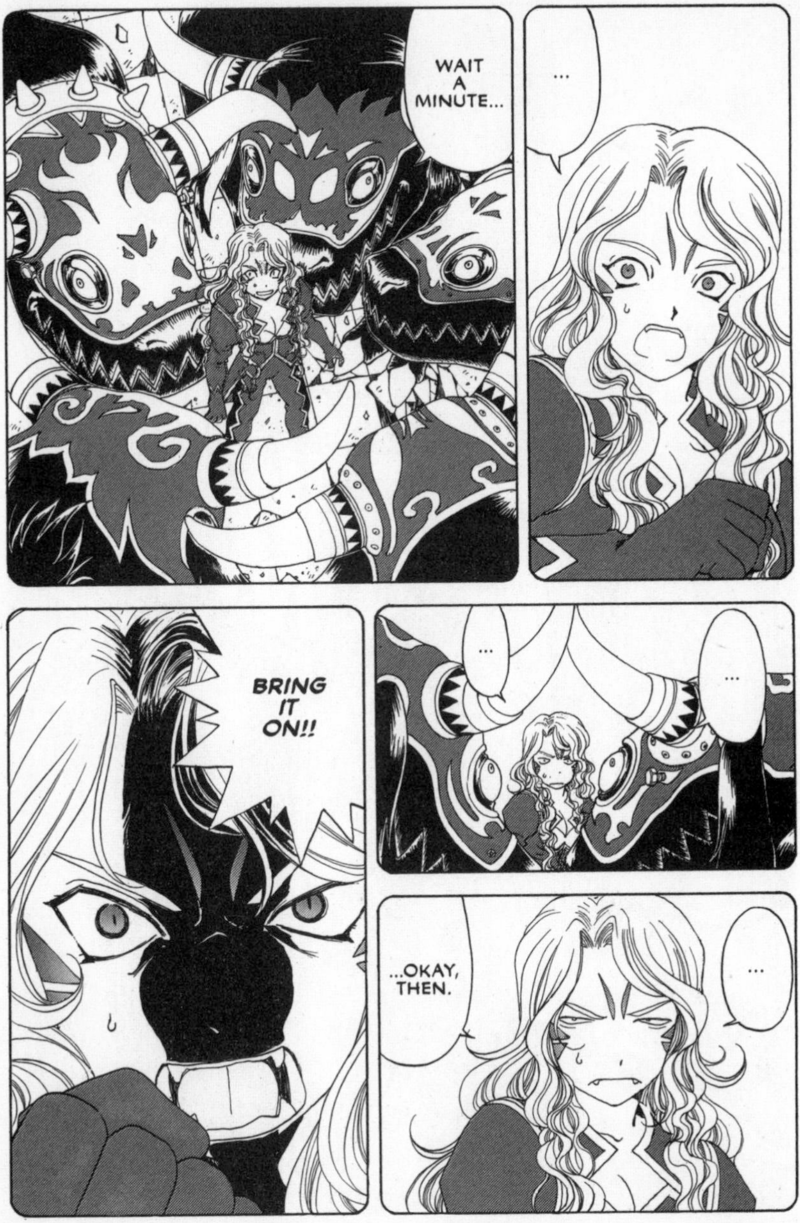
...
WAIT A MINUTE...
...
...
...
...OKAY, THEN.
BRING IT ON!!

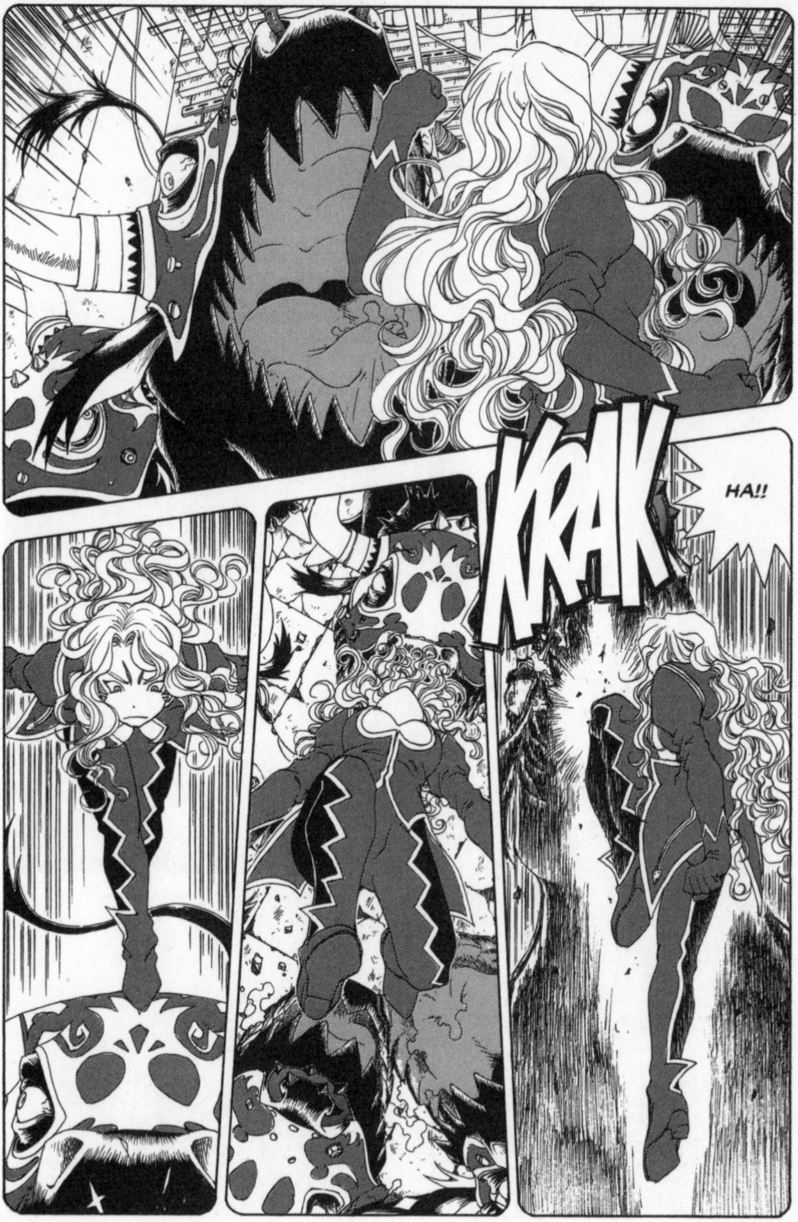
KRAK
HA!!

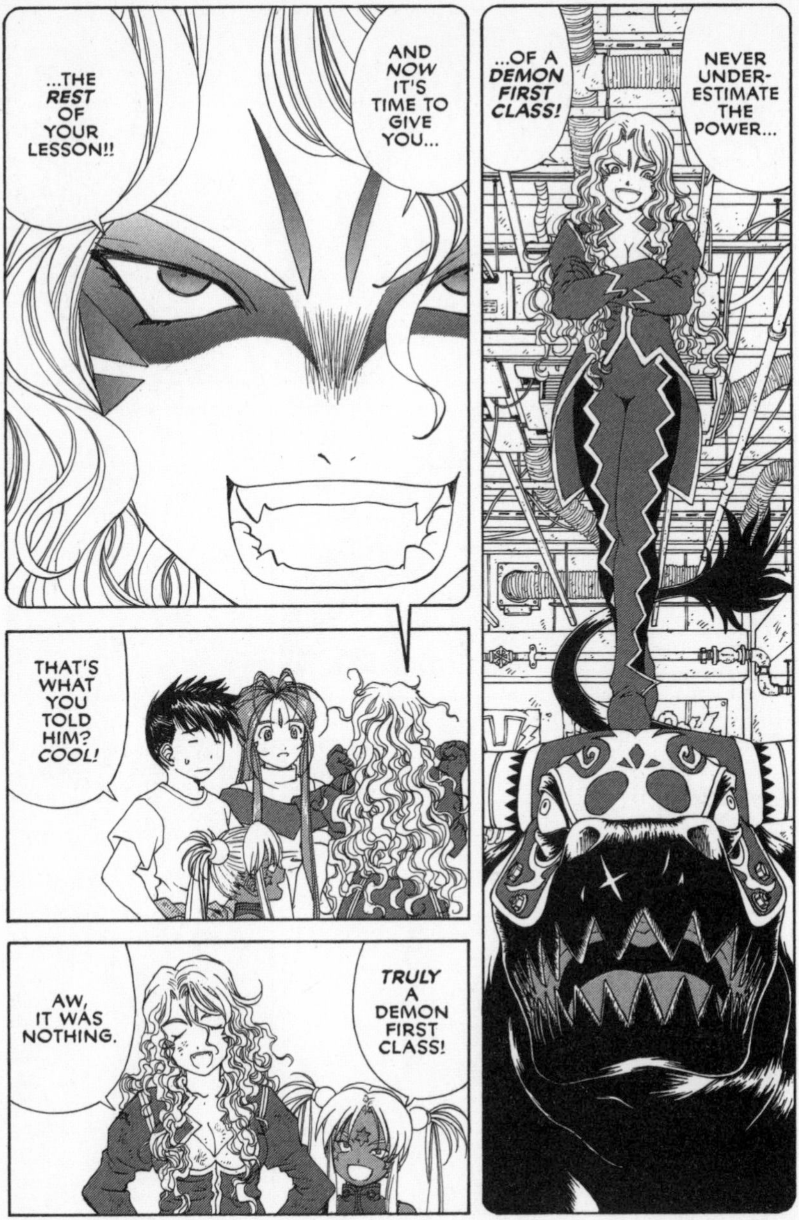
NEVER UNDER-ESTIMATE THE POWER...
...OF A DEMON FIRST CLASS!
AND NOW IT'S TIME TO GIVE YOU...
...THE REST OF YOUR LESSON!!
THAT'S WHAT YOU TOLD HIM? COOL!
TRULY A DEMON FIRST CLASS!
AW, IT WAS NOTHING.

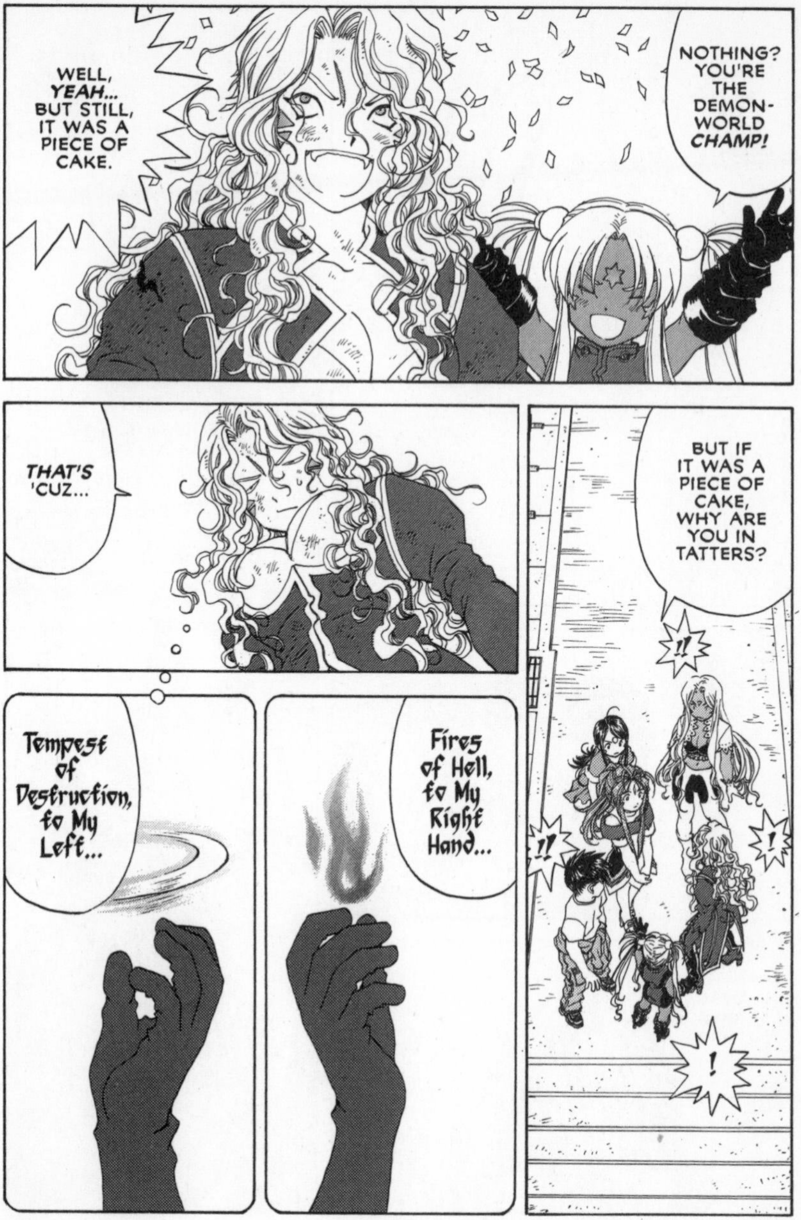
NOTHING? YOU'RE THE DEMON-WORLD *CHAMP!*
WELL, *YEAH*... BUT STILL, IT WAS A PIECE OF CAKE.
BUT IF IT WAS A PIECE OF CAKE, WHY ARE YOU IN TATTERS?
!!
!
!!
!
THAT'S 'CUZ...
Fires of Hell, to My Right Hand...
Tempest of Destruction, to My Left...

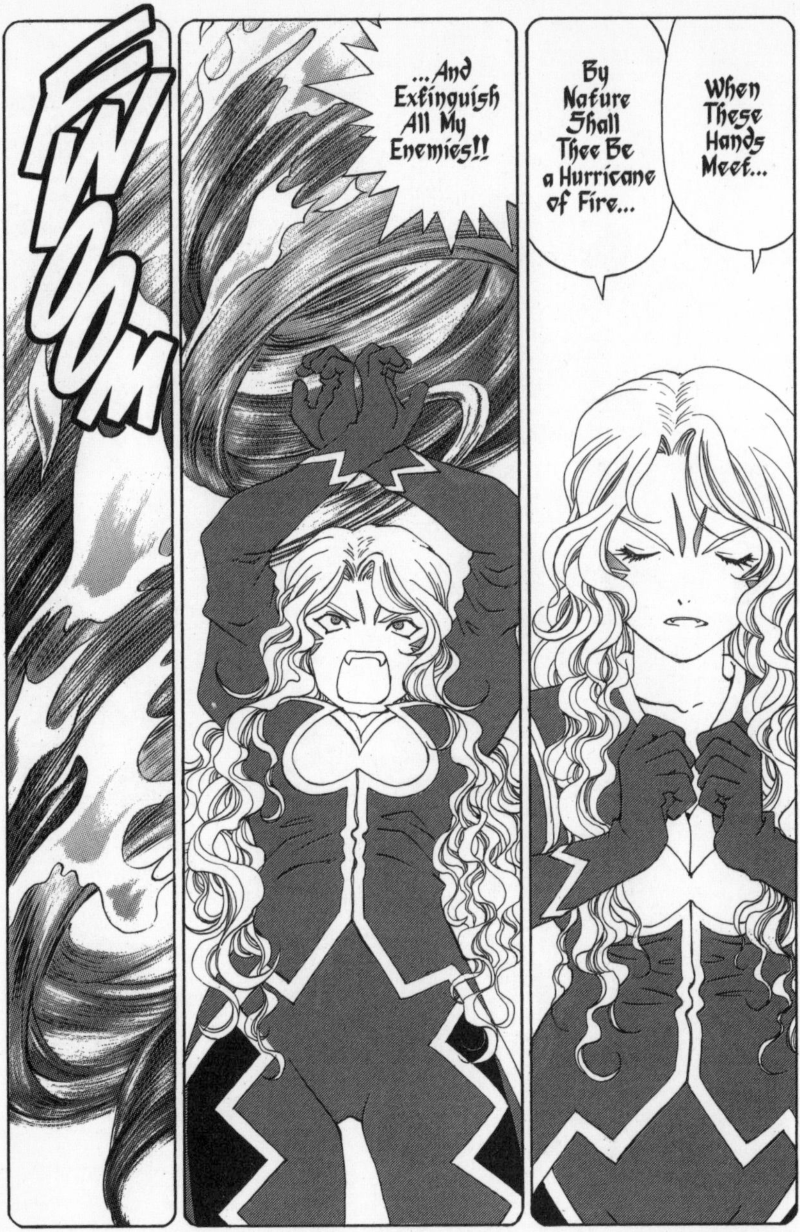
When These Hands Meet...
By Nature Shall Thee Be a Hurricane of Fire...
...And Extinguish All My Enemies!!
VWOOOM

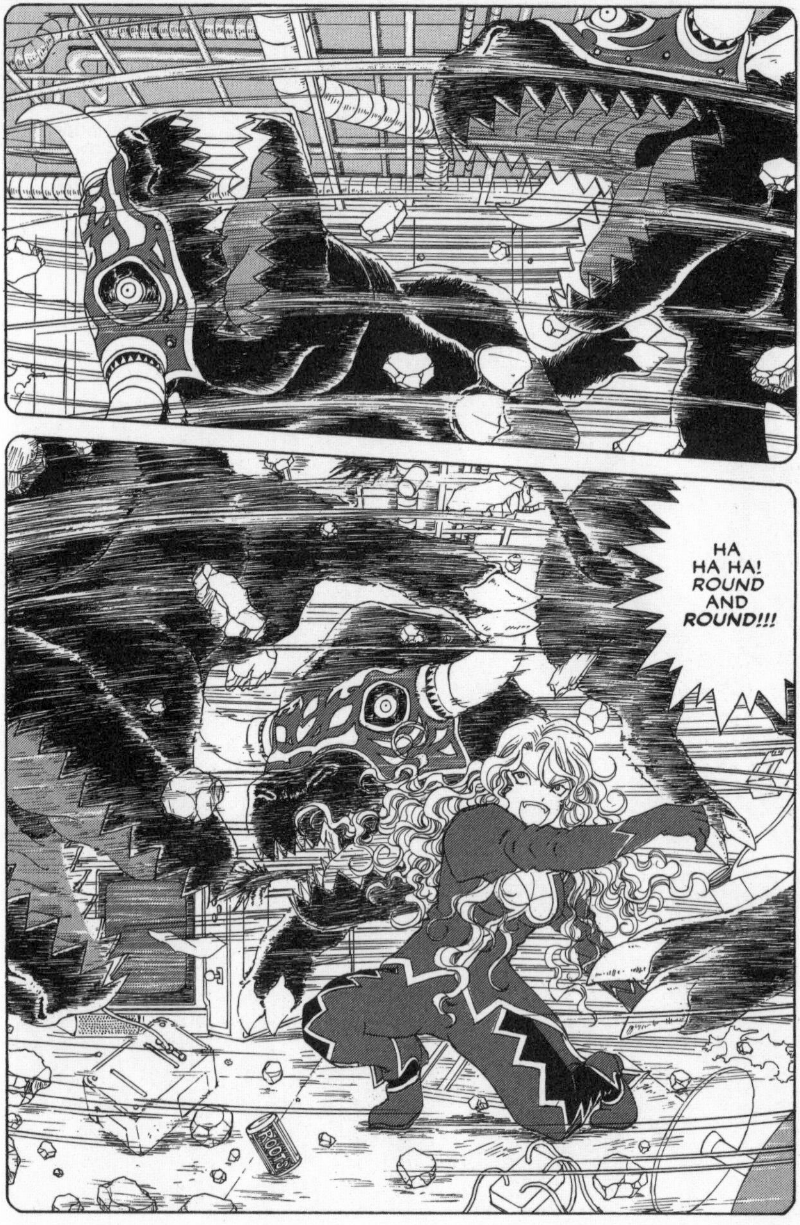
HA HA HA! ROUND AND ROUND!!!
ROOTS

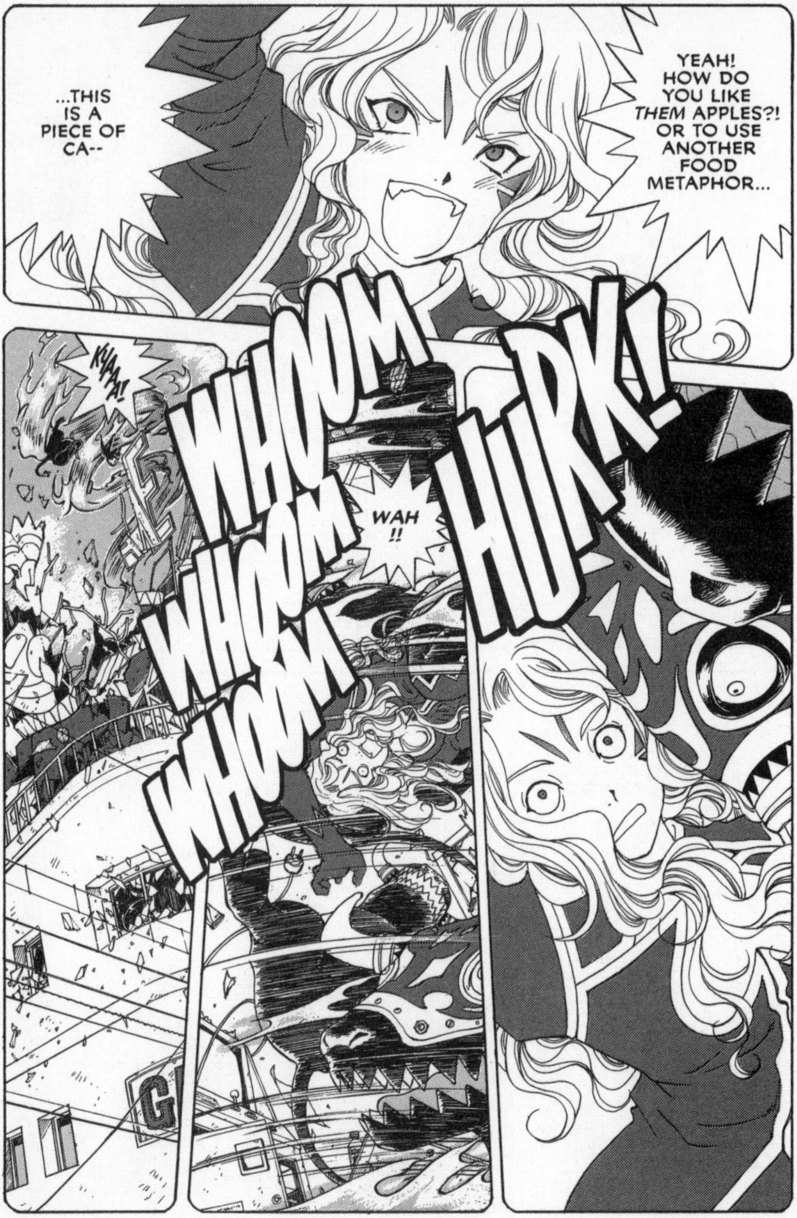
YEAH! HOW DO YOU LIKE *THEM* APPLES?! OR TO USE ANOTHER FOOD METAPHOR...
...THIS IS A PIECE OF CA--
HURK!!
WHOOM WHOOM WHOOM
WAH !!
KYAAA!

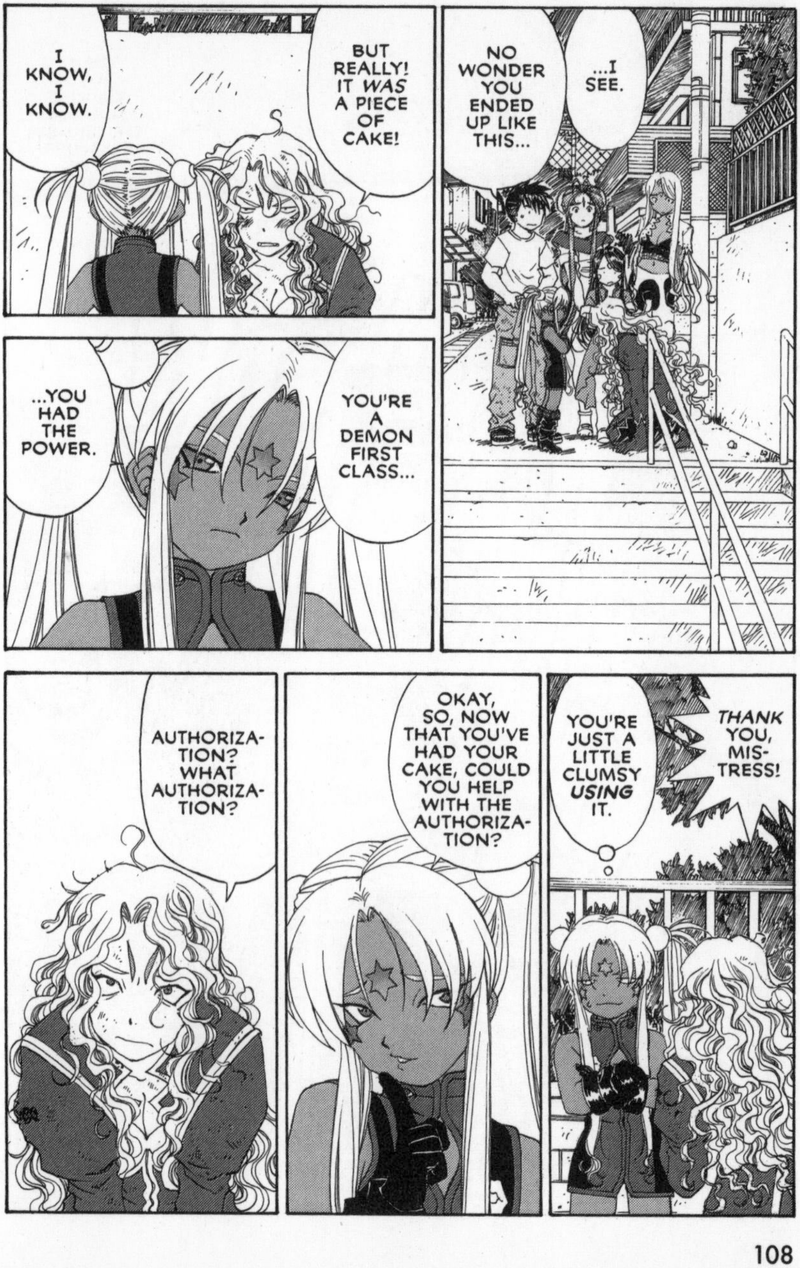
...I SEE.
NO WONDER YOU ENDED UP LIKE THIS...
BUT REALLY! IT *WAS* A PIECE OF CAKE!
I KNOW, I KNOW.
YOU'RE A DEMON FIRST CLASS...
...YOU HAD THE POWER.
THANK YOU, MISTRESS!
YOU'RE JUST A LITTLE CLUMSY *USING* IT.
OKAY, SO, NOW THAT YOU'VE HAD YOUR CAKE, COULD YOU HELP WITH THE AUTHORIZATION?
AUTHORIZATION? WHAT AUTHORIZATION?

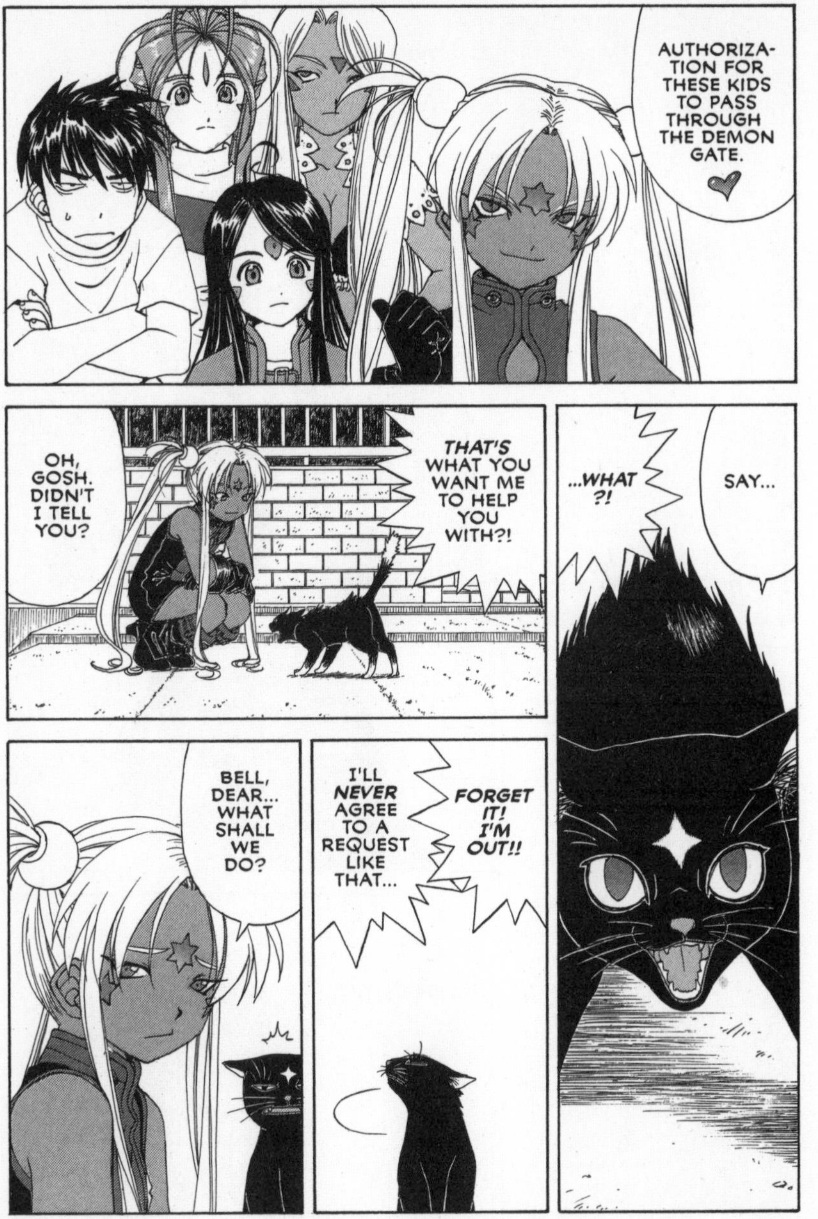
AUTHORIZATION FOR THESE KIDS TO PASS THROUGH THE DEMON GATE. ♥
SAY...
...WHAT ?!
THAT'S WHAT YOU WANT ME TO HELP YOU WITH?!
OH, GOSH. DIDN'T I TELL YOU?
FORGET IT! I'M OUT!!
I'LL NEVER AGREE TO A REQUEST LIKE THAT...
BELL, DEAR... WHAT SHALL WE DO?

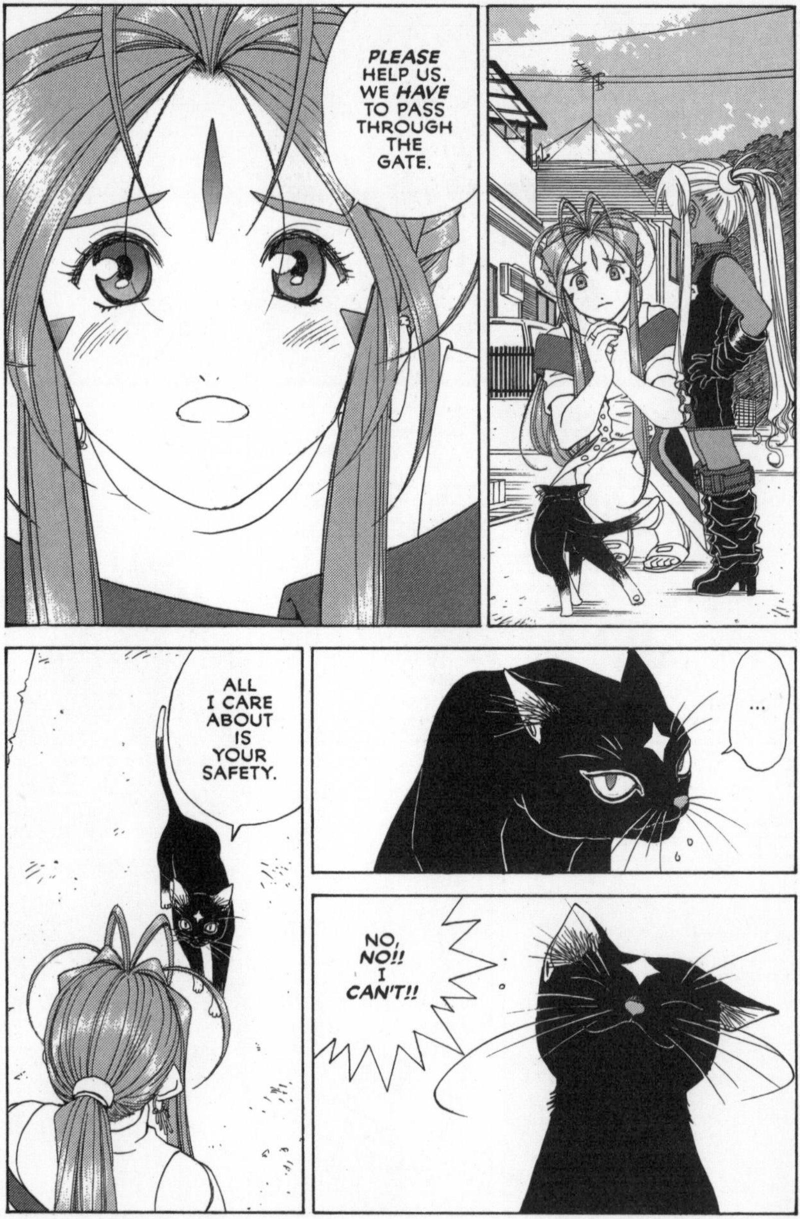
PLEASE HELP US. WE *HAVE* TO PASS THROUGH THE GATE.
...
NO, *NO!!* I *CAN'T!!*
ALL I CARE ABOUT IS YOUR SAFETY.

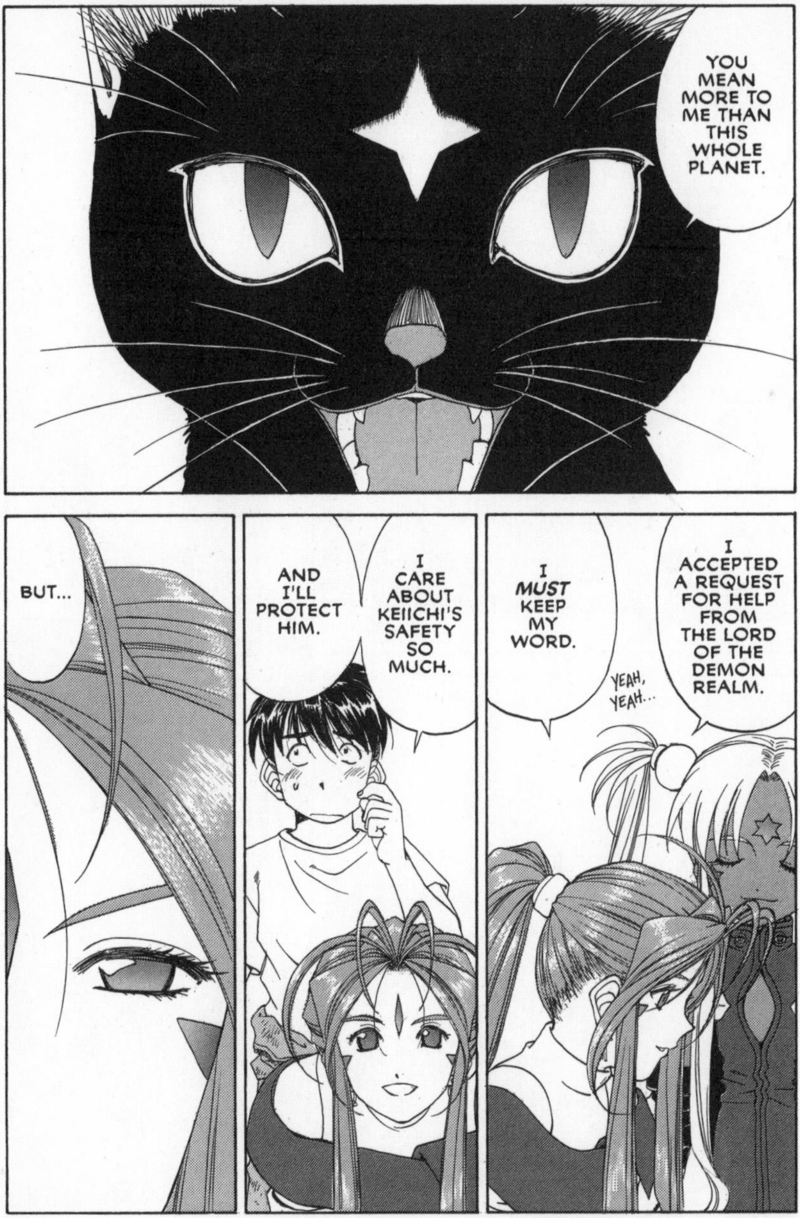
YOU MEAN MORE TO ME THAN THIS WHOLE PLANET.
I ACCEPTED A REQUEST FOR HELP FROM THE LORD OF THE DEMON REALM.
YEAH, YEAH...
I *MUST* KEEP MY WORD.
I CARE ABOUT KEIICHI'S SAFETY SO MUCH.
AND I'LL PROTECT HIM.
BUT...

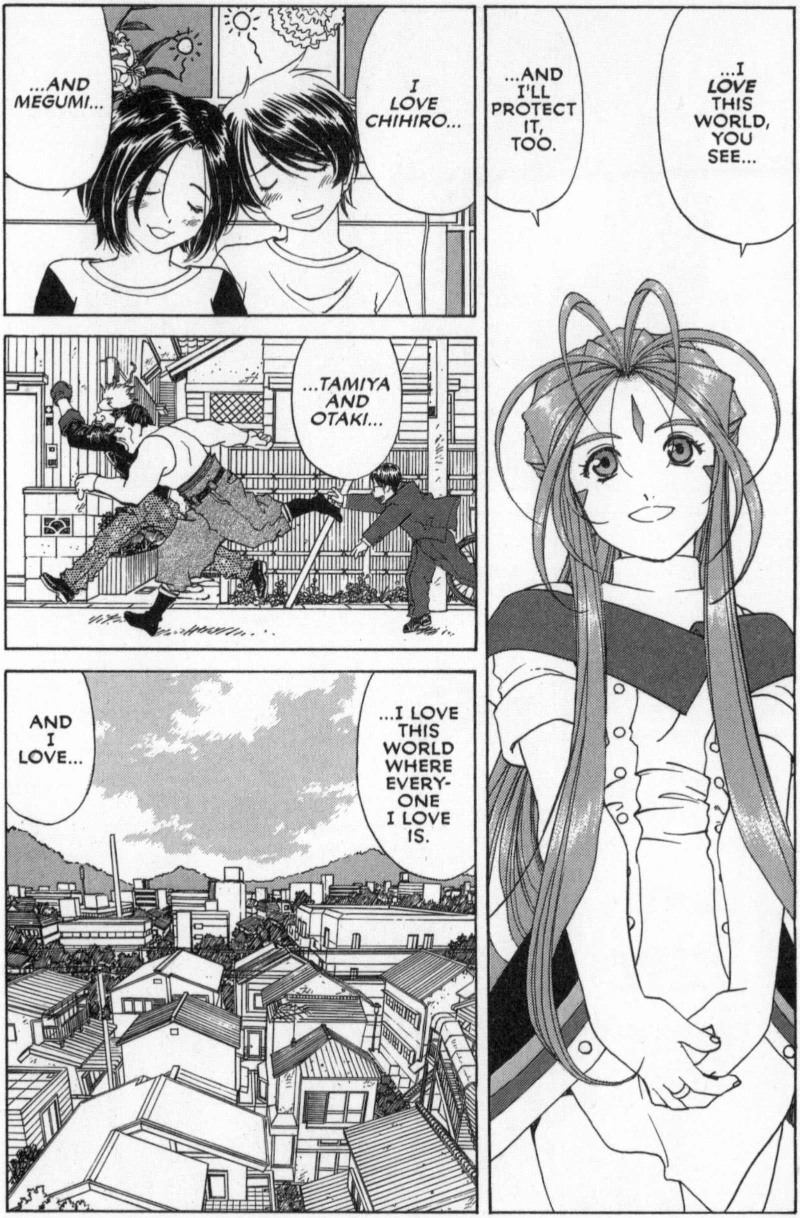
...I LOVE THIS WORLD, YOU SEE...
...AND I'LL PROTECT IT, TOO.
I LOVE CHIHIRO...
...AND MEGUMI...
...TAMIYA AND OTAKI...
...I LOVE THIS WORLD WHERE EVERY-ONE I LOVE IS.
AND I LOVE...

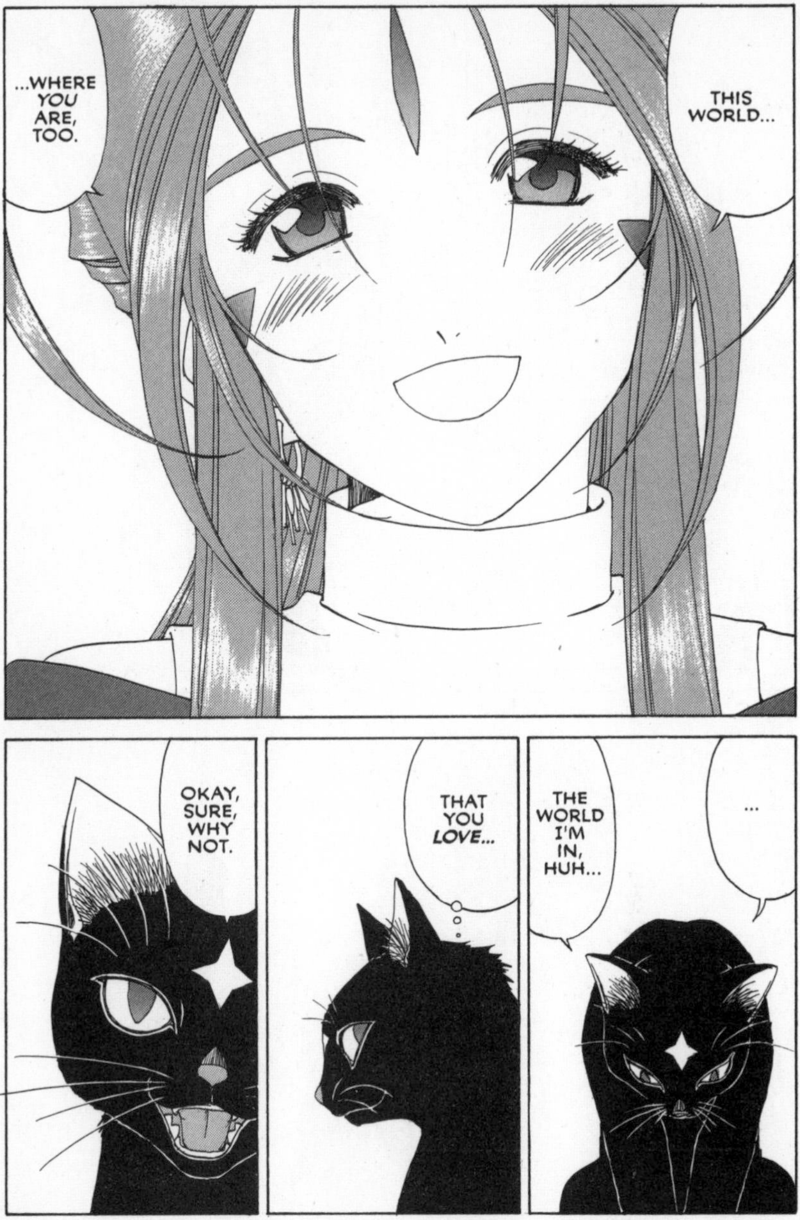
THIS WORLD...
...WHERE *YOU* ARE, TOO.
...
THE WORLD I'M IN, HUH...
THAT YOU ***LOVE***...
OKAY, SURE, WHY NOT.

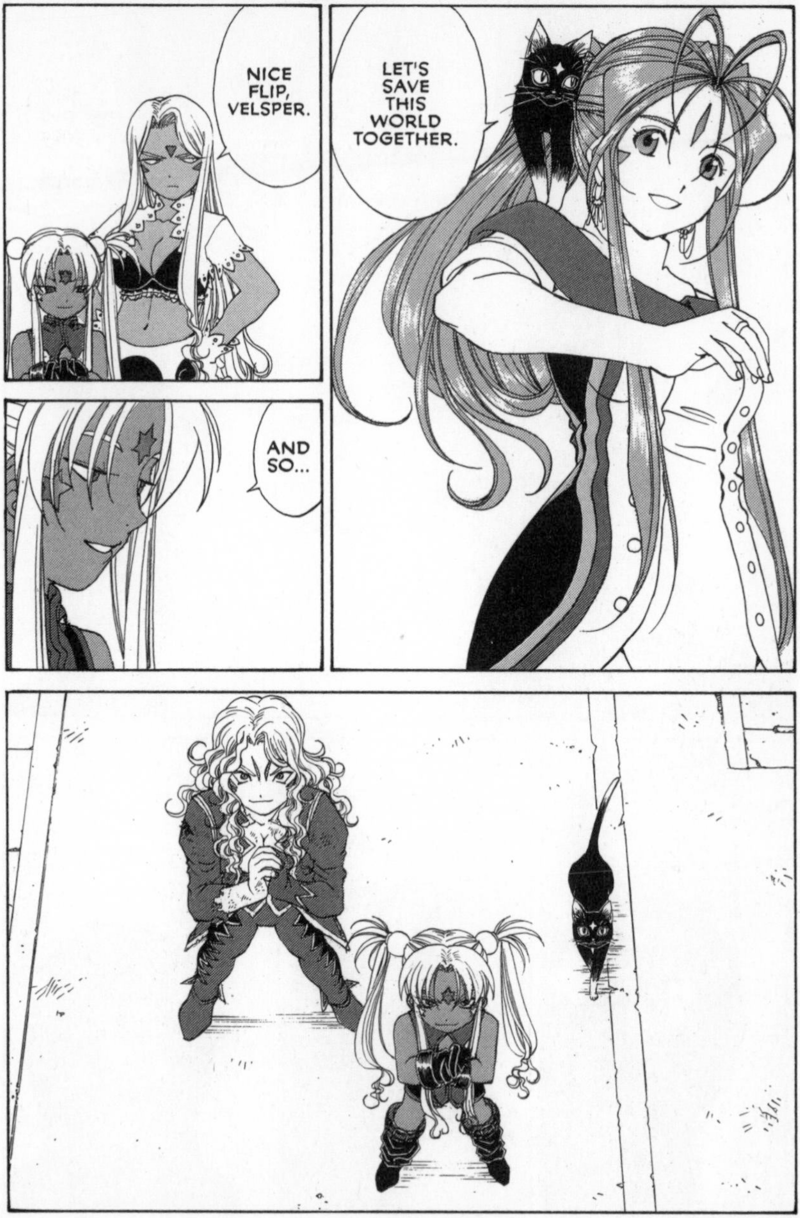
LET'S SAVE THIS WORLD TOGETHER.
NICE FLIP, VELSPER.
AND SO...

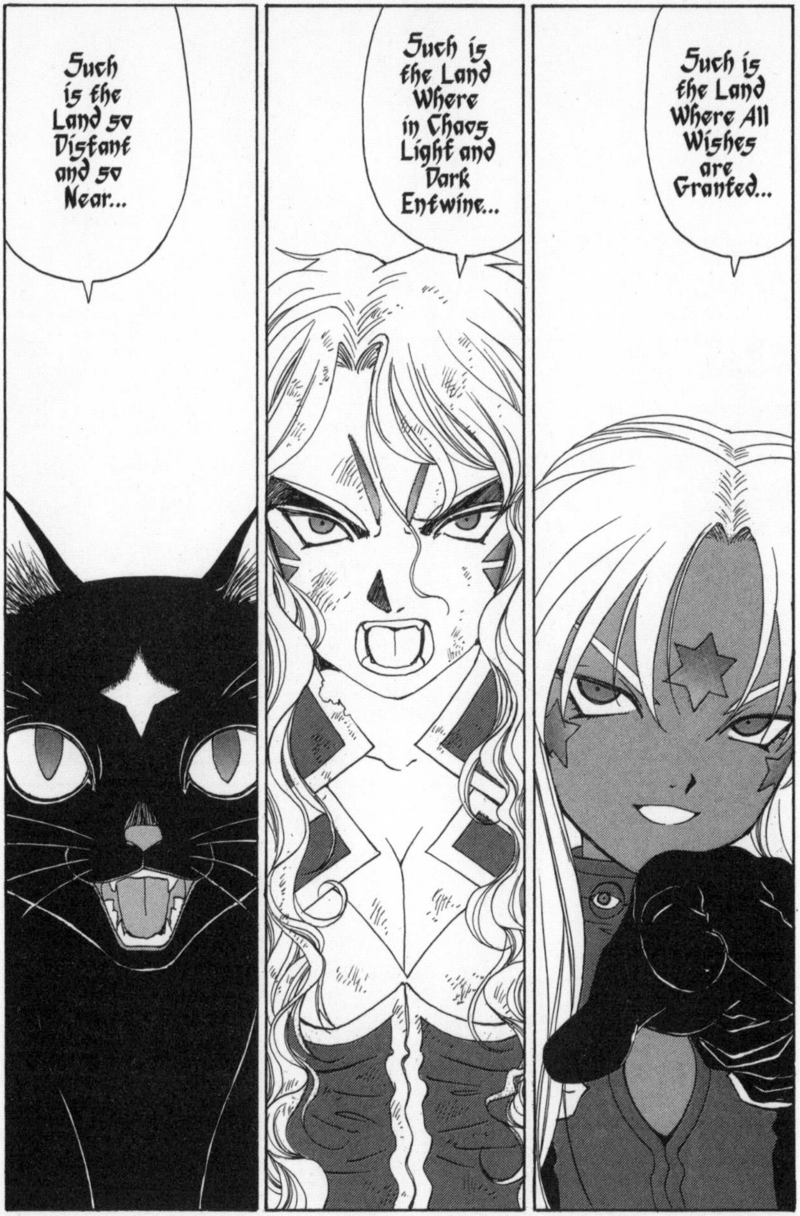
Such is the Land Where All Wishes are Granted...
Such is the Land Where in Chaos Light and Dark Entwine...
Such is the Land so Distant and so Near...

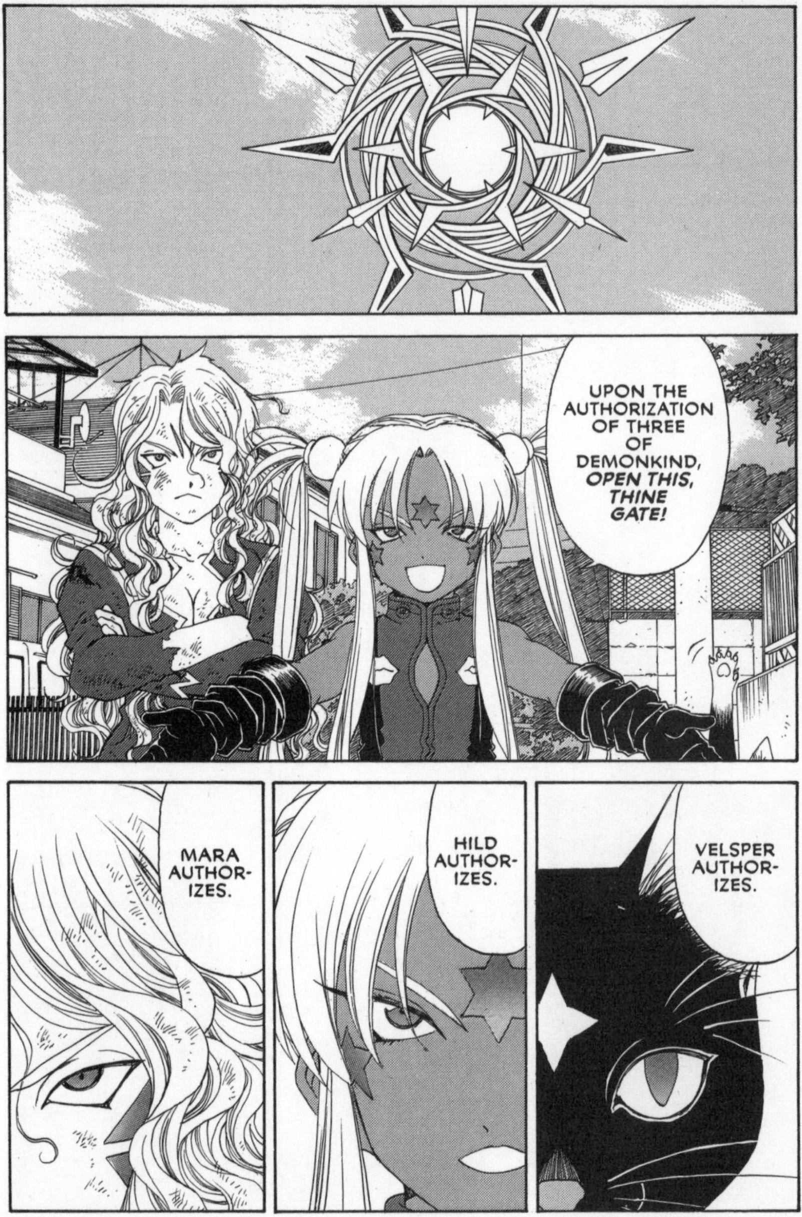
UPON THE AUTHORIZATION OF THREE OF DEMONKIND, *OPEN THIS, THINE GATE!*
VELSPER AUTHOR-IZES.
HILD AUTHOR-IZES.
MARA AUTHOR-IZES.

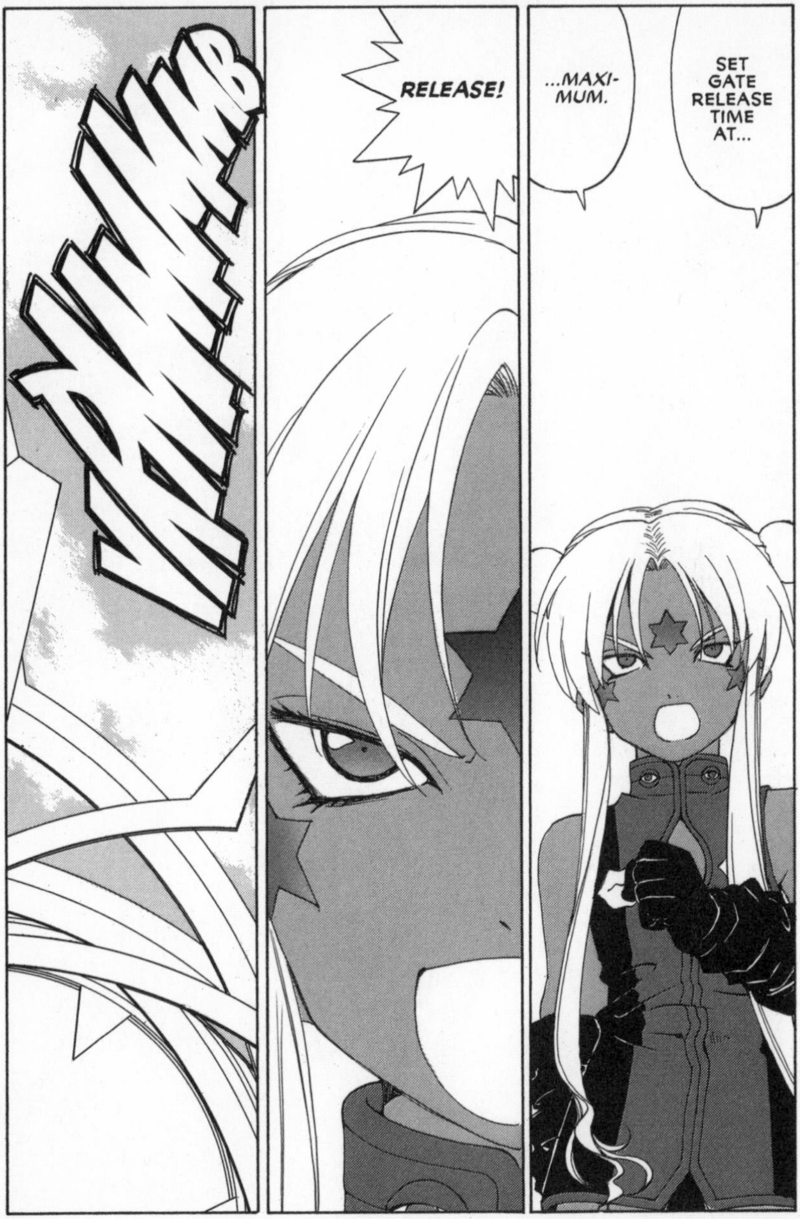
SET GATE RELEASE TIME AT...
...MAXI-MUM.
RELEASE!

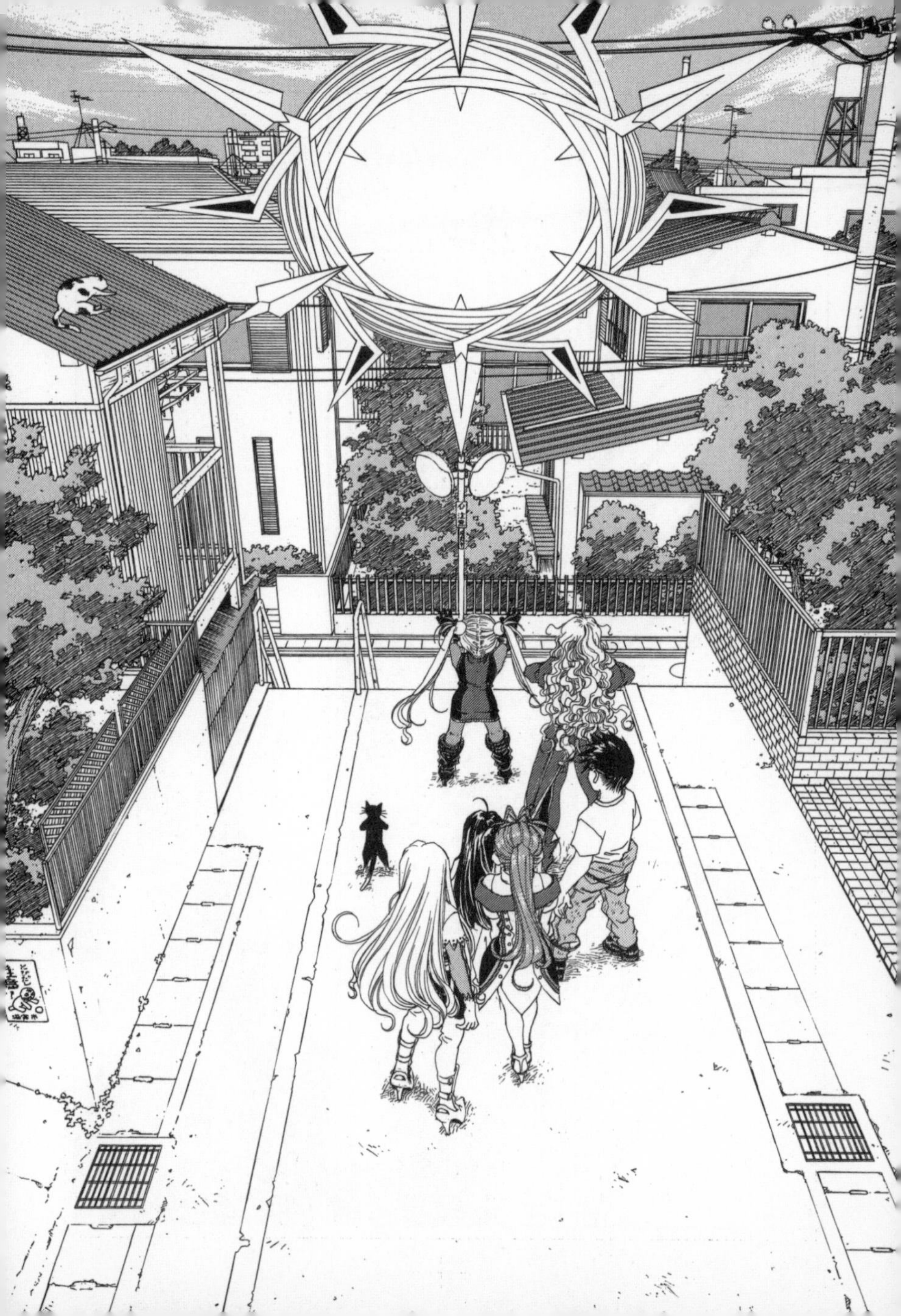

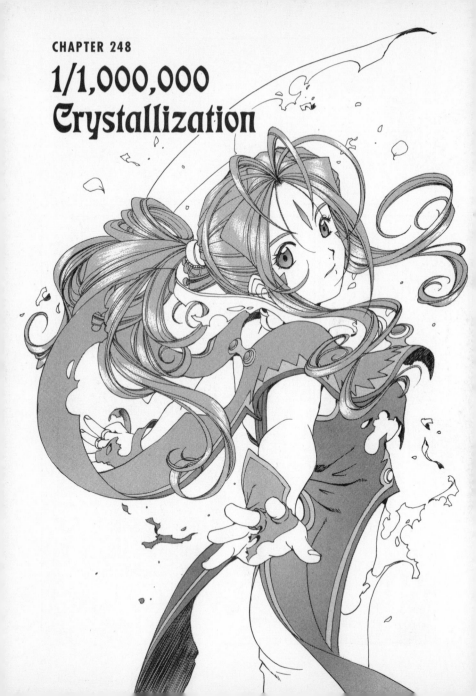

CHAPTER 248
1/1,000,000
Crystallization

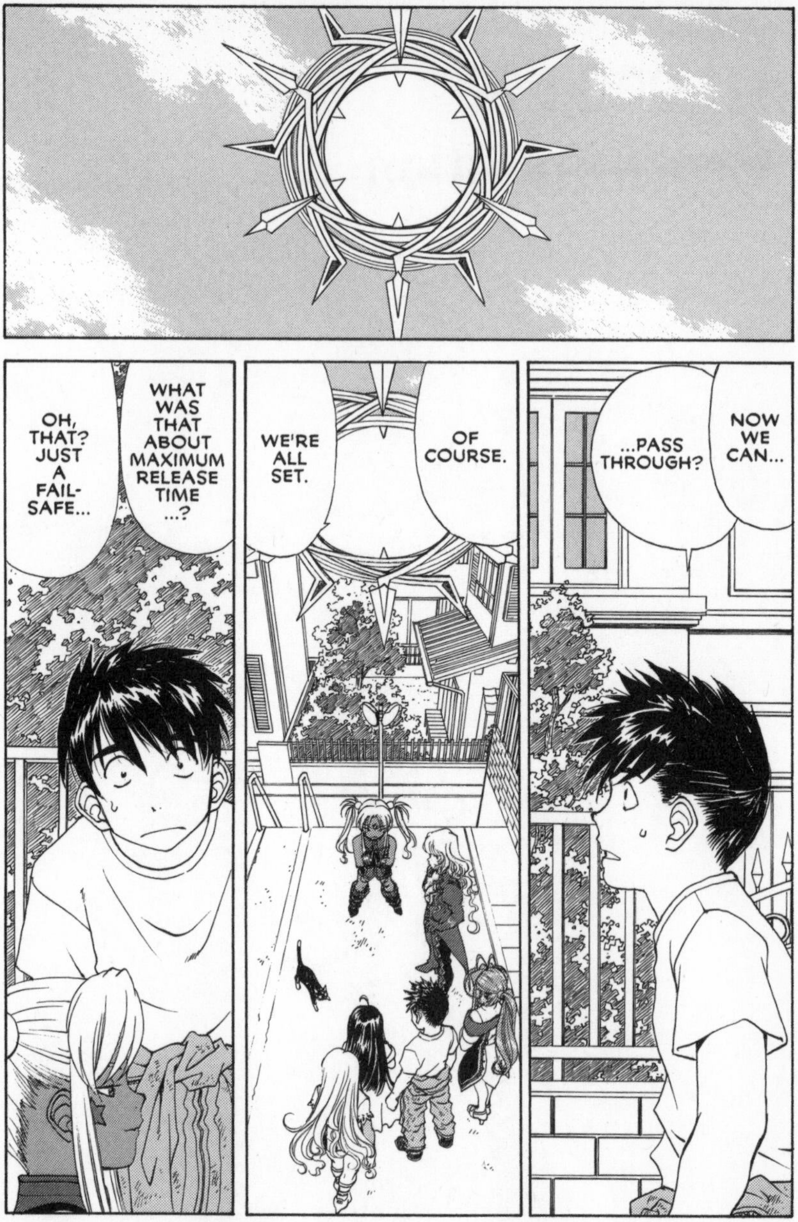
NOW WE CAN...
...PASS THROUGH?
OF COURSE.
WE'RE ALL SET.
WHAT WAS THAT ABOUT MAXIMUM RELEASE TIME ...?
OH, THAT? JUST A FAIL-SAFE...

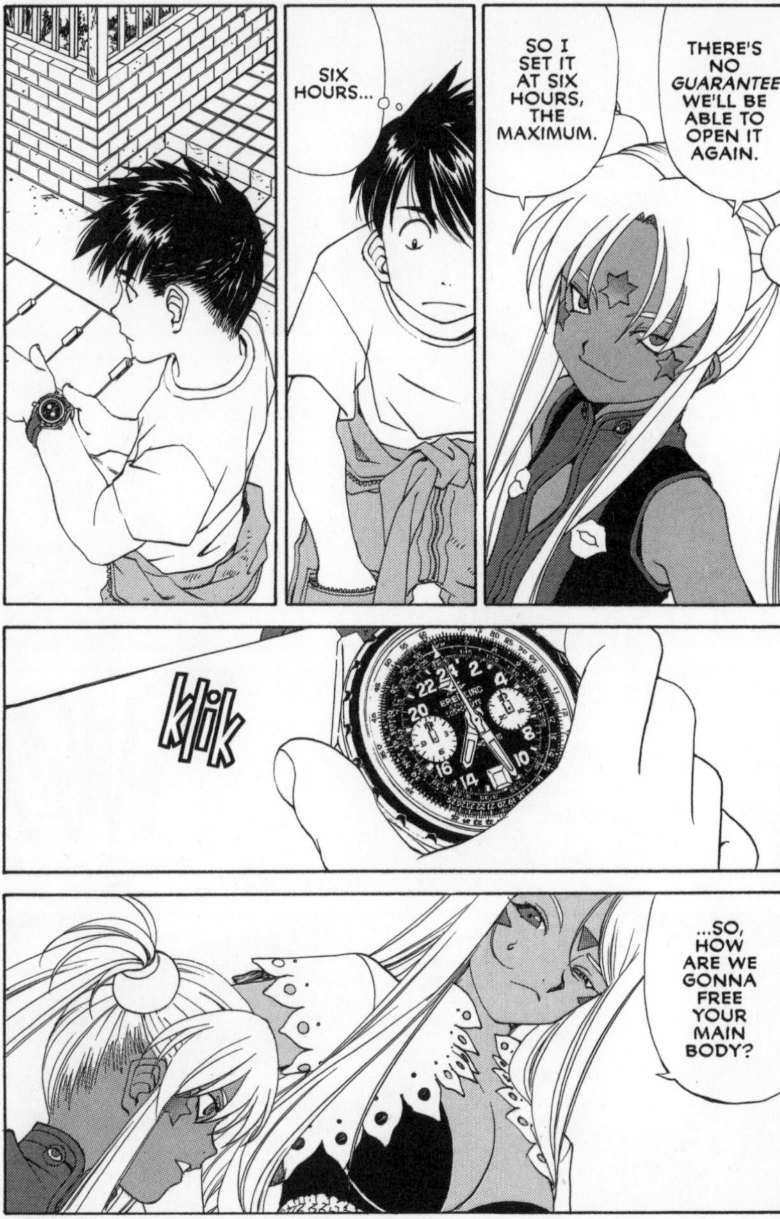
THERE'S NO *GUARANTEE* WE'LL BE ABLE TO OPEN IT AGAIN.
SO I SET IT AT SIX HOURS, THE MAXIMUM.
SIX HOURS...
klik
...SO, HOW ARE WE GONNA FREE YOUR MAIN BODY?

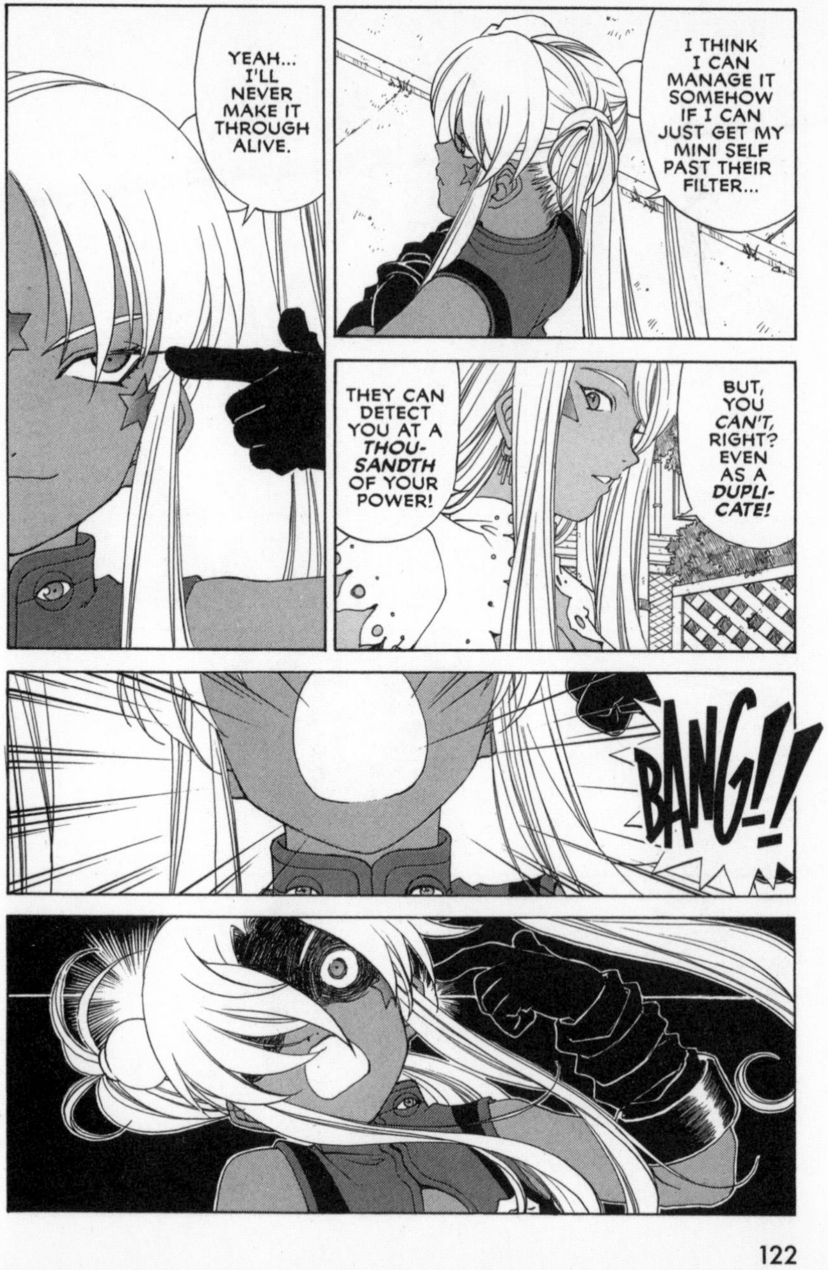
I THINK I CAN MANAGE IT SOMEHOW IF I CAN JUST GET MY MINI SELF PAST THEIR FILTER...
BUT, YOU *CAN'T*, RIGHT? EVEN AS A *DUPLICATE!*
THEY CAN DETECT YOU AT A *THOUSANDTH* OF YOUR POWER!
YEAH... I'LL NEVER MAKE IT THROUGH ALIVE.
BANG!!

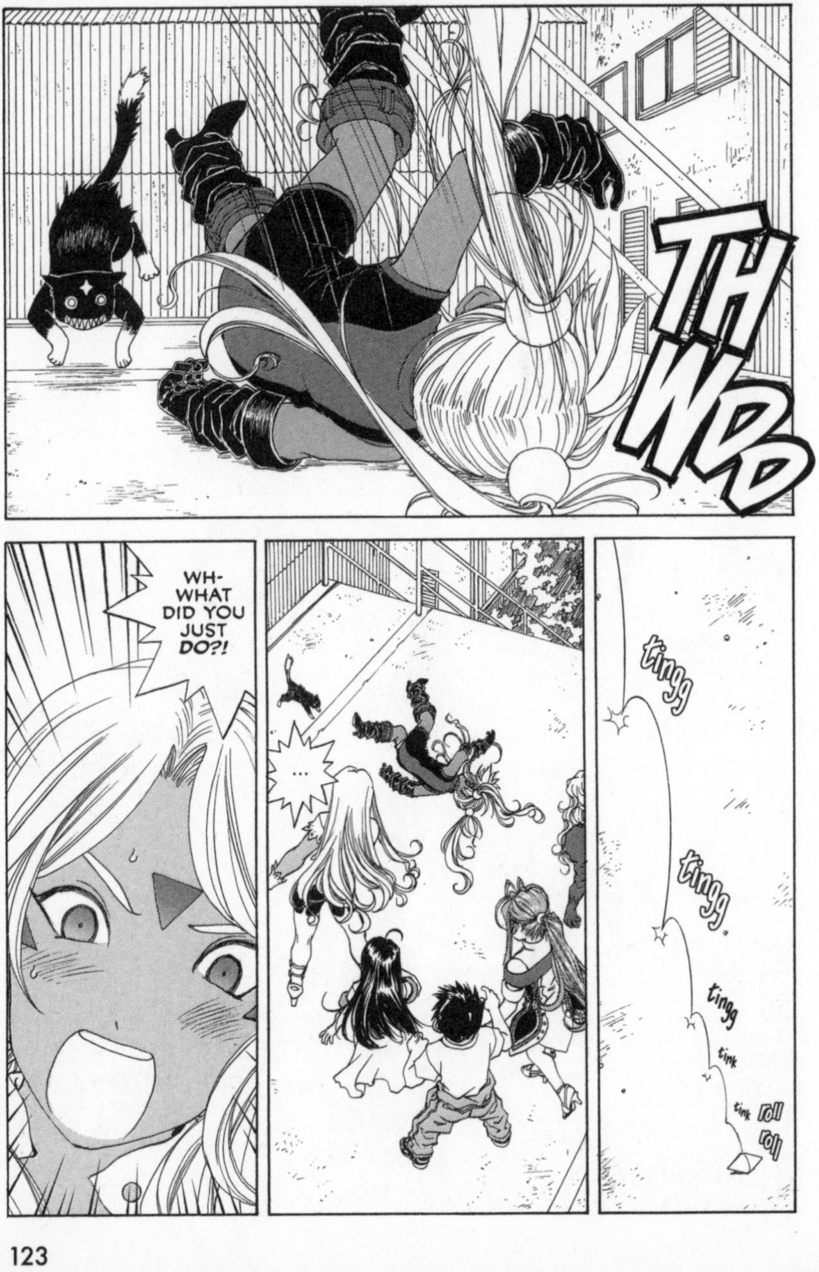
THWDD
tingg
tingg.
tingg
tink
tink
roll
roll
...
WH-WHAT DID YOU JUST DO?!

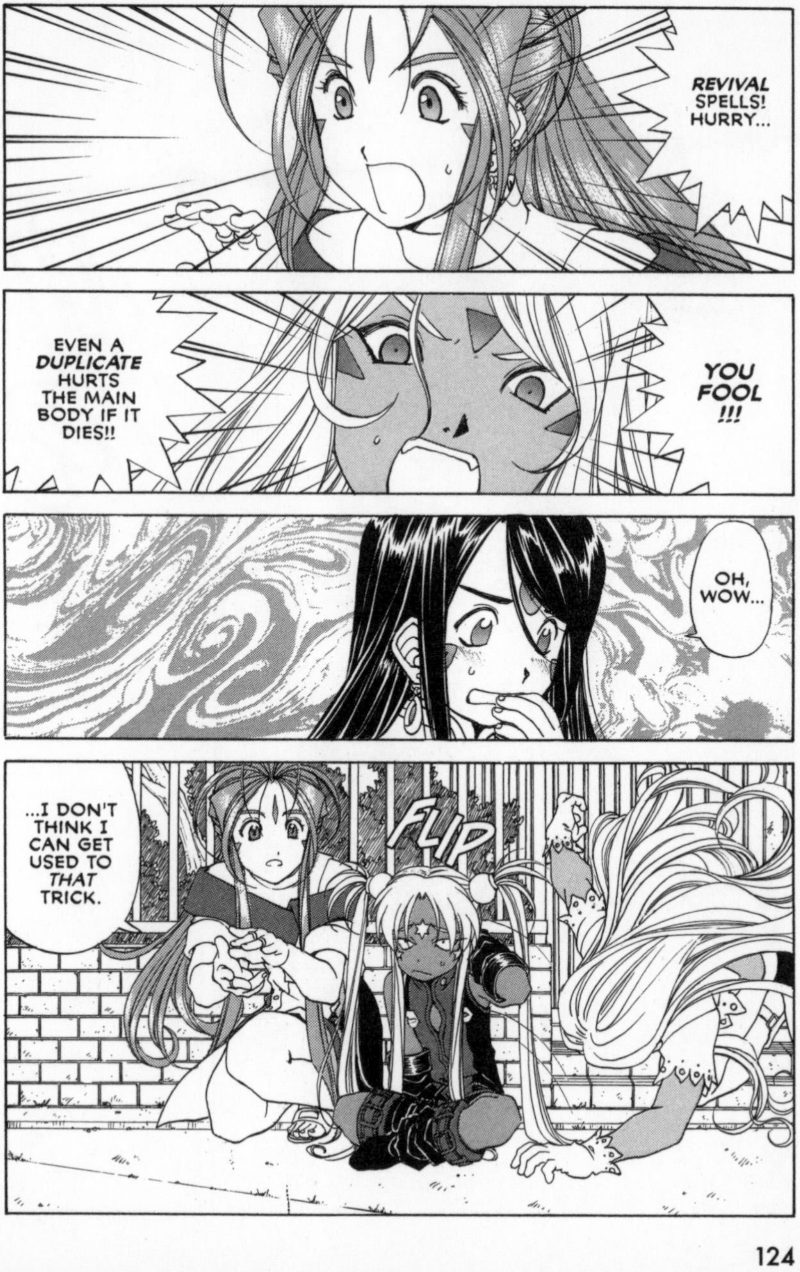
REVIVAL SPELLS! HURRY...
YOU FOOL!!!
EVEN A DUPLICATE HURTS THE MAIN BODY IF IT DIES!!
OH, WOW...
FLIP
...I DON'T THINK I CAN GET USED TO THAT TRICK.

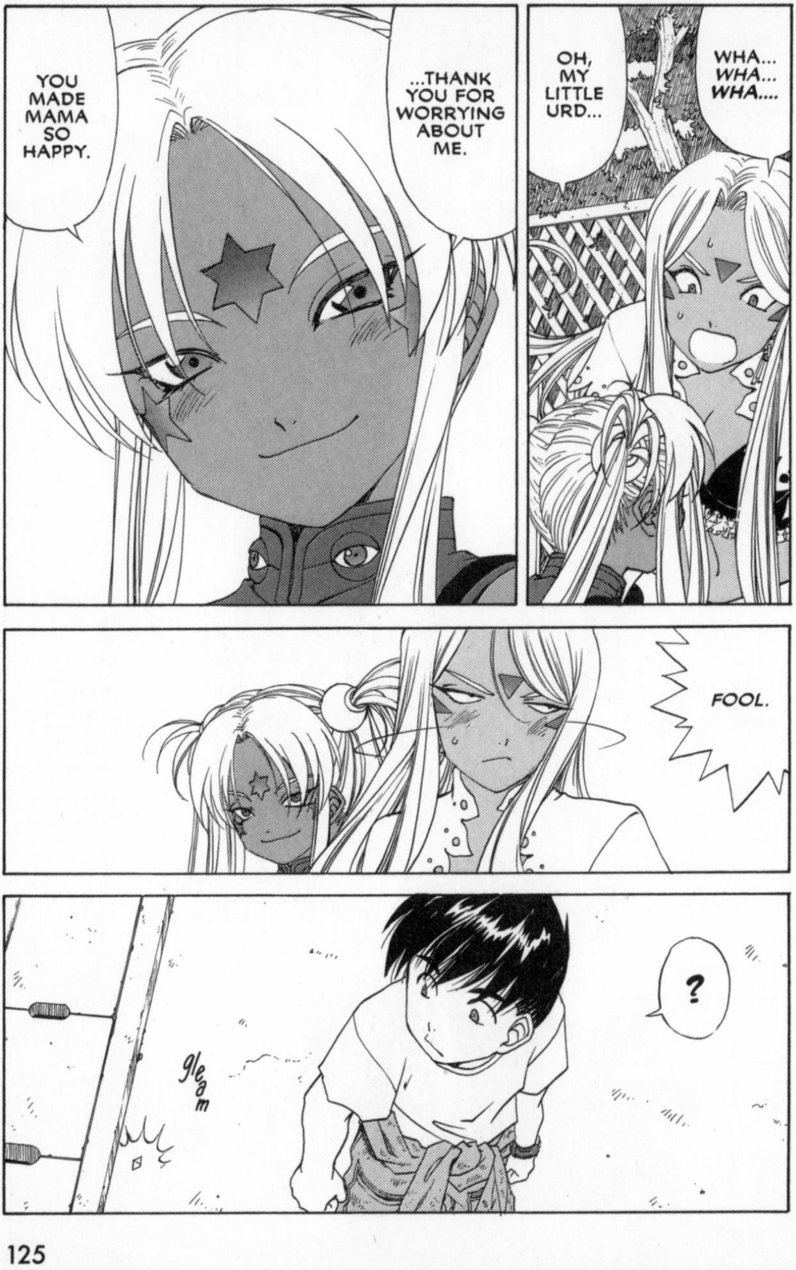
WHA... WHA... WHA....
OH, MY LITTLE URD...
...THANK YOU FOR WORRYING ABOUT ME.
YOU MADE MAMA SO HAPPY.
FOOL.
?
gleam

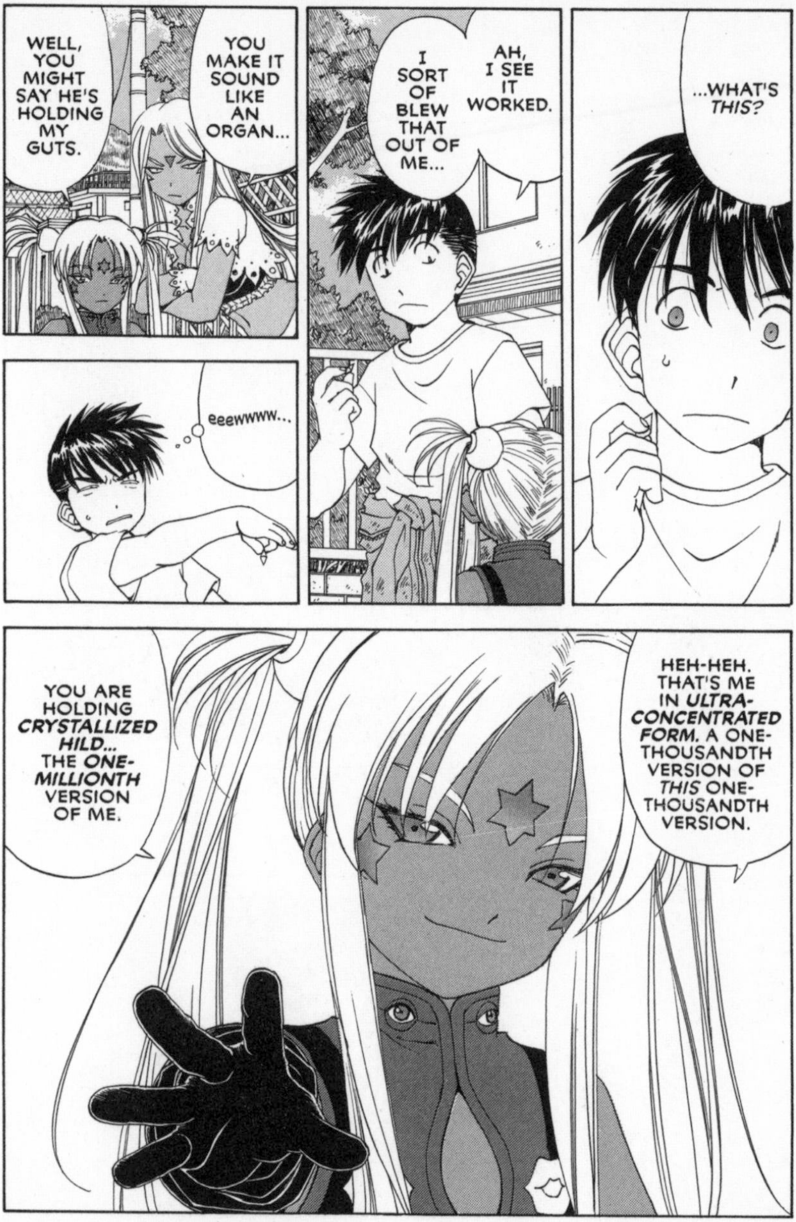
...WHAT'S *THIS?*
AH, I SEE IT WORKED.
I SORT OF BLEW THAT OUT OF ME...
YOU MAKE IT SOUND LIKE AN ORGAN...
WELL, YOU MIGHT SAY HE'S HOLDING MY GUTS.
eeewwww...
HEH-HEH. THAT'S ME IN ***ULTRA-CONCENTRATED FORM.*** A ONE-THOUSANDTH VERSION OF *THIS* ONE-THOUSANDTH VERSION.
YOU ARE HOLDING ***CRYSTALLIZED HILD...*** THE ***ONE-MILLIONTH*** VERSION OF ME.

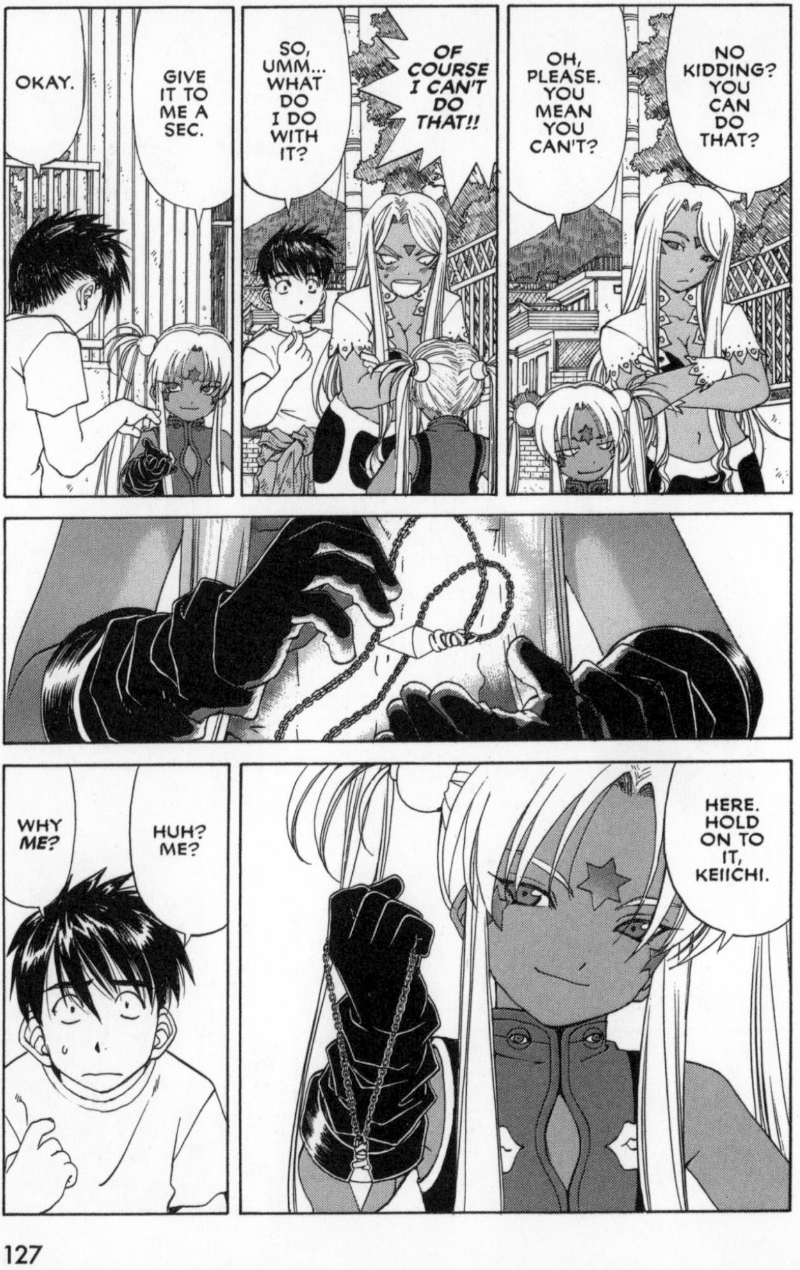
NO KIDDING? YOU CAN DO THAT?
OH, PLEASE. YOU MEAN YOU CAN'T?
OF COURSE I CAN'T DO THAT!!
SO, UMM... WHAT DO I DO WITH IT?
GIVE IT TO ME A SEC.
OKAY.
HERE. HOLD ON TO IT, KEIICHI.
HUH? ME?
WHY *ME?*

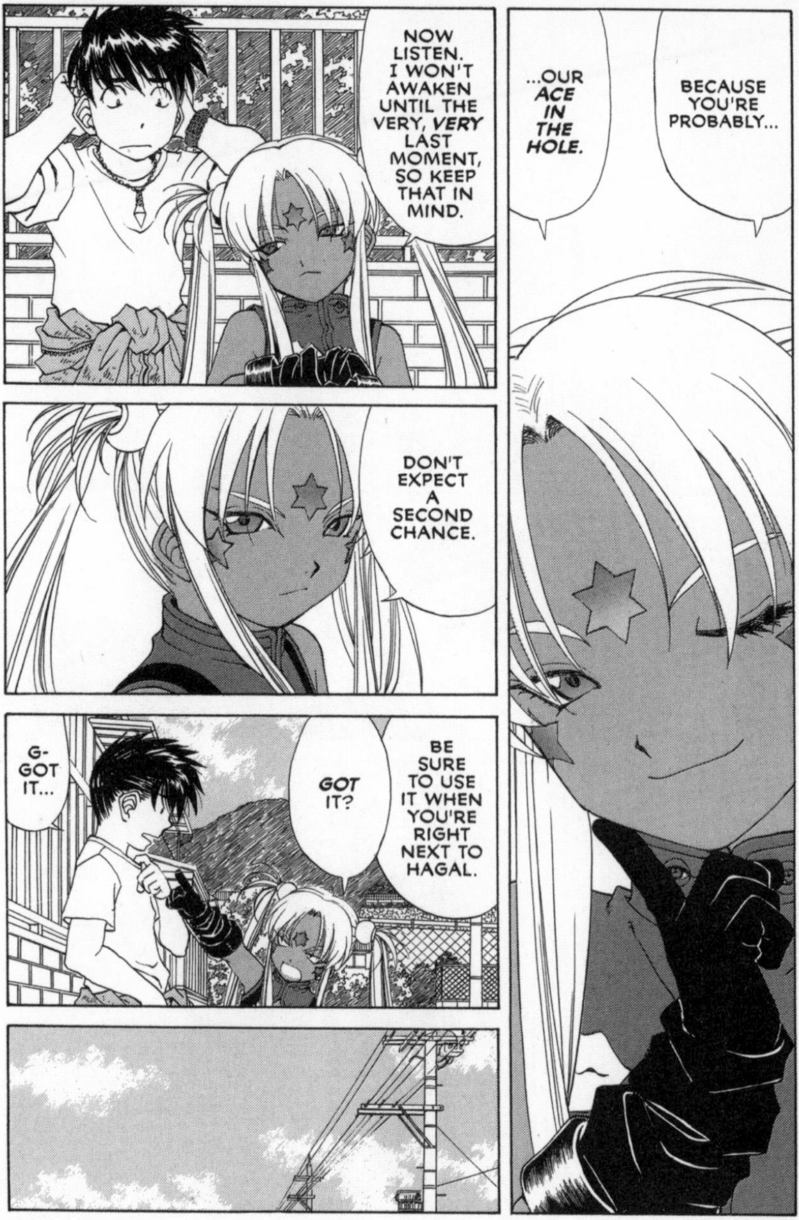
BECAUSE YOU'RE PROBABLY...
...OUR *ACE IN THE HOLE.*
NOW LISTEN. I WON'T AWAKEN UNTIL THE VERY, *VERY* LAST MOMENT, SO KEEP THAT IN MIND.
DON'T EXPECT A SECOND CHANCE.
BE SURE TO USE IT WHEN YOU'RE RIGHT NEXT TO HAGAL.
GOT IT?
G- GOT IT...

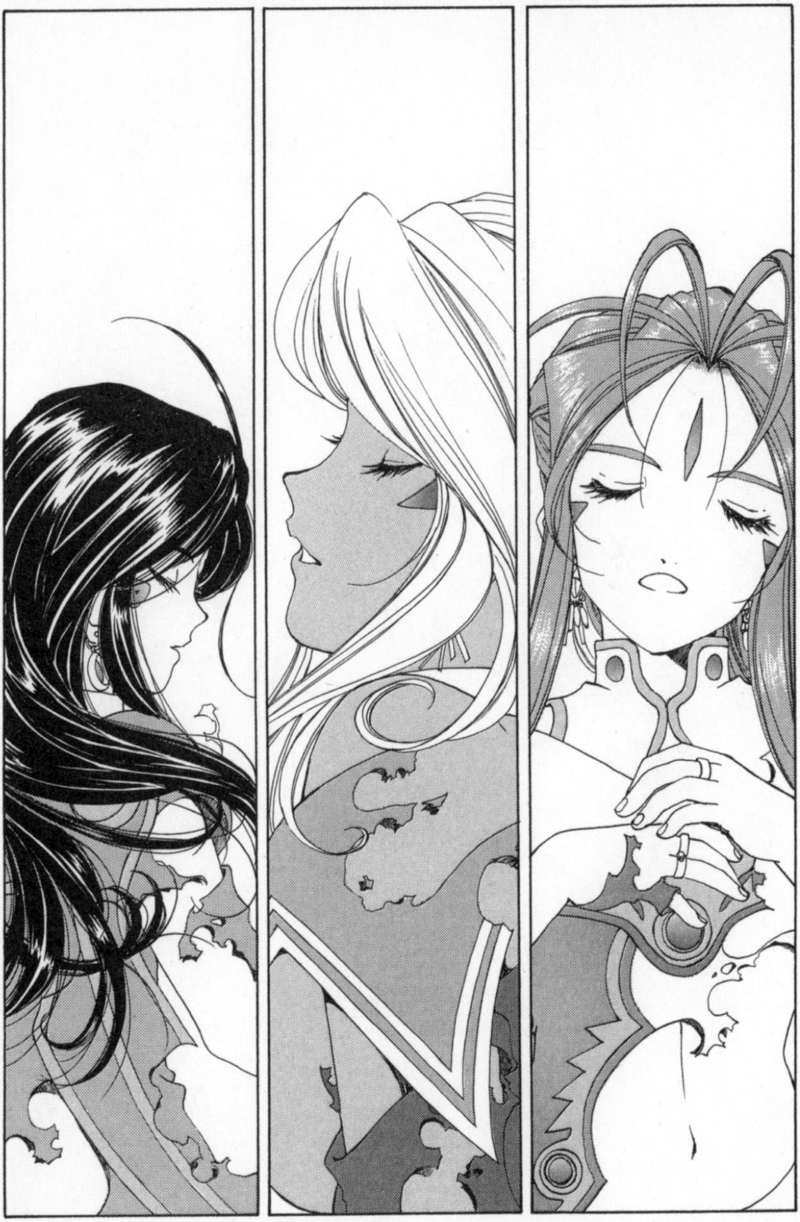

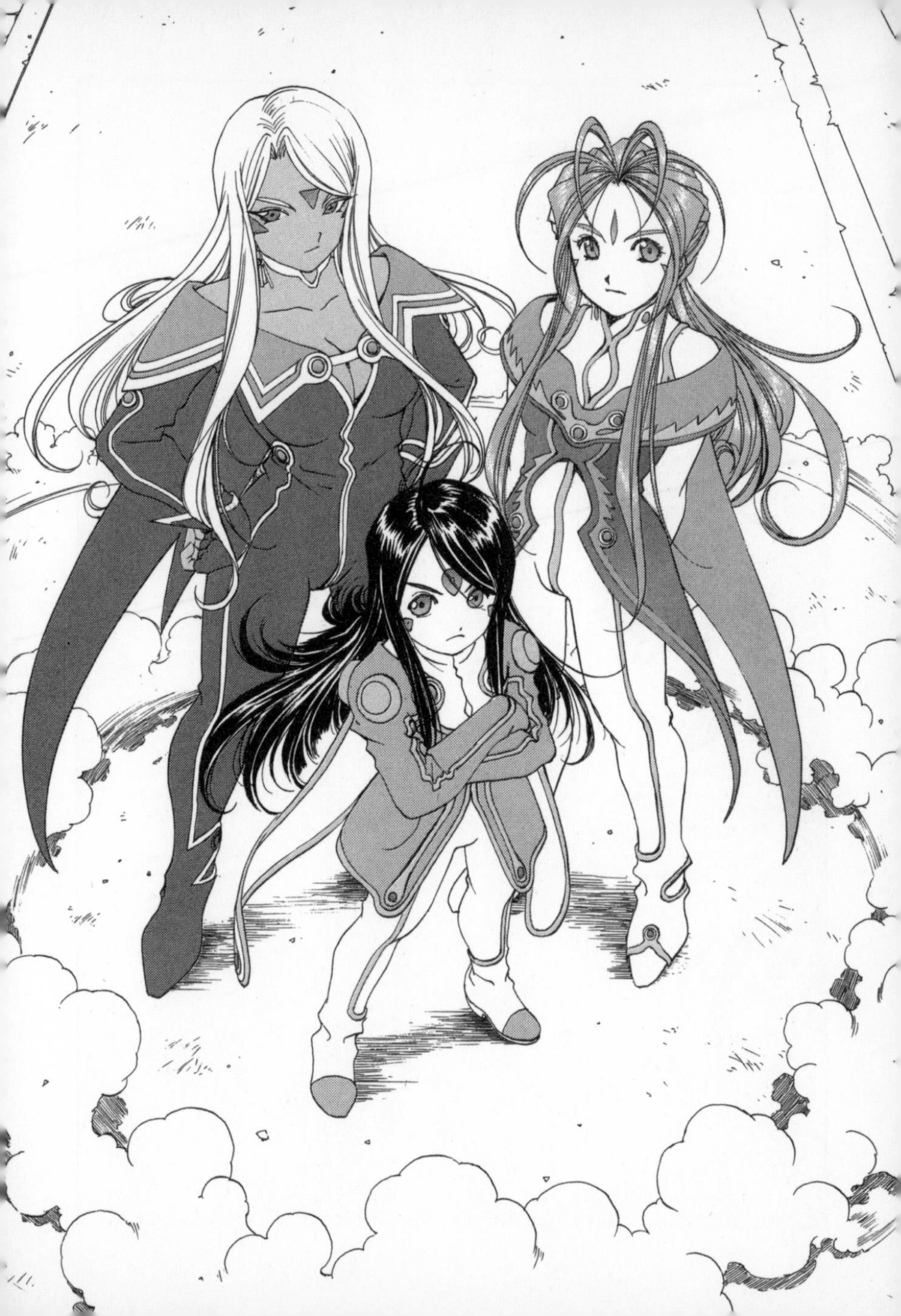

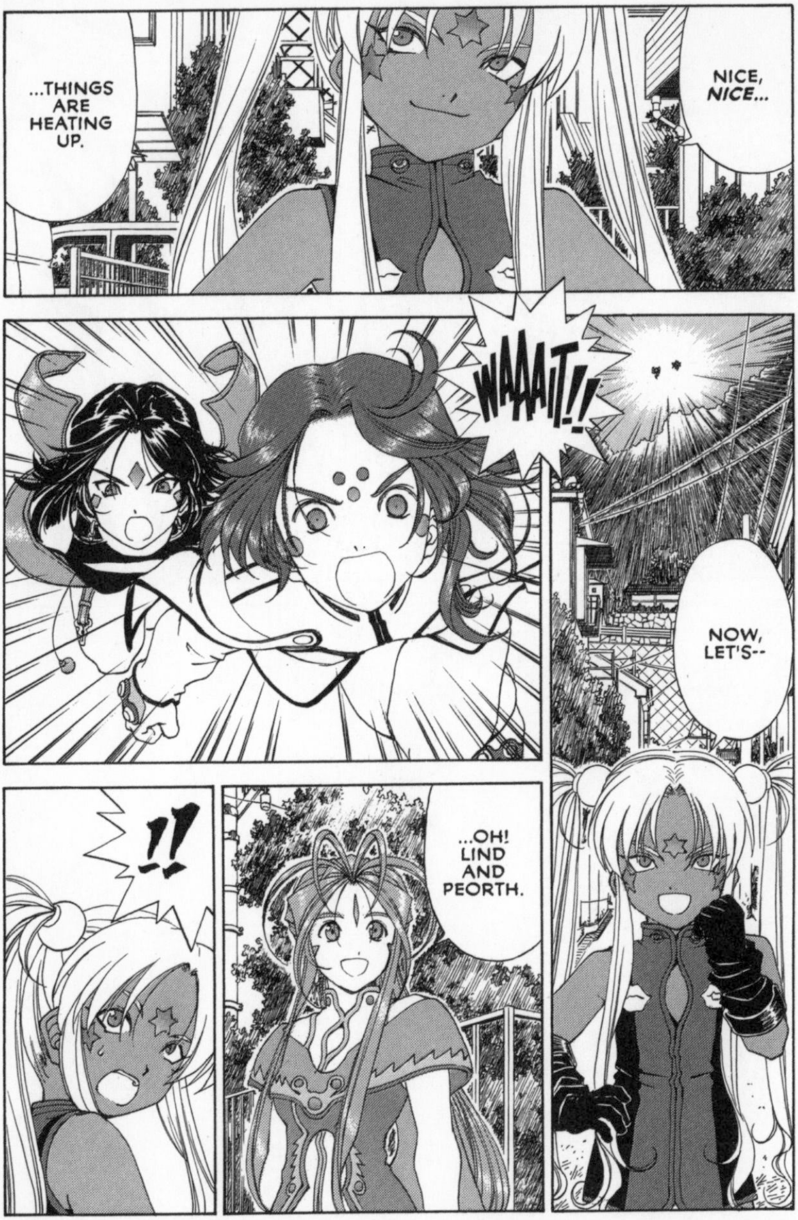
NICE, NICE...
...THINGS ARE HEATING UP.
NOW, LET'S--
WAAAIT!!
...OH! LIND AND PEORTH.
!!

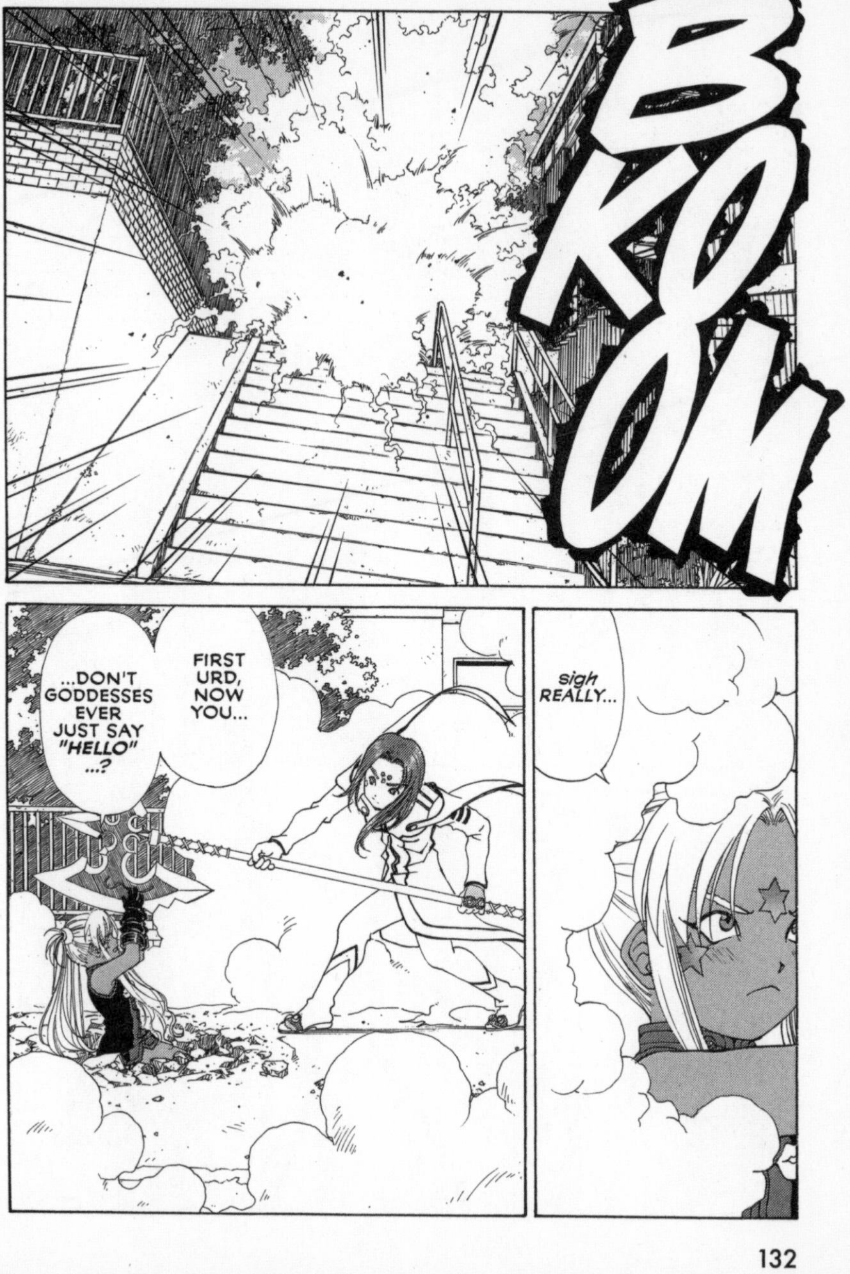
BKOOM
sigh REALLY...
FIRST URD, NOW YOU...
...DON'T GODDESSES EVER JUST SAY "HELLO" ...?

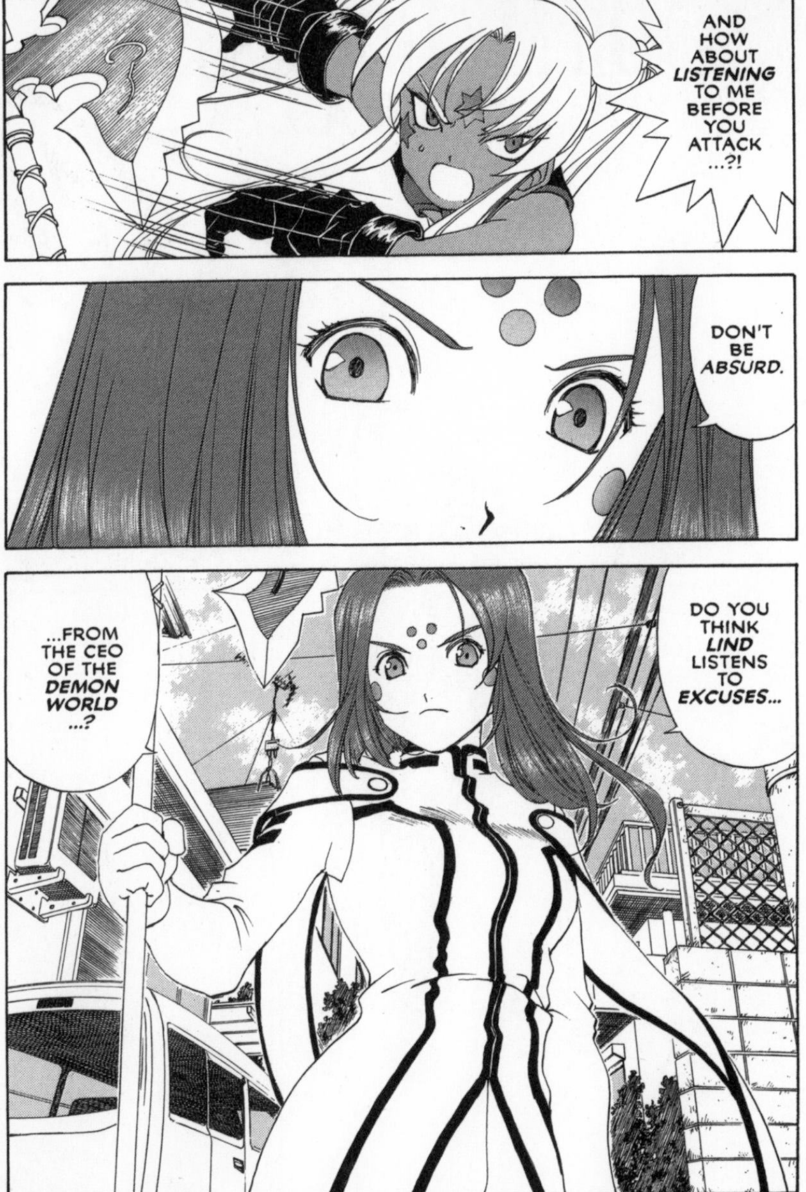
AND HOW ABOUT LISTENING TO ME BEFORE YOU ATTACK ...?!
DON'T BE ABSURD.
DO YOU THINK LIND LISTENS TO EXCUSES...
...FROM THE CEO OF THE DEMON WORLD ...?

OH MY GODDESS!
MARA

CHAPTER 249

The Benefits of Misunderstanding

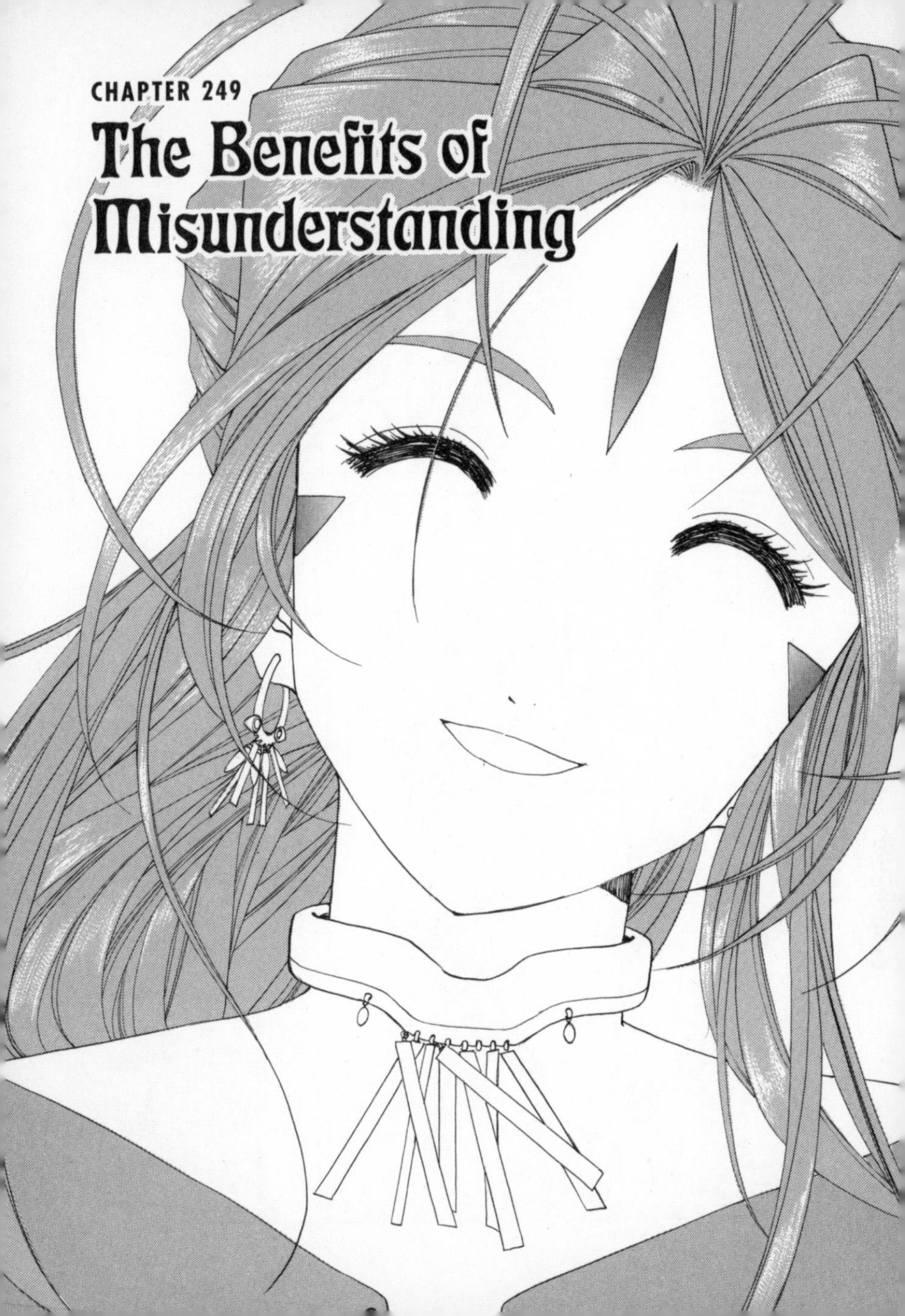

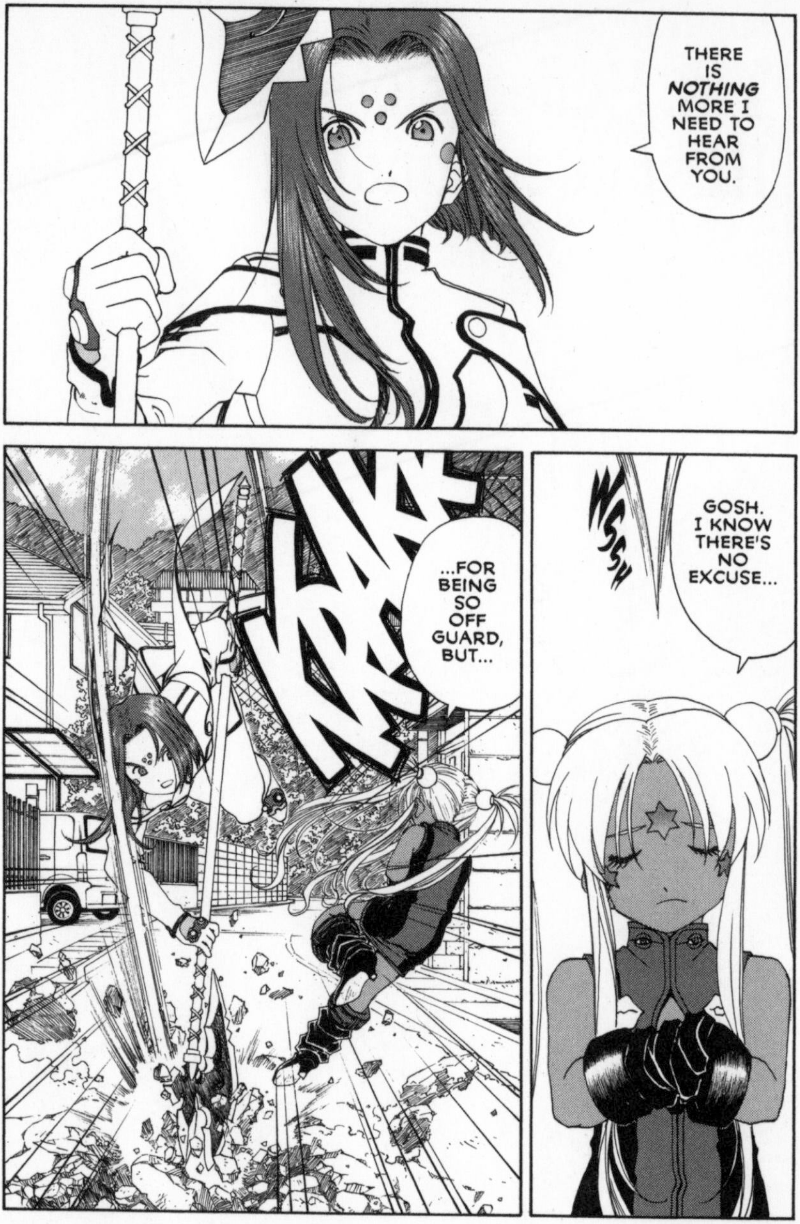
THERE IS NOTHING MORE I NEED TO HEAR FROM YOU.
WSSH
GOSH. I KNOW THERE'S NO EXCUSE...
...FOR BEING SO OFF GUARD, BUT...

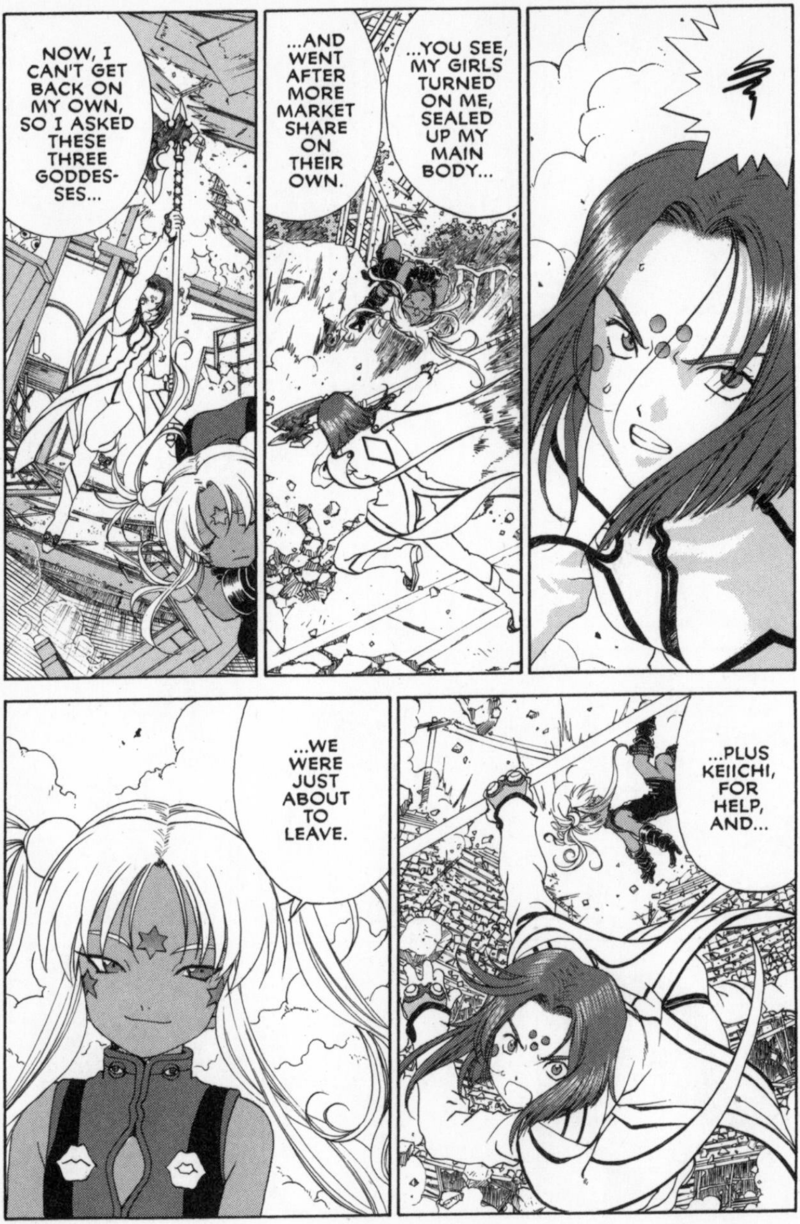
...YOU SEE, MY GIRLS TURNED ON ME, SEALED UP MY MAIN BODY...
...AND WENT AFTER MORE MARKET SHARE ON THEIR OWN.
NOW, I CAN'T GET BACK ON MY OWN, SO I ASKED THESE THREE GODDES-SES...
...PLUS KEIICHI, FOR HELP, AND...
...WE WERE JUST ABOUT TO LEAVE.

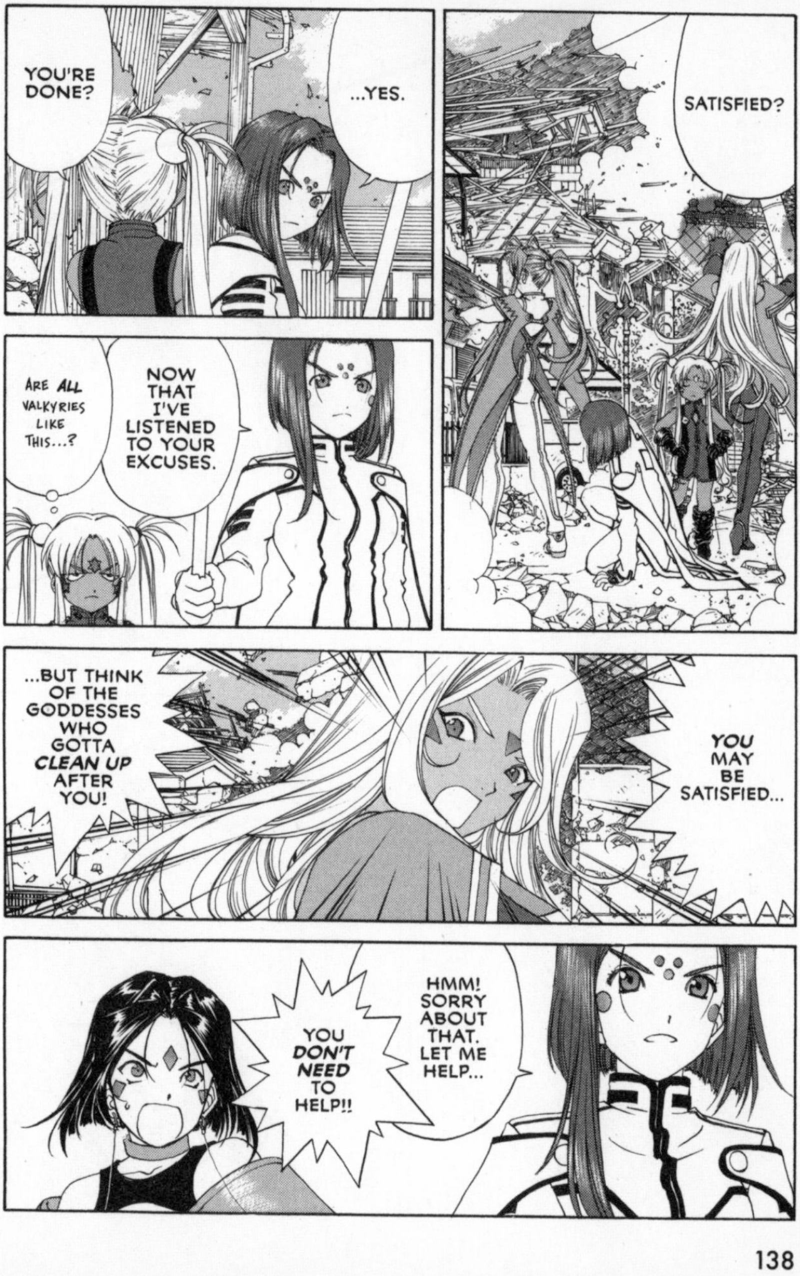
SATISFIED?
YOU'RE DONE?
...YES.
NOW THAT I'VE LISTENED TO YOUR EXCUSES.
Are *ALL* valkyries like this...?
YOU MAY BE SATISFIED...
...BUT THINK OF THE GODDESSES WHO GOTTA *CLEAN UP* AFTER YOU!
HMM! SORRY ABOUT THAT. LET ME HELP...
YOU *DON'T NEED* TO HELP!!

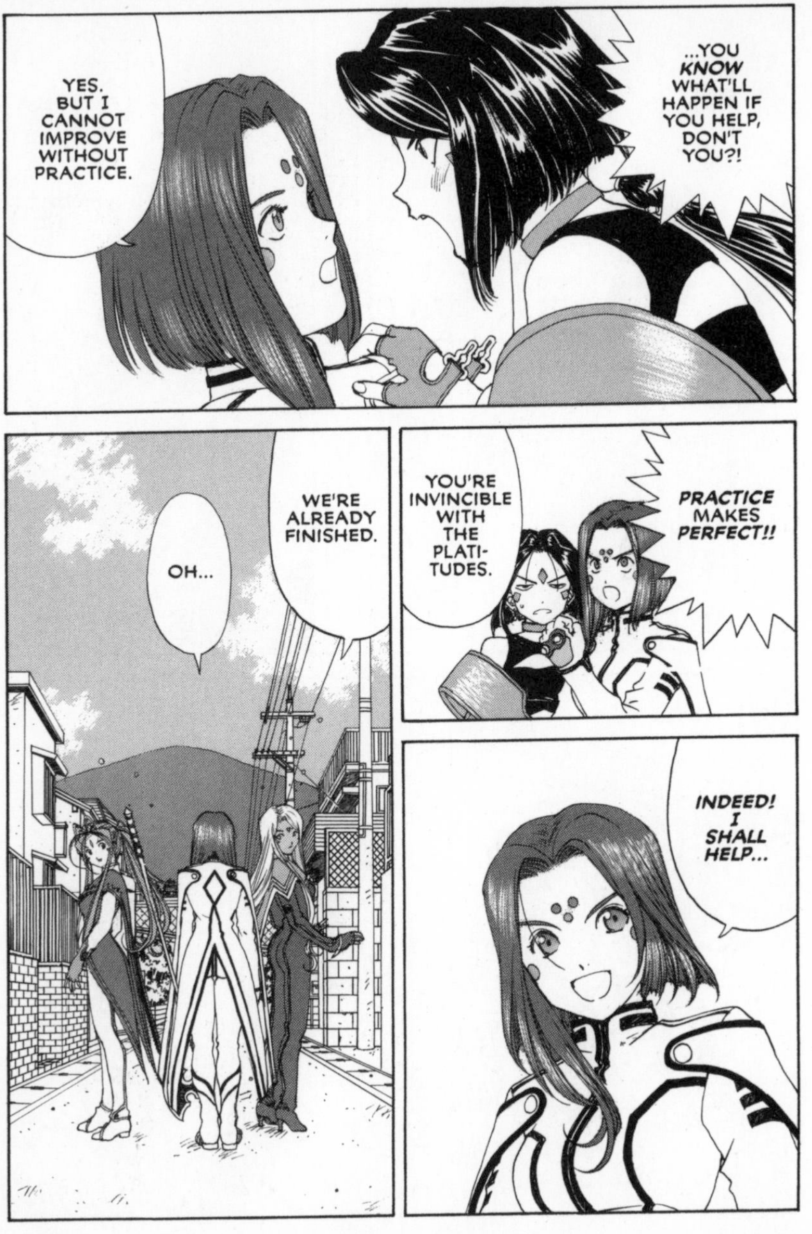
...YOU *KNOW* WHAT'LL HAPPEN IF YOU HELP, DON'T YOU?!
YES. BUT I CANNOT IMPROVE WITHOUT PRACTICE.
PRACTICE MAKES *PERFECT!!*
YOU'RE INVINCIBLE WITH THE PLATI-TUDES.
INDEED! I SHALL HELP...
WE'RE ALREADY FINISHED.
OH...

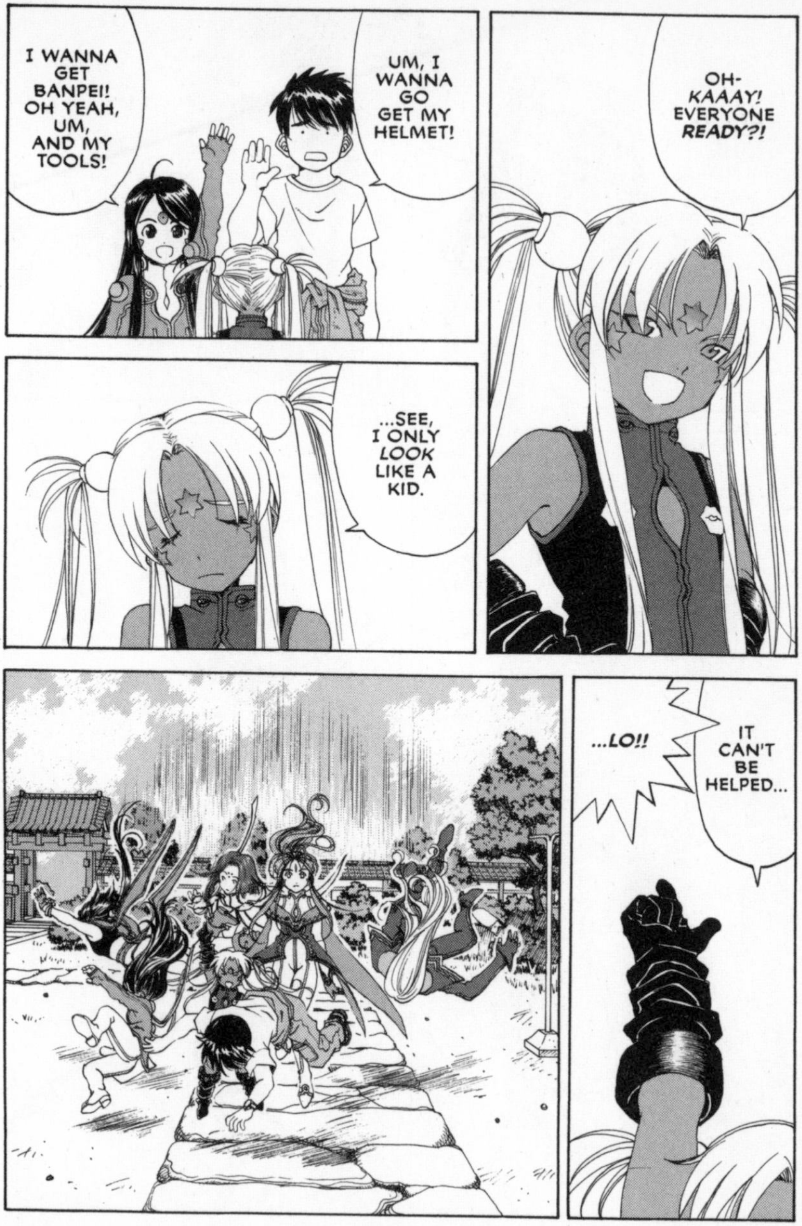
OH-KAAAY! EVERYONE *READY?!*
UM, I WANNA GO GET MY HELMET!
I WANNA GET BANPEI! OH YEAH, UM, AND MY TOOLS!
...SEE, I ONLY *LOOK* LIKE A KID.
IT CAN'T BE HELPED...
...LO!!

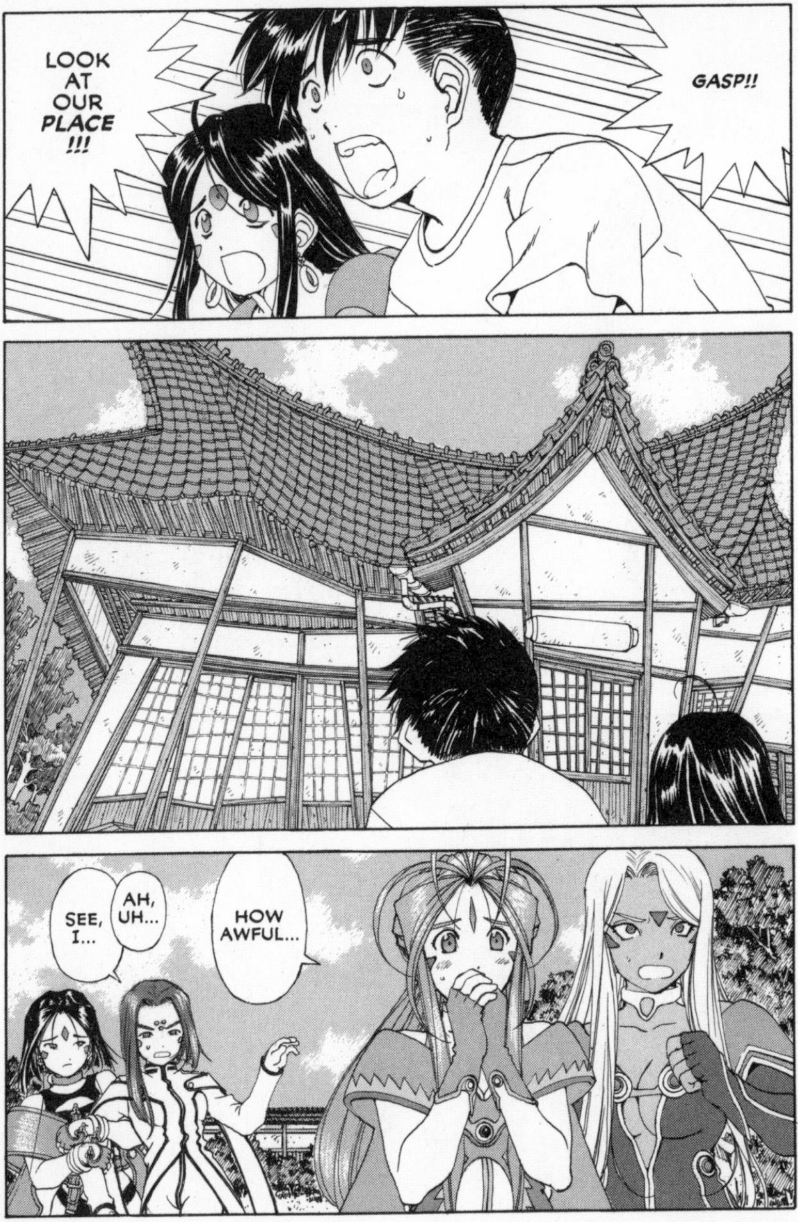
GASP!!
LOOK AT OUR PLACE!!!
HOW AWFUL...
AH, UH...
SEE, I...

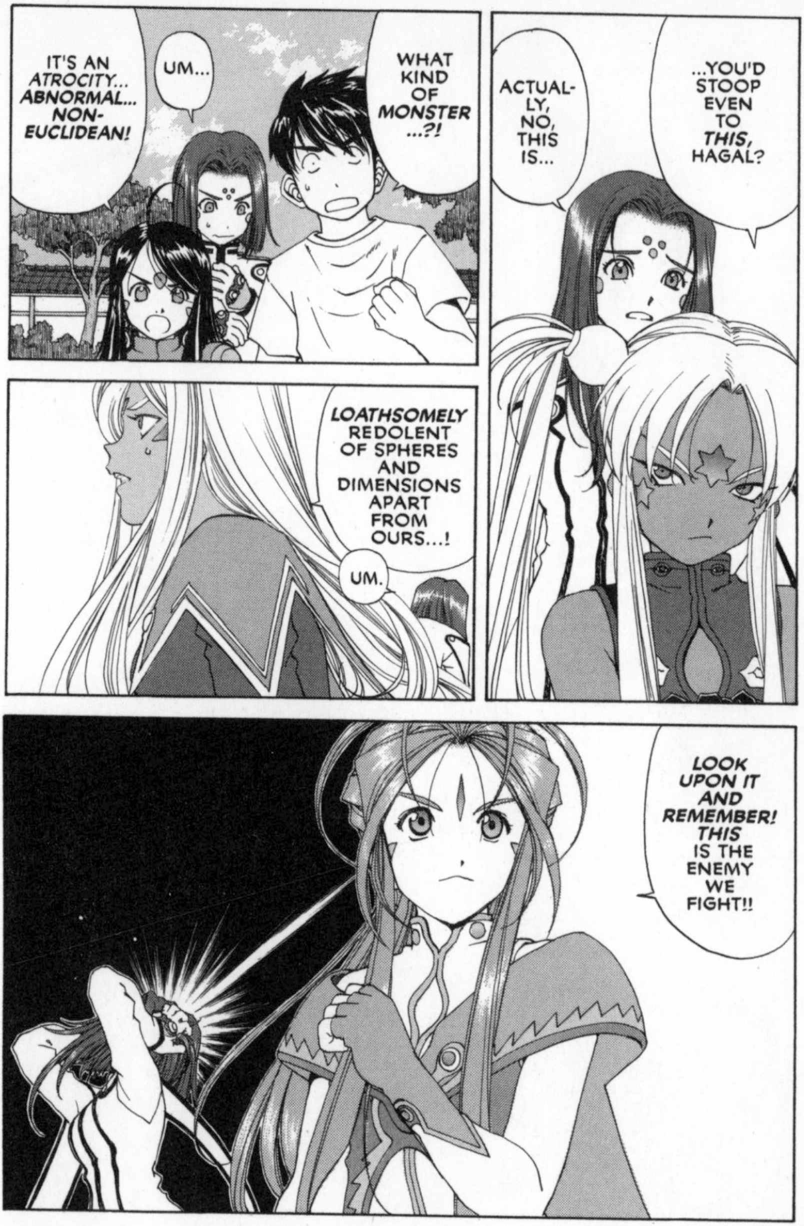
...YOU'D STOOP EVEN TO *THIS*, HAGAL?
ACTUAL-LY, NO, THIS IS...
WHAT KIND OF ***MONSTER*** ...?!
UM...
IT'S AN *ATROCITY*... ***ABNORMAL...*** ***NON-EUCLIDEAN!***
LOATHSOMELY REDOLENT OF SPHERES AND DIMENSIONS APART FROM OURS...!
UM.
LOOK UPON IT AND REMEMBER! THIS IS THE ENEMY WE FIGHT!!

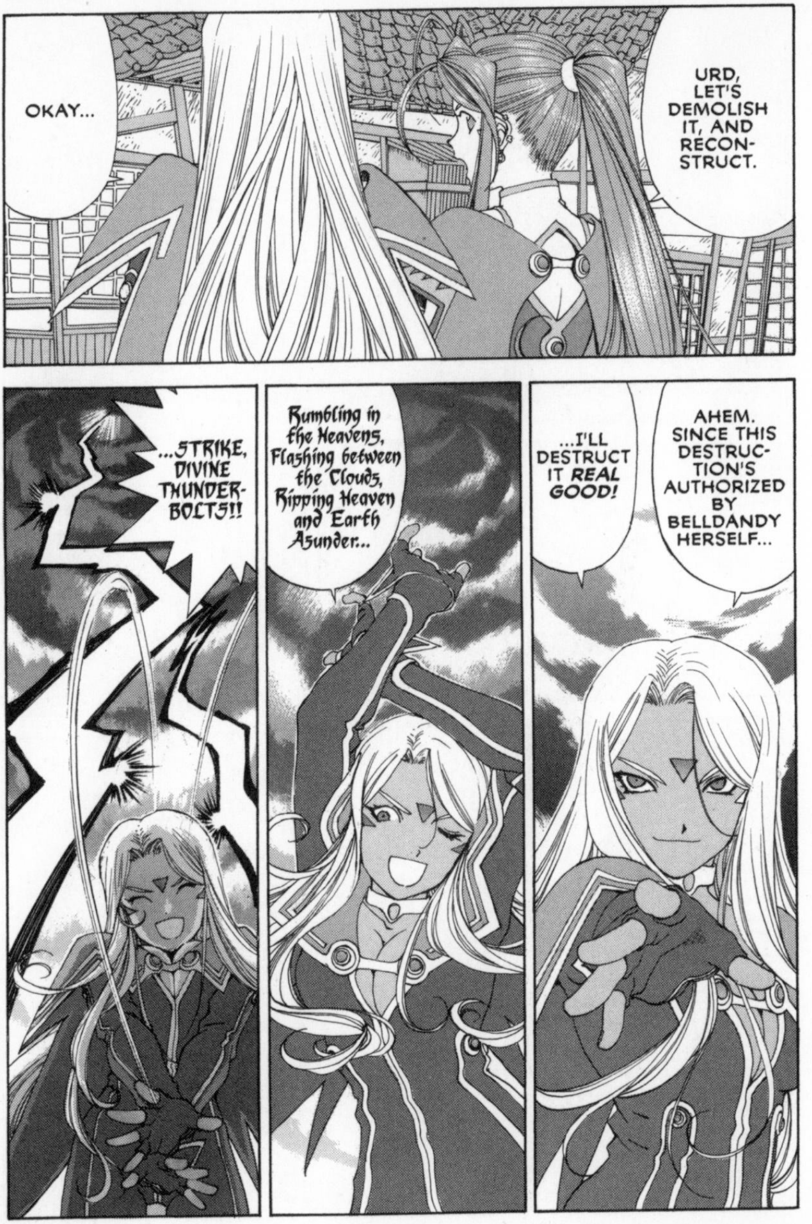
URD, LET'S DEMOLISH IT, AND RECONSTRUCT.
OKAY...
AHEM. SINCE THIS DESTRUCTION'S AUTHORIZED BY BELLDANDY HERSELF...
...I'LL DESTRUCT IT *REAL GOOD!*
Rumbling in the Heavens, Flashing between the Clouds, Ripping Heaven and Earth Asunder...
...STRIKE, DIVINE THUNDERBOLTS!!

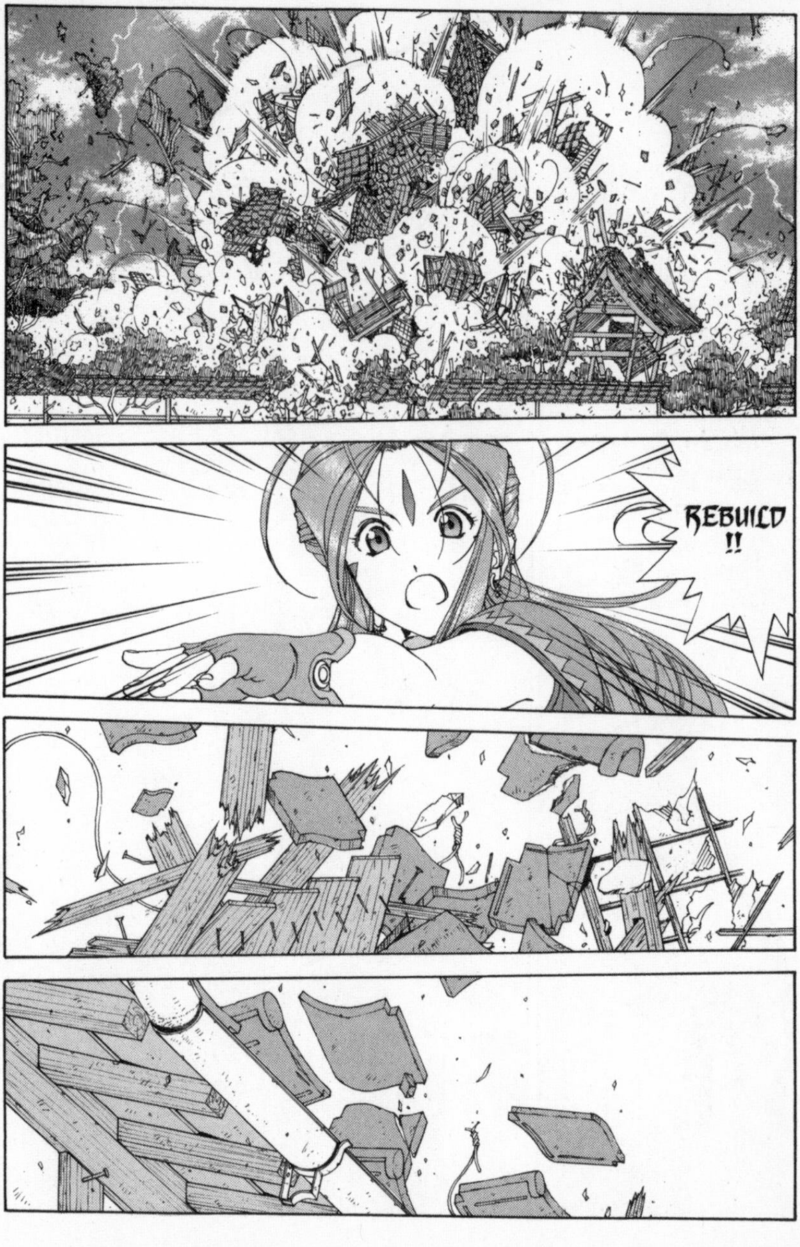
REBUILD
!!

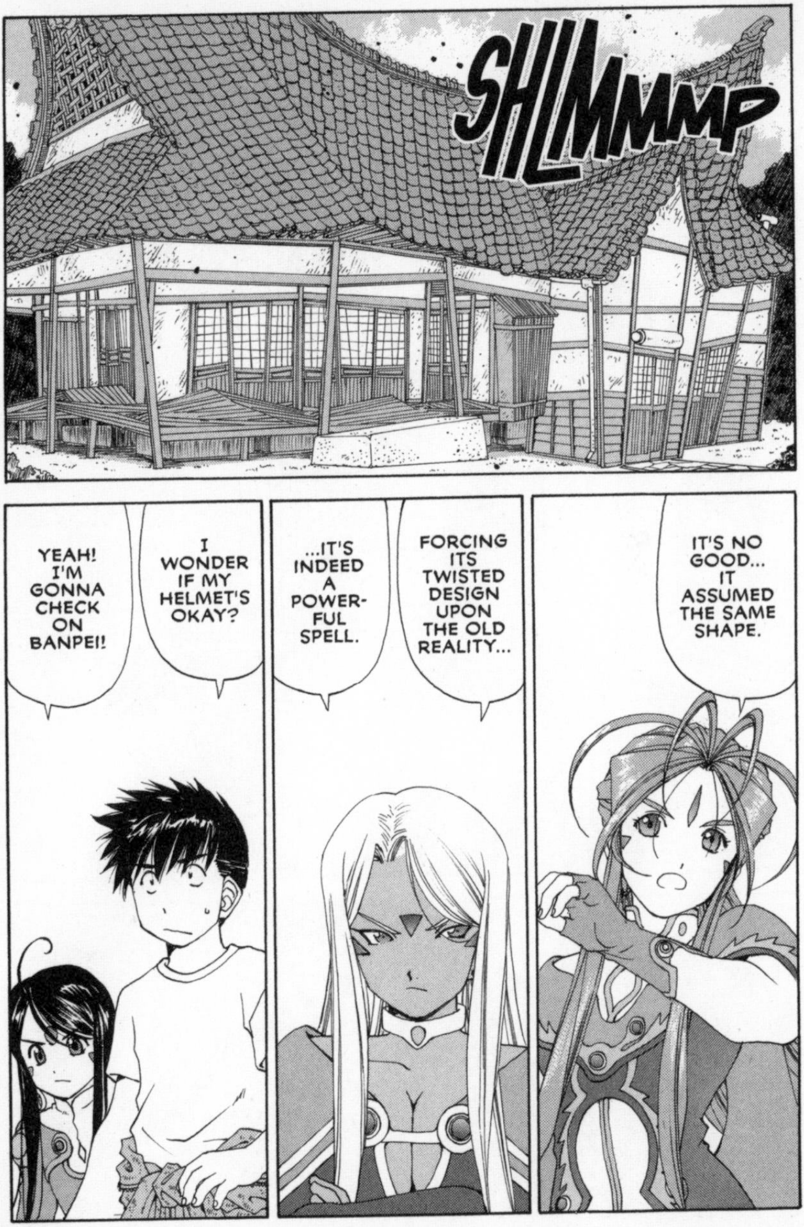
SHLIMMMP
IT'S NO GOOD... IT ASSUMED THE SAME SHAPE.
FORCING ITS TWISTED DESIGN UPON THE OLD REALITY...
...IT'S INDEED A POWER-FUL SPELL.
I WONDER IF MY HELMET'S OKAY?
YEAH! I'M GONNA CHECK ON BANPEI!

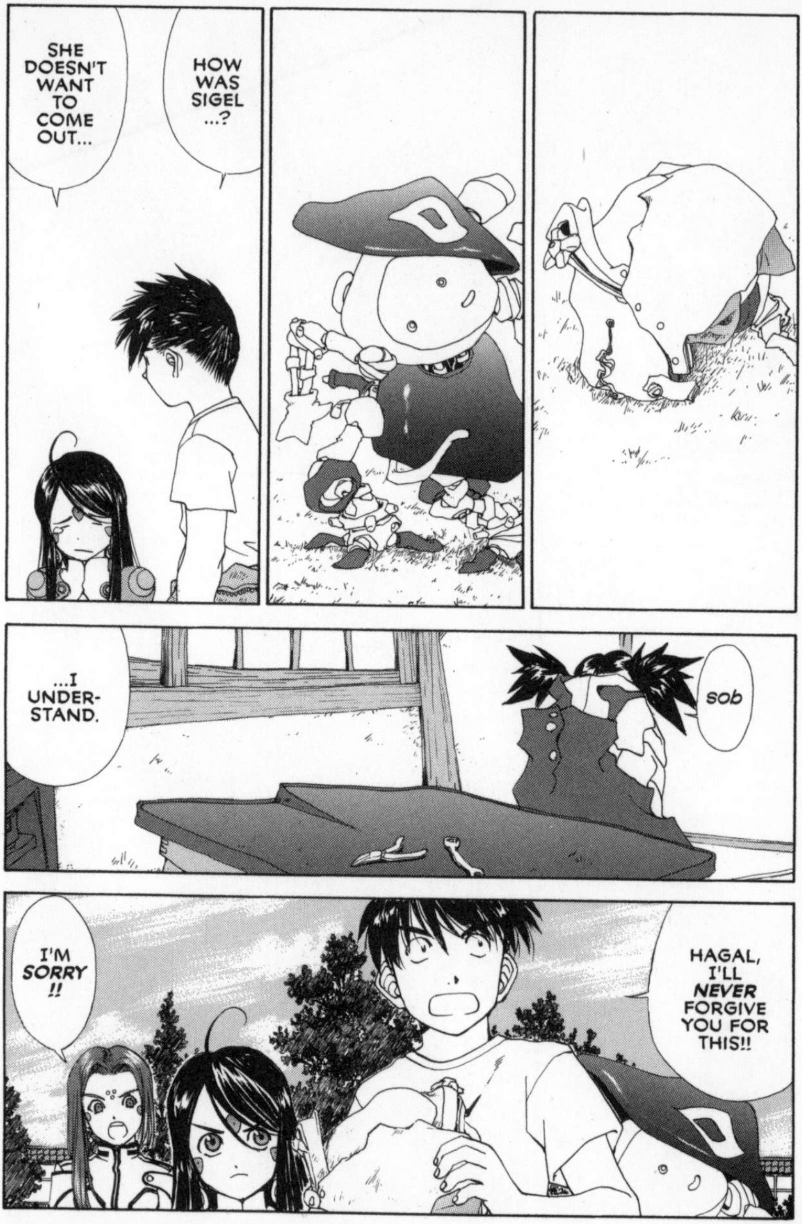
HOW WAS SIGEL ...?
SHE DOESN'T WANT TO COME OUT...
sob
...I UNDER-STAND.
HAGAL, I'LL *NEVER* FORGIVE YOU FOR THIS!!
I'M *SORRY* !!

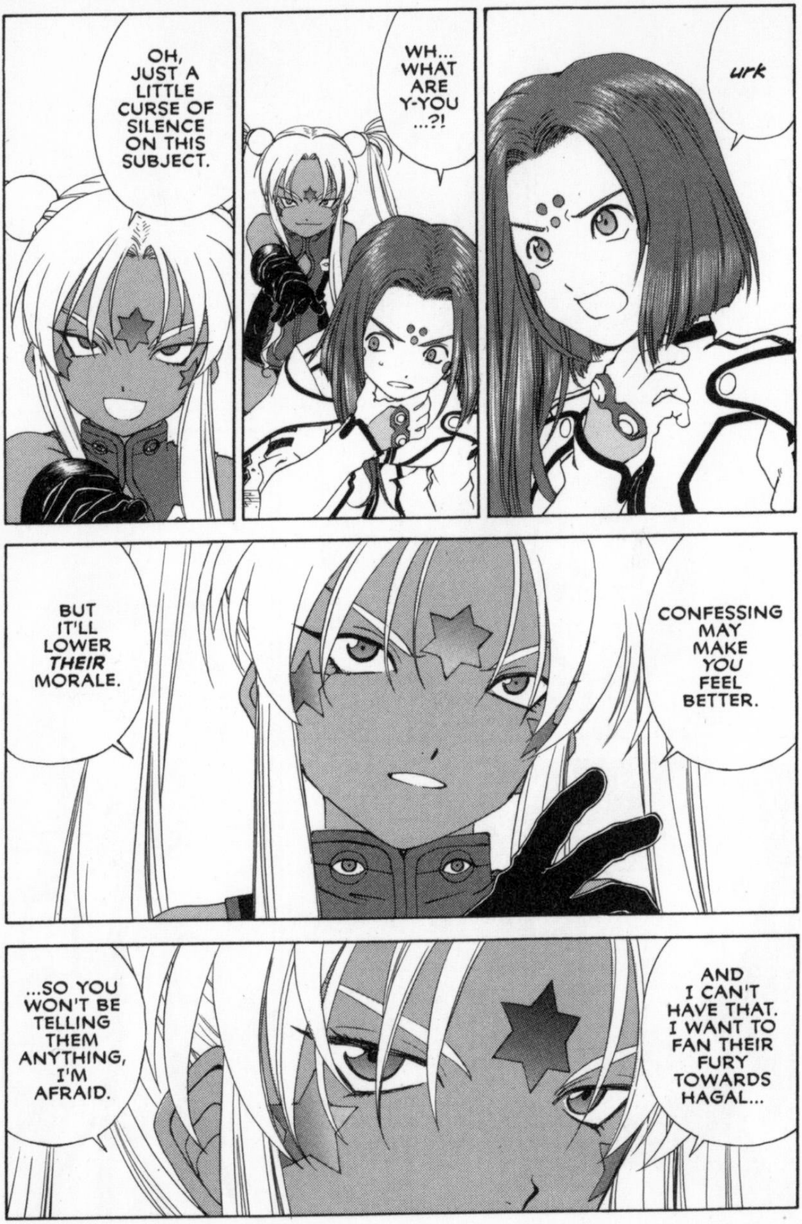
urk
WH... WHAT ARE Y-YOU ...?!
OH, JUST A LITTLE CURSE OF SILENCE ON THIS SUBJECT.
CONFESSING MAY MAKE *YOU* FEEL BETTER.
BUT IT'LL LOWER *THEIR* MORALE.
AND I CAN'T HAVE THAT. I WANT TO FAN THEIR FURY TOWARDS HAGAL...
...SO YOU WON'T BE TELLING THEM ANYTHING, I'M AFRAID.

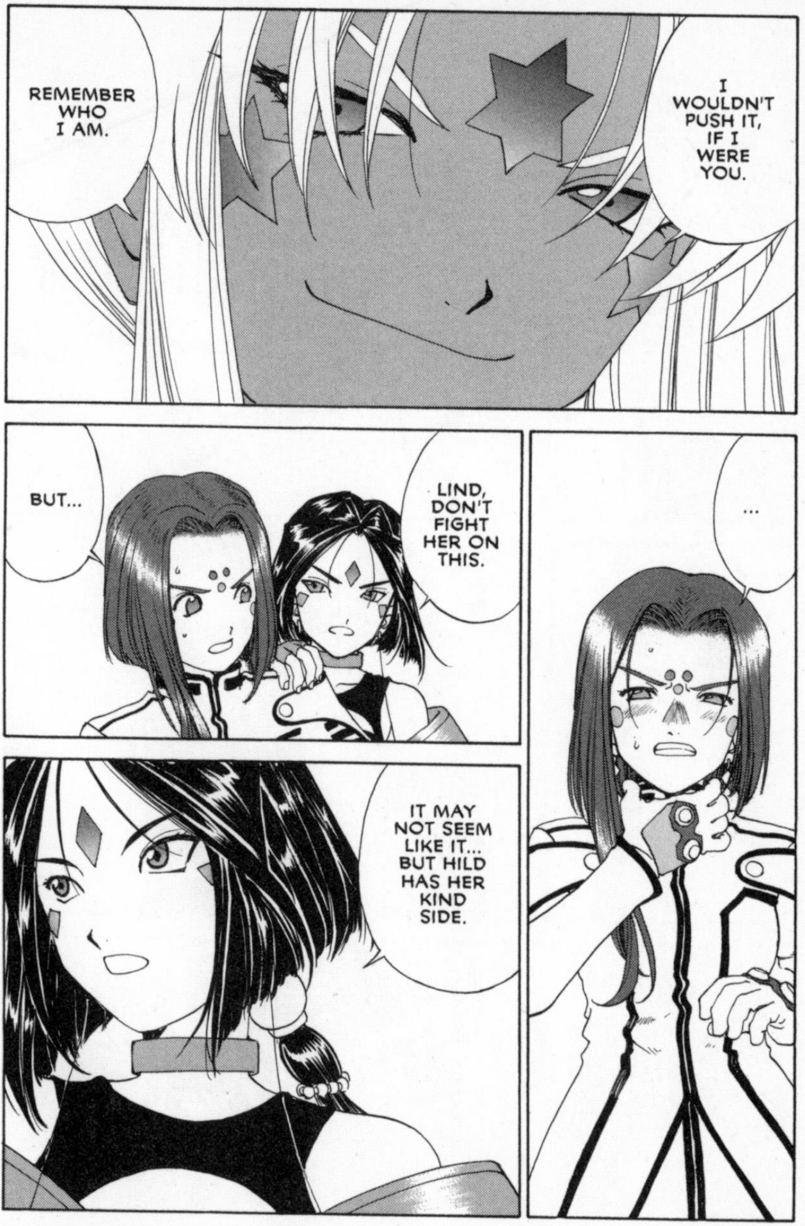

I WOULDN'T PUSH IT, IF I WERE YOU.
REMEMBER WHO I AM.
...
LIND, DON'T FIGHT HER ON THIS.
BUT...
IT MAY NOT SEEM LIKE IT... BUT HILD HAS HER KIND SIDE.

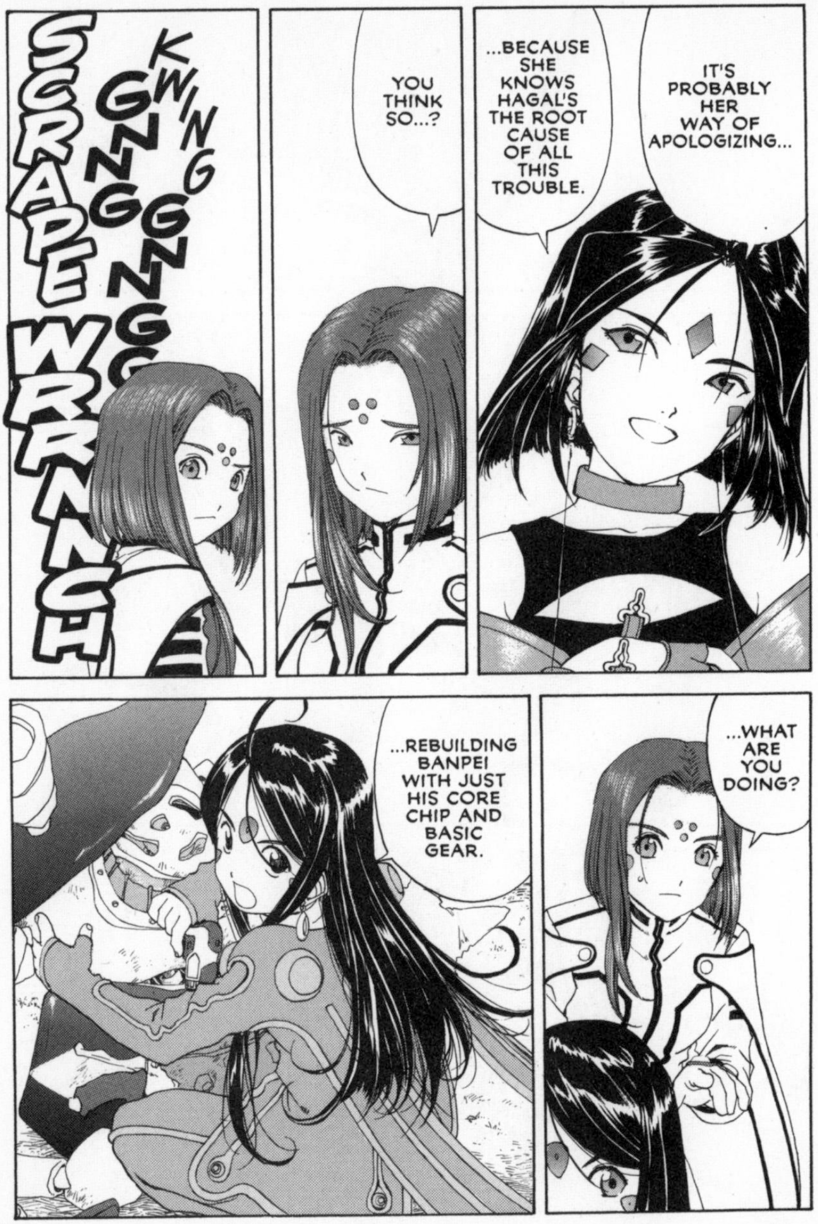
IT'S PROBABLY HER WAY OF APOLOGIZING...
...BECAUSE SHE KNOWS HAGAL'S THE ROOT CAUSE OF ALL THIS TROUBLE.
YOU THINK SO...?
KWING
GNNGG
SCRAPE
WRRNNCH
...WHAT ARE YOU DOING?
...REBUILDING BANPEI WITH JUST HIS CORE CHIP AND BASIC GEAR.

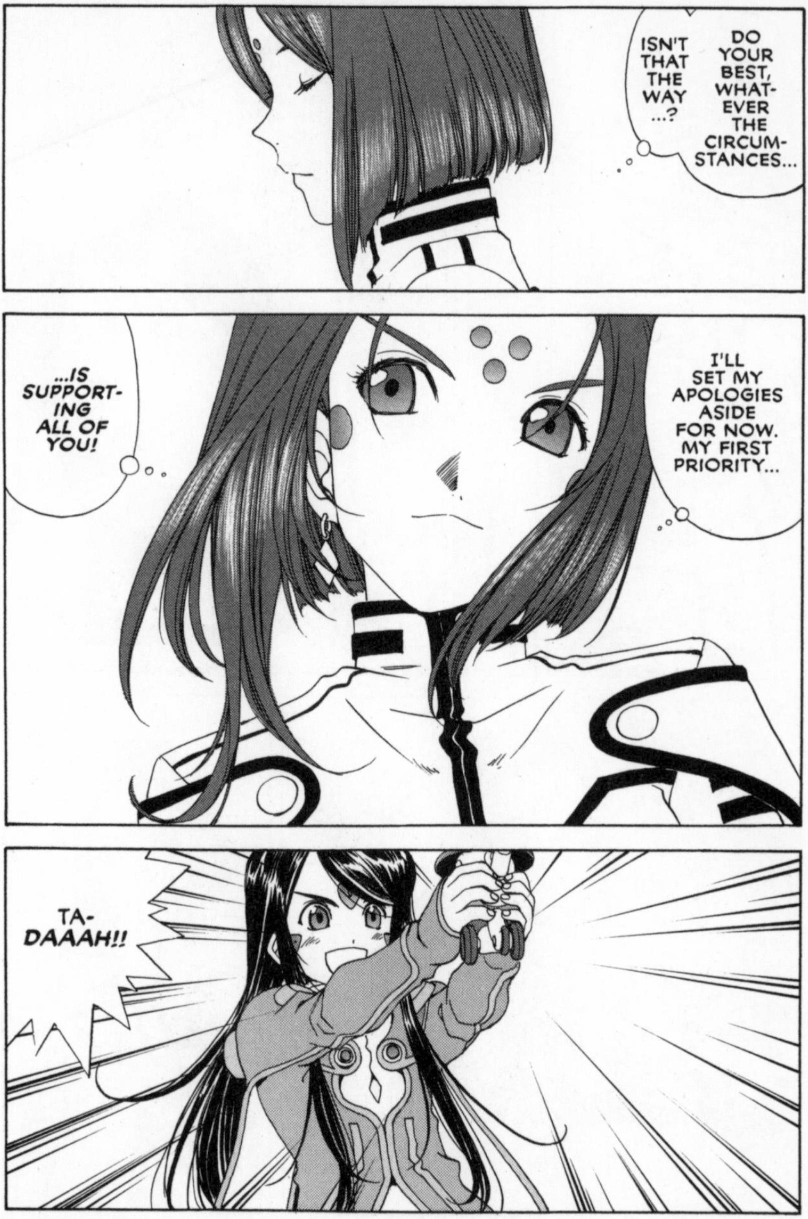
DO YOUR BEST, WHATEVER THE CIRCUMSTANCES...
ISN'T THAT THE WAY...?
I'LL SET MY APOLOGIES ASIDE FOR NOW. MY FIRST PRIORITY...
...IS SUPPORTING ALL OF YOU!
TA-DAAAH!!

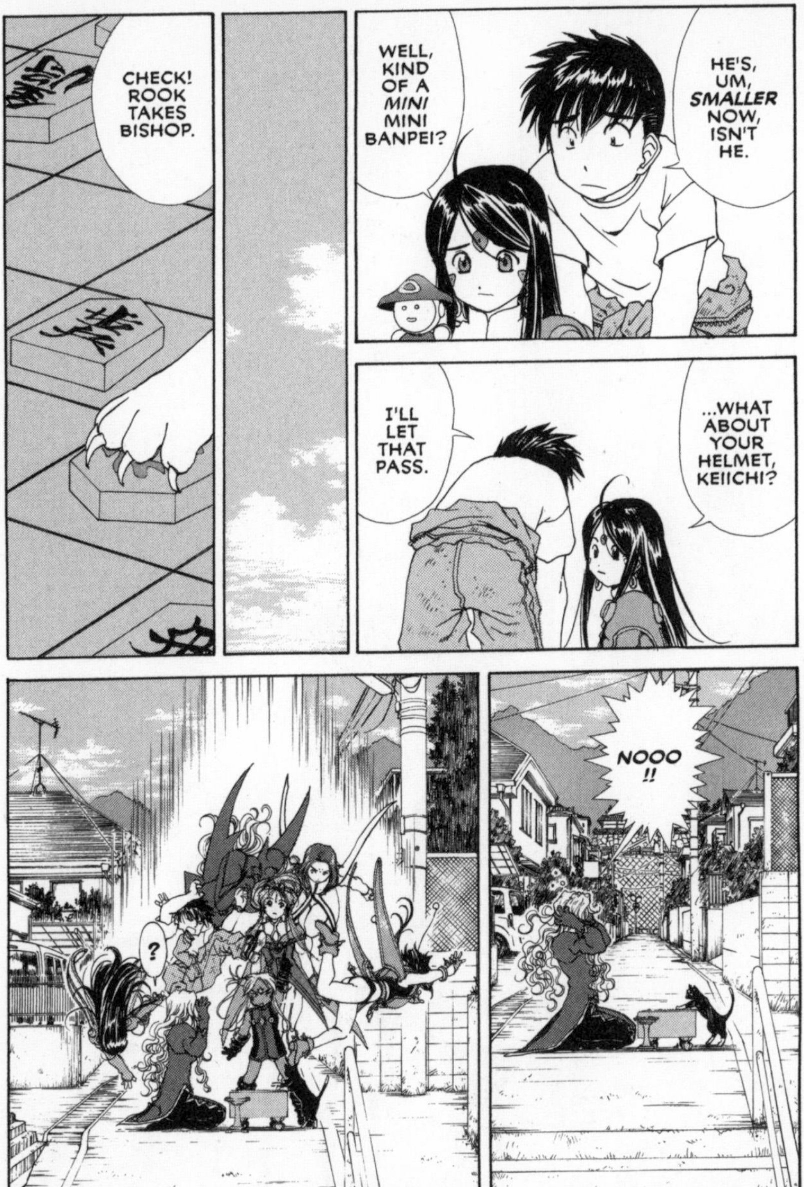
HE'S, UM, SMALLER NOW, ISN'T HE.
WELL, KIND OF A MINI MINI BANPEI?
...WHAT ABOUT YOUR HELMET, KEIICHI?
I'LL LET THAT PASS.
CHECK! ROOK TAKES BISHOP.
NOOO !!
?

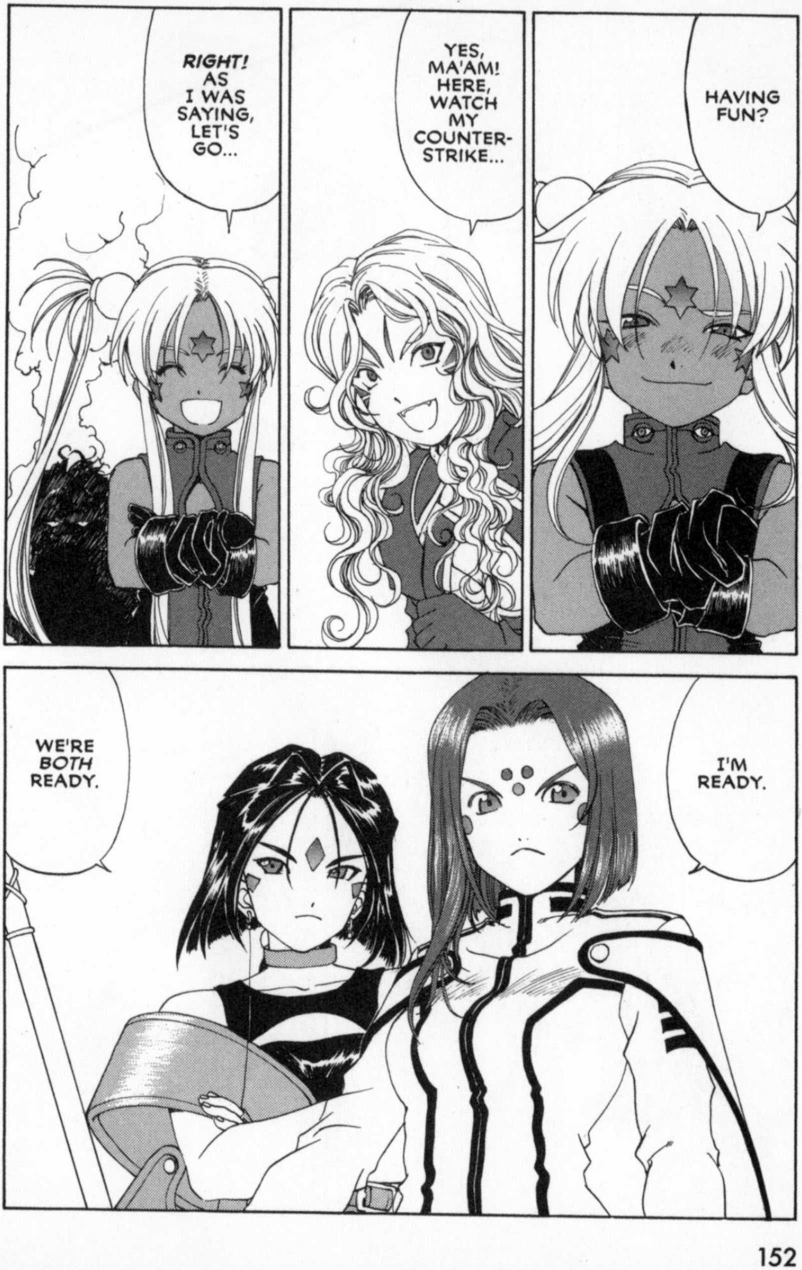
HAVING FUN?
YES, MA'AM! HERE, WATCH MY COUNTER-STRIKE...
RIGHT! AS I WAS SAYING, LET'S GO...
I'M READY.
WE'RE *BOTH* READY.

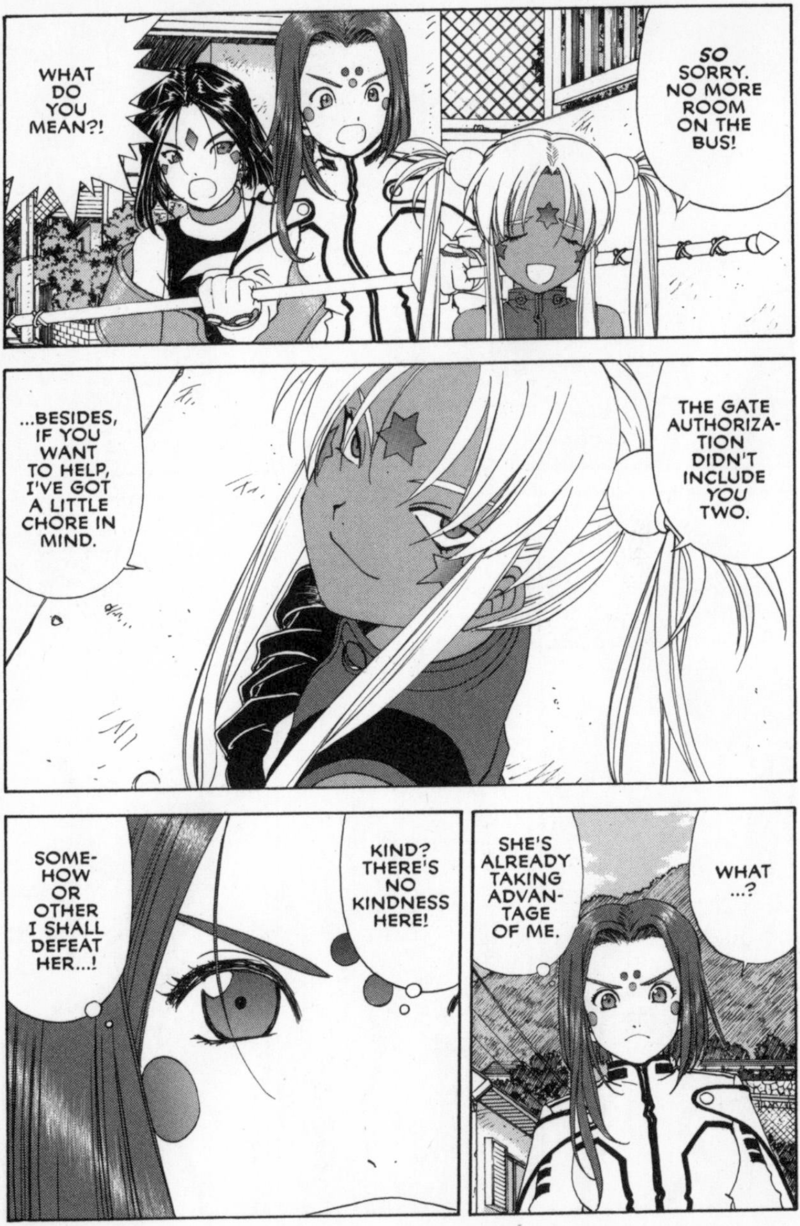
SO SORRY. NO MORE ROOM ON THE BUS!
WHAT DO YOU MEAN?!
THE GATE AUTHORIZA-TION DIDN'T INCLUDE *YOU* TWO.
...BESIDES, IF YOU WANT TO HELP, I'VE GOT A LITTLE CHORE IN MIND.
WHAT ...?
SHE'S ALREADY TAKING ADVAN-TAGE OF ME.
KIND? THERE'S NO KINDNESS HERE!
SOME-HOW OR OTHER I SHALL DEFEAT HER...!

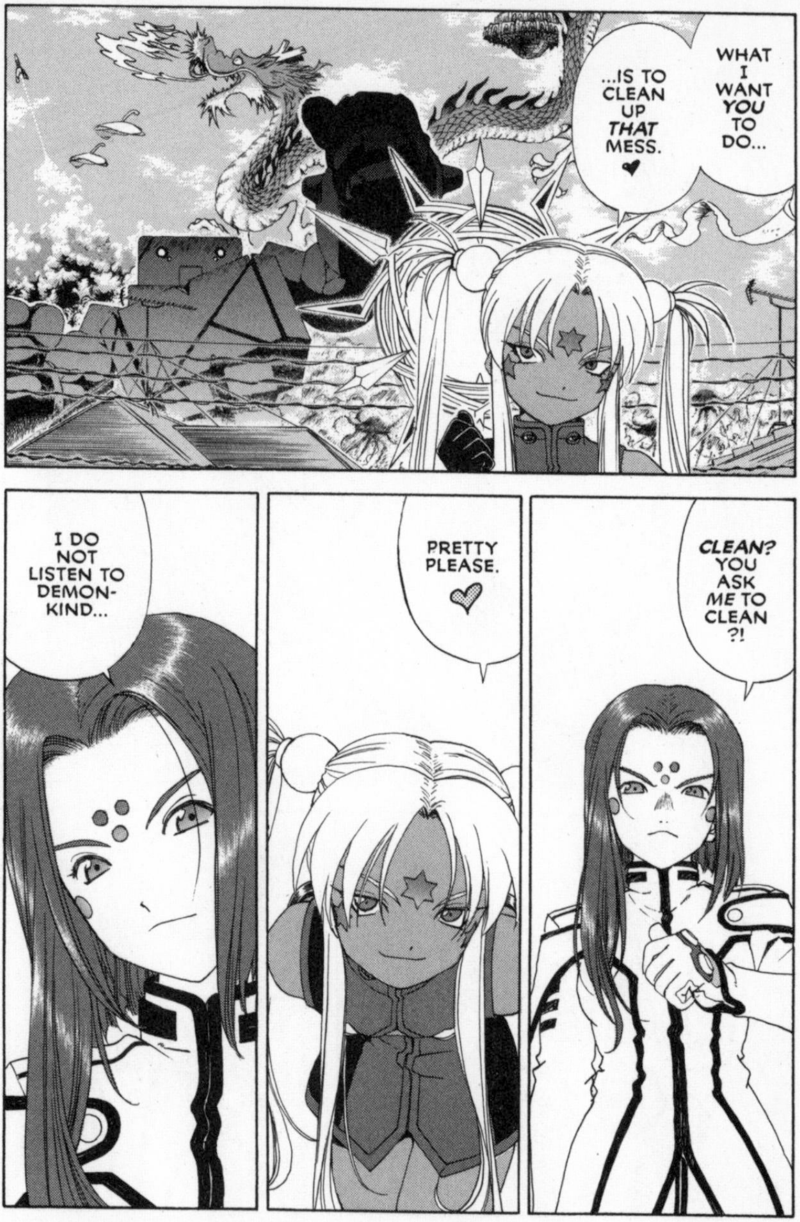
WHAT I WANT *YOU* TO DO...
...IS TO CLEAN UP *THAT* MESS. ♥
CLEAN? YOU ASK *ME* TO CLEAN ?!
PRETTY PLEASE. ♥
I DO NOT LISTEN TO DEMON-KIND...

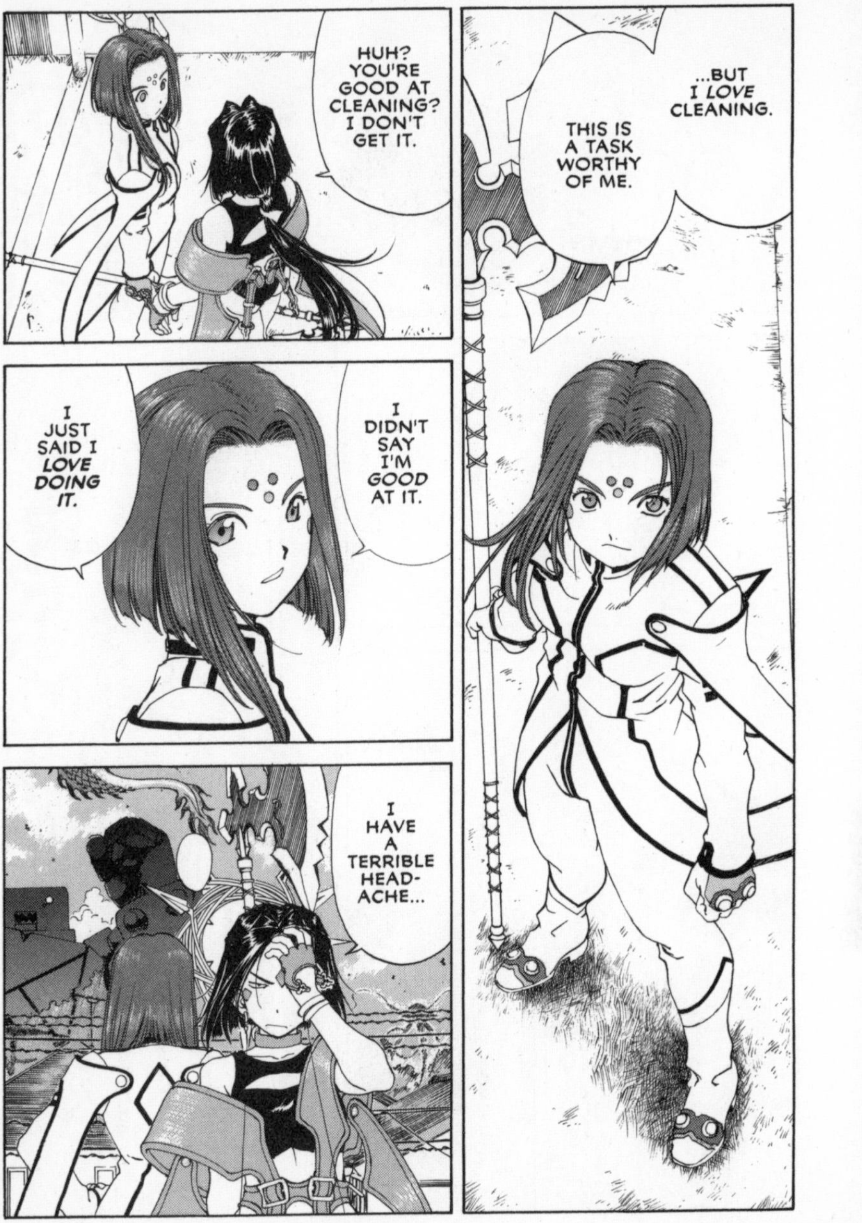
THIS IS A TASK WORTHY OF ME.
...BUT I *LOVE* CLEANING.
HUH? YOU'RE GOOD AT CLEANING? I DON'T GET IT.
I DIDN'T SAY I'M *GOOD* AT IT.
I JUST SAID I *LOVE DOING IT.*
I HAVE A TERRIBLE HEAD-ACHE...

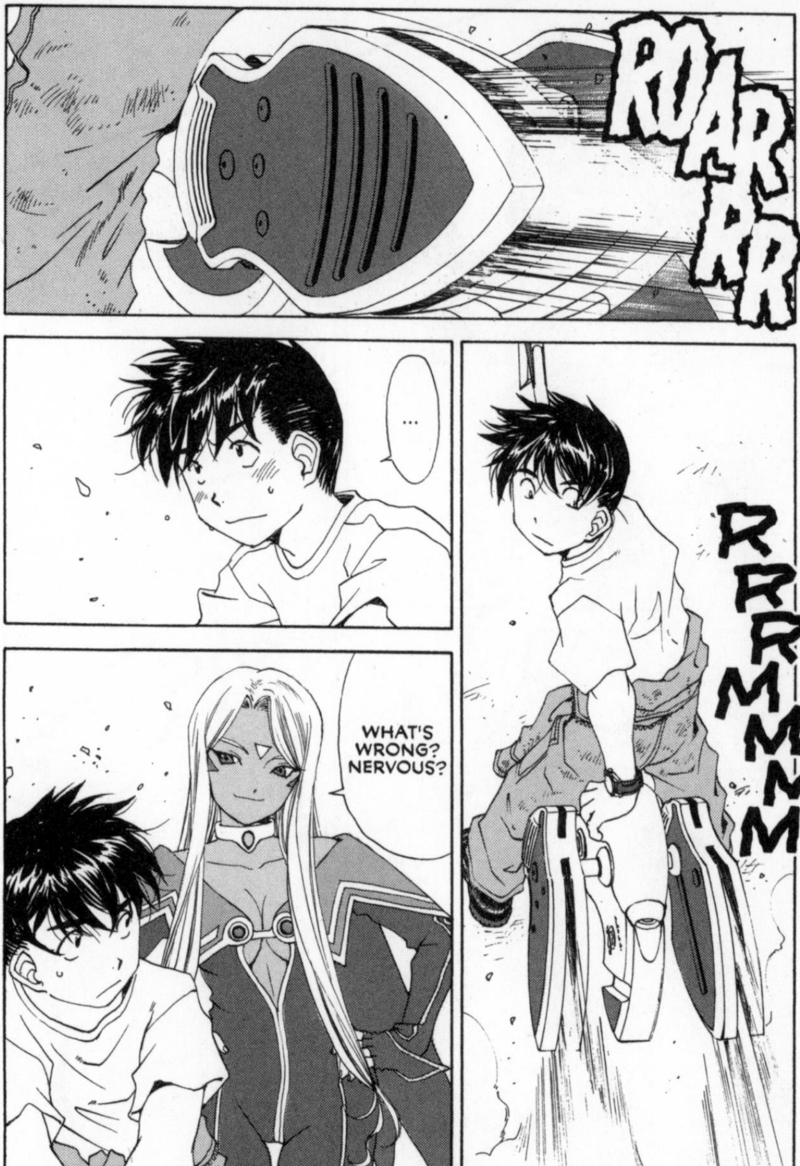
ROARRR
RRRMMMM
...
WHAT'S WRONG? NERVOUS?

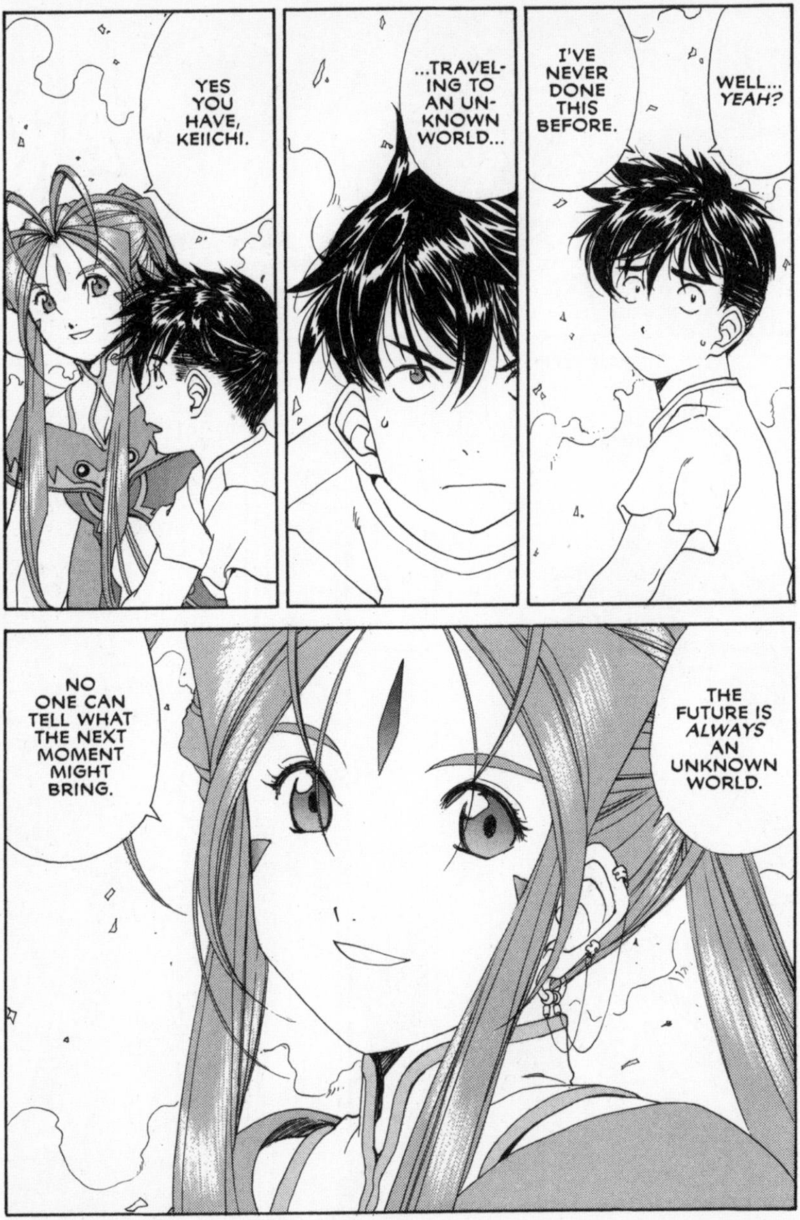
WELL... *YEAH?*
I'VE NEVER DONE THIS BEFORE.
...TRAVELING TO AN UNKNOWN WORLD...
YES YOU HAVE, KEIICHI.
THE FUTURE IS *ALWAYS* AN UNKNOWN WORLD.
NO ONE CAN TELL WHAT THE NEXT MOMENT MIGHT BRING.

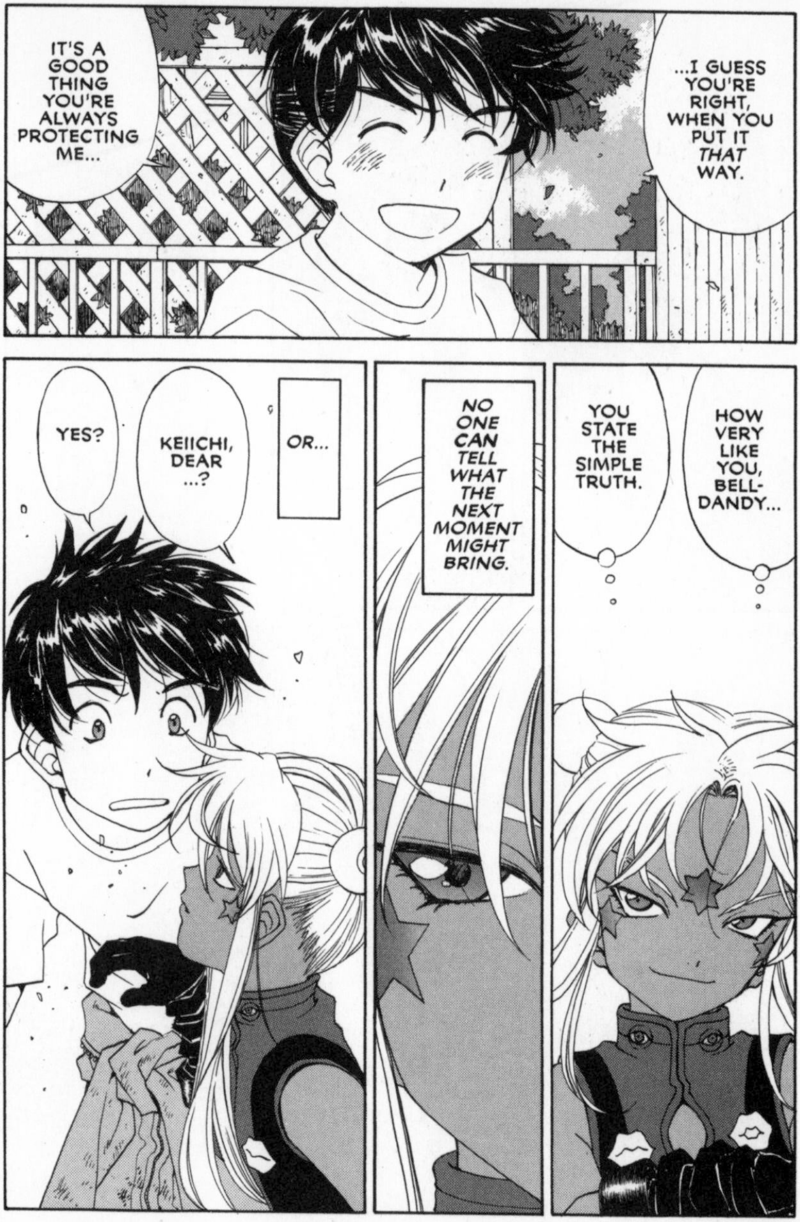

...I GUESS YOU'RE RIGHT, WHEN YOU PUT IT *THAT* WAY.
IT'S A GOOD THING YOU'RE ALWAYS PROTECTING ME...
HOW VERY LIKE YOU, BELL-DANDY...
YOU STATE THE SIMPLE TRUTH.
NO ONE CAN TELL WHAT THE NEXT MOMENT MIGHT BRING.
OR...
KEIICHI, DEAR ...?
YES?

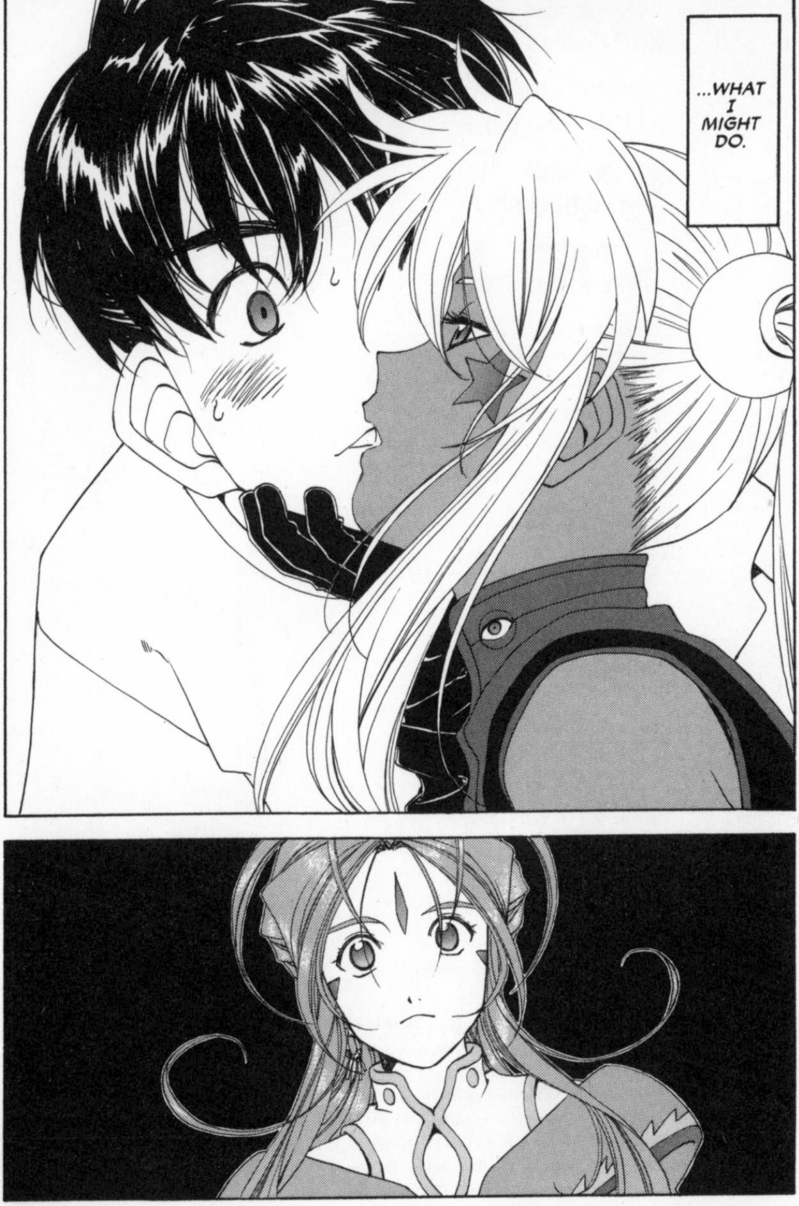
...WHAT I MIGHT DO.

EDITOR
Carl Gustav Horn

EDITORIAL ASSISTANT
Annie Gullion

DESIGNER
Kat Larson

PUBLISHER
Mike Richardson

English-language version
produced by Dark Horse Comics

OH MY GODDESS! Vol. 39

Published by Dark Horse Manga
A division of Dark Horse Comics, Inc.
10956 SE Main Street
Milwaukie, OR 97222
DarkHorse.com

To find a comics shop in your area,
call the Comic Shop Locator Service
toll-free at 1-888-266-4226

First edition: August 2011
ISBN 978-1-59582-795-1

1 3 5 7 9 10 8 6 4 2

Printed at Transcontinental Gagné,
Louiseville, QC, Canada

MIKE RICHARDSON president and publisher **NEIL HANKERSON** executive vice president **TOM WEDDLE**
chief financial officer **RANDY STRADLEY** vice president of publishing **MICHAEL MARTENS** vice
president of book trade sales **ANITA NELSON** vice president of business affairs **MICHA HERSHMAN** vice
president of marketing **DAVID SCROGGY** vice president of product development **DALE LAFOUNTAIN**
vice president of information technology **DARLENE VOGEL** senior director of print, design, and
production **KEN LIZZI** general counsel **DAVEY ESTRADA** editorial director **SCOTT ALLIE** senior
managing editor **CHRIS WARNER** senior books editor **DIANA SCHUTZ** executive editor **CARY GRAZZINI**
director of print and development **LIA RIBACCHI** art director **CARA NIECE** director of scheduling

letters to the ENCHANTRESS

10956 SE Main Street, Milwaukie, Oregon 97222
OMG@DarkHorse.com • DarkHorse.com

NOTE: Full addresses and e-mail addresses will not be printed, unless you ask! All fan artwork, letters, and e-mails submitted become the property of Dark Horse Comics.

As always, welcome back! We've been receiving some really nice letters recently, so once again I want to let you know that if your letter hasn't shown up in one of the "newer" *Oh My Goddess!* volumes (vols. 37, 38, 39, etc.) look out for it in one of the "older" ones instead, such as the upcoming vol. 19 in October 2011 and vol. 20 in February 2012. Actually, vol. 20 will be the last of the "older" volumes to be reissued in Japanese format reading format, since we made the switch from Western to Japanese with vol. 21. We will, of course, continue to release newer volumes of *Oh My Goddess!* even after we complete the reissue of the older ones. So vol. 40 in December 2011 will come between vols. 19 and 20, but after 20 comes out, we'll then proceed with 41, 42, etc.

Let's return to the feature we've run in recent newer volumes of *Oh My Goddess!*—Kosuke Fujishima's remarks to readers from the early days of the story. Note that of two of the *OMG!* illustrations referenced in the comments below, "Urd in Moonlight" and "Belldandy Riding on the Back of a Goldfish in a *Yukata*," the first appeared as the double-page chapter 37 title spread at the beginning of *Oh My Goddess!* Vol. 6, and the second was done as a special piece not included in either the Japanese or the American graphic novels of *Oh My Goddess!* The Japanese editor of *OMG!* commented that both illustrations, as well as many others from the series, were finally reprinted in the December 25, 2008, release *Fujishima Kosuke Gashu Aa Megamisama 1998–2008*—you probably got most of that, ^_^ but it means *Kosuke Fujishima Art Book: Oh My Goddess! 1998–2008*.

Of course, this art book was published in celebration of the twentieth anniversary of *Oh My Goddess!*, the first chapter of which was published in the November 1988 issue of *Afternoon* magazine. *Afternoon* is still today, as it was then, a monthly publication, and longtime fans of the Dark Horse English-language version of *Oh My Goddess!* will remember that *OMG!* also used to be a monthly publication; that is, instead of being collected straight to graphic novel (*tankobon*) as is the norm today, Dark Horse, between August 1994 and September 2004, published the first 127 chapters (127 is the third-to-last chapter of vol. 20) of *Oh My Goddess!* one (or occasionally, two) chapters at a time, either as a monthly comic book, or (in the case of chapters 2–13 and 15–16) in our former monthly anthology magazine, *Super Manga Blast.*

What is this all leading up to? (You dearly hoped it was leading up to something ^_^) Well, one of the advantages of publishing *Oh My Goddess!* as a monthly comic was that you could read the story at the pace the creator intended. But one of the disadvantages for the publisher (i.e., Dark Horse, although it was also a common problem for all U.S. manga companies at the time) was the constant need to find cover art. If you stop to think about it, each issue of an American comic book has a separate cover illustration done for it. In fact, the cover illustration is considered such an important marketing tool in the US comics industry that it's often done by a different—and often more prestigious—artist, and in a different style, than the actual story inside.

The idea of having a different artist do the cover than the interior story would be a strange approach in Japan; the only creator I can think of offhand who does this on a regular basis is Eiji Otsuka (*The Kurosagi Corpse Delivery Service, MPD Psycho*). But (getting back to the point—oh, so near it! ^_^) there is simply less

demand for manga cover illustrations in general in Japan, because almost all manga are first published in anthology magazines, such as *Afternoon.* Even though *Oh My Goddess!* might be considered the flagship title of *Afternoon* (it is, not surprisingly, its longest-running series), it is, only one title among many in the magazine.

How many? Well, during the time the chapters you've just read (chapters 243–249) ran in *Afternoon* (to be exact, they were in the January through July 2009 issues), *Oh My Goddess!* was sharing space with thirty-eight other manga! No wonder *Afternoon's* motto is "MANGA AGGRESSION!"— each issue of the magazine is literally a thousand pages long. Naturally it would be inappropriate for every issue of *Afternoon* to put *Oh My Goddess!* on the cover, and in fact it only happens on occasion; otherwise, the cover spot is used for other *Afternoon* manga, such as *Blade of the Immortal, Genshiken, Vinland Saga,* or *Big Windup!*

Speaking of windups, this has certainly been a big one, but now the pitch—even though, as mentioned above, Dark Horse published well over a hundred issues of the *Oh My Goddess!* comic book, there was certainly never anything near like a hundred *Oh My Goddess!* cover paintings done by Fujishima-*sensei* for *Afternoon* magazine. So what *did* Dark Horse use for cover art? Well, fortunately, Fujishima did lots of color paintings of *OMG!* over the years that didn't get on the cover, but ran in the interior of *Afternoon* as pinups, or were done for other promotional purposes.

So while you've never seen the "Belldandy Riding on the Back of a Goldfish in a *Yukata*" piece on the cover or interior of an *Oh My Goddess!* graphic novel, if you're an old-school fan of the English edition, you *have* seen it as the cover of *Oh My Goddess!* Part II #8, published by Dark Horse in September 1995. This was the fourteenth monthly issue of the *Oh My Goddess!* comic book, even though it didn't contain *OMG!* chapter 14 as you might expect, but *OMG!* chapter 23! It's another long story, but the original Dark Horse *Oh My Goddess!* comic books, while they *did* start with the first chapter, ^_^ otherwise often skipped and re-arranged chapters—for example, the first six issues published contained chapters 1, 14, 20, and 26–28.

Why those particular ones? Well, in part, it was because that way Belldandy, Urd, and Skuld all got introduced to the readers in the first six issues, something you had to wait until vol. 4 to finish doing in the original Japanese. It was thought to be a good idea to bring in the entire main cast as soon as possible for the English-language edition, to hook reader interest. And in retrospect it seems like it *was* a good idea, for after all, it laid the foundation for a North American readership that is still going strong seventeen years later. And of course, today the current Dark Horse graphic- novel edition of *Oh My*

Goddess! (hey, you're holding it now!) reprints all the chapters in their original Japanese order.

Right . . . now let's get back to the nineties again, specifically (as always) October of 1991! Matthew Sweet had just released his third album, and the one that made him an indie star, *Girlfriend*. Back before most people had ever heard the term "AMV," Sweet was putting anime into his actual videos (like, on MTV—this was back when they showed videos, of course). It's not too surprising that his songs would be in the English version of *Oh My Goddess!* Vol. 18, including "I've Been Waiting," the second track off *Girlfriend* (the music video featured Lum from *Urusei Yatsura*—also not too surprising, as Sweet has her tattooed on his arm ^_^).

But no one was bringing the wickedness quite like Urd in the aforementioned moonlight picture, which was prompting reader questions like this in that month's issue of *Afternoon*:

"You ever dance with the devil in the pale moonlight?" asked Godzilla vs. the Yomiuri Giants (having signed their name thus, we must take them at their word), twenty-seven years old from Kochi Prefecture. *"It's a line from a movie, but it's as though it was written just for Urd."* The movie G v. YG quotes is, of course, Batman. Which Batman, you ask? It was the one before The Dark Knight, Batman Begins, Batman & Robin, Batman Forever, and Batman Returns, so it was just called, er, Batman. Twenty-

year-old Natsu Wa Kirai (meaning "I Hate Summer"—have you noticed by now that fans of the English-language Oh My Goddess! have a tendency to write in using their real names, whereas in Japan . . . ? ^_^) of Saitama Prefecture reflected, "Urd and the full moon . . . Her bewitching beauty is good. But she really **is** mysterious!"

Fujishima replied in that same October 1991 issue of Afternoon, "I rendered Urd in relatively darker colors for that piece, reflecting the fact that it's a night scene and the moon is behind her. The moon itself is a bewitching motif, so I think it was a perfect combination. But what do you all think of the illustration ("Belldandy Riding on the Back of a Goldfish in a Yukata") I did for this month's Afternoon cover? I'll be waiting to hear from you!"

Of course, the readers liked it, even if they showed their usual discretion in doing so—in the November 1991 issue of Afternoon that featured chapter 39 (the conclusion of the "Lord of Terror" story arc, by the way), reader Gokuraku Yarou (meaning "Mr. Paradise"), nineteen years old from Hyogo Prefecture, said, "The cool summer-night atmosphere of the painting was really nice," whereas twenty-three-year-old Sake Nomitai ("I Want to Drink Sake") from Ibaraki Prefecture thought Belldandy looked great in the yukata, "but gosh, that goldfish sure was realistic! I was astonished."

"There was surprisingly little reference material on goldfish," answered Fujishima, "although there was tons of material on tropical fish . . . As I've said before, typically I seem to only find good reference material after I've already finished the illustration, but this time, my editor got me some good material in time, and it was a great help." Mr. Fujishima's remark, of course, shows the difference between doing research twenty years ago and today. Image search wouldn't have been an option, as in the fall of 1991 the web had literally just been invented by Tim Berners-Lee, and at the start there were only five images on it. I don't mean five images of goldfish—I mean, five images, total, on the entire World Wide Web. Mind-boggling, isn't it? By the way, for inventing the web, the queen eventually made Berners-Lee a Knight Commander of the Order of the British Empire. Very Hellsing.

Fujishima also mentioned in the November 1991 issue that in September, he attached an extra-large fuel tank to his Suzuki DR250S and finally got the chance to take a trip to the seaside. He was expecting "girls in bathing suits, seaside stalls selling kakigori [shaved ice with flavored syrup], grilled corn on the cob . . . " but what he got was "Zilch. Beaches empty of people, and nothing left but garbage." By September, everyone was gone, so he sadly reflected that 1991 would be another year without a summer for him.

Later that year, in December, Fujishima went to a video arcade, also for the first time in a long while, and was surprised at how many games now featured cockpits or seats that moved as you play, as opposed to the standard "cabinet" games that had dominated arcades since the 1970s. He and his friends got so excited playing that they did a lot of shouting and screaming, which earned them strange looks from the rest of the patrons. "Isn't it stranger to play those games in silence?" asked Fujishima.

Loyal reader Godzilla vs. the Giants, commenting on the end of the "Lord of Terror" story, wrote of his admiration for "that attitude of hers, after all she's done. Whether goddess or demon, I'm impressed how Urd never loses herself." From Saitama Prefecture, reader Mo Karada Boroboro ("My Body's Tired Out"), a student aged nineteen, noted that this was also the first anniversary of Mini-Urd's first appearance (the Mini-Goddess strips were originally known as the Mini-Urd strips, as at first they were all about her ^_^).

"It's been a whole year?" replied Fujishima. "I started it just thinking it'd be good filler for the graphic-novel collections, but I never dreamed it'd last this long. Thank you for your support, by the way. Like Urd, I've never lost my self-control, as I don't drink and I certainly don't do drugs. But there may be times when I don't know who I am, when I wonder, 'Maybe I'm not the **me** I think I am . . . ?!' For me, that's where the risk of 'losing myself' lies."

The creator's Japanese editor commented at this point, "How like Mr. Fujishima to say this so very calmly. Even if it were the end of the world, Mr. Fujishima would look as though he wasn't panicked at all." The creator's English-language editor reflects that the true reason Urd never loses self-control may be that she never had any to begin with. ^_^

In the December 1991 issue of Afternoon (chapter 40), a seventeen-year-old reader named "M93R-AUTO9" from Ibaraki Prefecture wrote, "Regarding Mr. Fujishima's comments of last month about losing himself, I feel it showed he's a man of high caliber. And I think it shows in the style of his work and in his stories' themes." Fujishima replied, "I said I've never lost myself, but probably it's just that I haven't been in a lot of critical situations. If something bad were to really happen, I'd probably panic. I'm a timid guy really!"

Fujishima's editor also noted that the end of the "Lord of Terror" story arc prompted Afternoon to receive many letters like fourteen-year-old Koutenei's from Miyagi Prefecture: "The story got so intense, I thought the manga itself was coming to an end, but it didn't! So strong is a true manga artist's spirit!" The creator replied, "Dear readers, I'm sorry I worried you. There is still time before the final episode. Please stick with me just a little while longer." We still don't know when the final episode of Oh My Goddess! will be, but as you can see, readers did stick with Fujishima-sensei a little while longer . . . as in twenty years! See you all in vol. 40!

—CGH

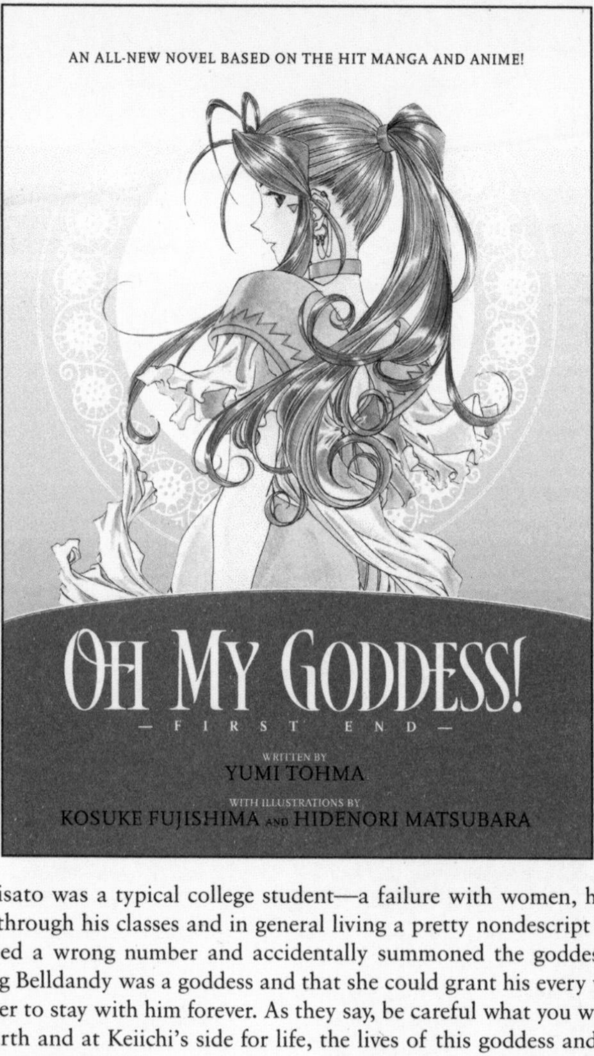
AN ALL-NEW NOVEL BASED ON THE HIT MANGA AND ANIME!
OH MY GODDESS!
—FIRST END—
WRITTEN BY
YUMI TOHMA
WITH ILLUSTRATIONS BY
KOSUKE FUJISHIMA AND HIDENORI MATSUBARA

Keiichi Morisato was a typical college student—a failure with women, he was struggling to get through his classes and in general living a pretty nondescript life. That is, until he dialed a wrong number and accidentally summoned the goddess Belldandy. Not believing Belldandy was a goddess and that she could grant his every wish, Keiichi wished for her to stay with him forever. As they say, be careful what you wish for! Now bound to Earth and at Keiichi's side for life, the lives of this goddess and human will never be the same again!

ISBN 978-1-59582-137-9 | $14.95

AVAILABLE AT YOUR LOCAL COMICS SHOP OR BOOKSTORE

To find a comics shop in your area, call 1.888.266.4226. For more information or to order direct: •On the web: darkhorse.com •E-mail: mailorder@darkhorse.com •Phone: 1.800.862.0052 Mon.–Fri. 9 AM to 5 PM Pacific Time.

darkhorse.com

NEON GENESIS EVANGELION

Dark Horse Manga is proud to present two new original series based on the wildly popular *Neon Genesis Evangelion* manga and anime! Continuing the rich story lines and complex characters, these new visions of *Neon Genesis Evangelion* provide extra dimensions for understanding one of the greatest series ever made!

**STORY AND ART
BY OSAMU TAKAHASHI**

VOLUME 1
ISBN 978-1-59582-321-2 | $9.99

VOLUME 2
ISBN 978-1-59582-377-9 | $9.99

VOLUME 3
ISBN 978-1-59582-447-9 | $9.99

VOLUME 4
ISBN 978-1-59582-454-7 | $9.99

VOLUME 5
ISBN 978-1-59582-520-9 | $9.99

VOLUME 6
ISBN 978-1-59582-580-3 | $9.99

VOLUME 7
ISBN 978-1-59582-595-7 | $9.99

VOLUME 8
ISBN 978-1-59582-694-7 | $9.99

VOLUME 9
ISBN 978-1-59582-800-2 | $9.99

**STORY AND ART
BY MINGMING**

VOLUME 1
ISBN 978-1-59582-530-8 | $10.99

VOLUME 2
ISBN 978-1-59582-661-9 | $10.99

VOLUME 3
ISBN 978-1-59582-680-0 | $10.99

VOLUME 4
ISBN 978-1-59582-689-3 | $10.99

**Each volume of *Neon Genesis Evangelion* features bonus color pages,
your *Evangelion* fan art and letters, and special reader giveaways!**

AVAILABLE AT YOUR LOCAL COMICS SHOP OR BOOKSTORE
To find a comics shop in your area, call 1-888-266-4226 • For more information or to order direct: • On the web: darkhorse.com
E-mail: mailorder@darkhorse.com • Phone: 1-800-862-0052 Mon.–Fri. 9 AM to 5 PM Pacific Time.

DarkHorse.com

STOP! This is the back of the book!

This manga collection is translated into English, but arranged in right-to-left reading format to maintain the artwork's visual orientation as originally drawn and published in Japan. If you've never read comics this way before, take a look at the diagram below to give yourself an idea of how to go about it. Basically, you'll be starting in the upper right-hand corner, and will read each word balloon and panel moving right to left. It may take a little getting used to, but you should get the hang of it very quickly. Have fun! If this is the millionth manga you've read this way, never mind. ^_^

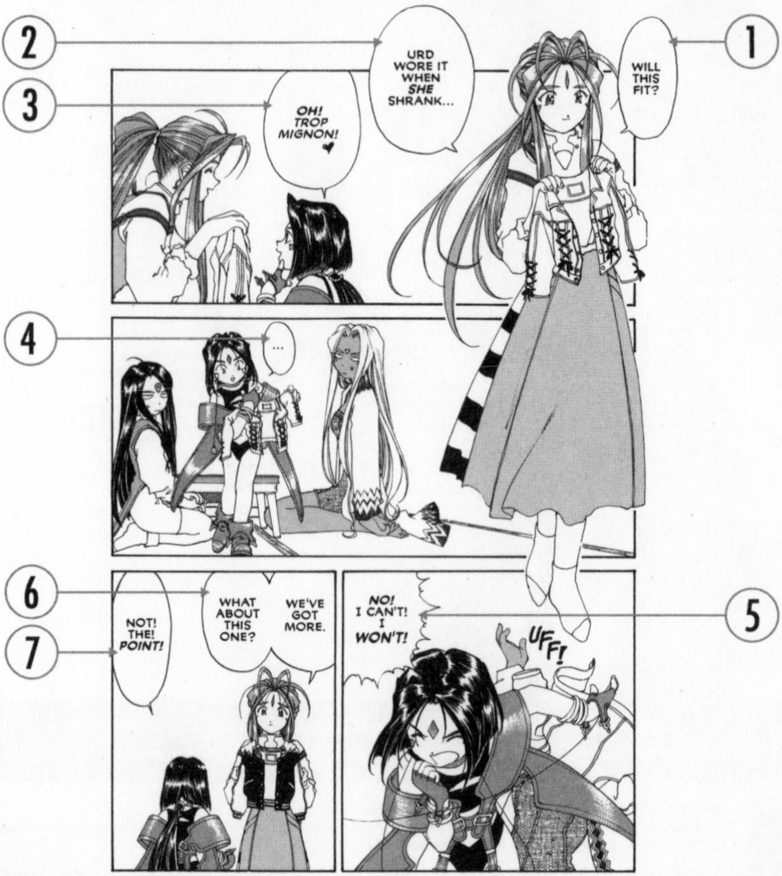
1
WILL THIS FIT?
2
URD WORE IT WHEN SHE SHRANK...
3
OH! TROP MIGNON!
4
...
5
NO! I CAN'T! I WON'T!
UFF!
6
WE'VE GOT MORE.
WHAT ABOUT THIS ONE?
7
NOT! THE! POINT!